Capitol Kid:

A Baby Boomer Grows Up In Washington, D.C.

GARY C. DREIBELBIS

ISBN-13: 978-1-63535-449-2 (Digital)
ISBN-13: 978-1-63535-421-8 (Paperback)
ISBN-13: 978-1-63535-411-9 (Hardback)
Library of Congress Control Number: 2018935529

Front cover photography by David Blackwell

Permissions and credits for all images displayed in this book were obtained.
Photography Credits as follows:
David Blackwell
Don Burgess courtesy of the Harper's Ferry Historical Society
District Department of Transportation Archives
Tom Buckley, WUSA
John Consoli, University of Maryland
Tom Buckley, Milt Grant

Printed in the United States of America.

First print edition 2018.

Neely Worldwide Publishing
Neely Productions Inc.
3811 Suitland Rd SE
Washington D.C. 20020

www.neelyproductionsinc.com
www.neelyworldwidepublishing.com

TABLE OF CONTENTS

ACKNOWLEDGEMENTS

First of all thanks to my wife Eileen for her patience and encouragement during the process.

Cris Lee, Bill Knight, and Marlyn Knight Cunningham all gave valuable advice as to editing.

Don Burgess of the Harpers Ferry Historical Society, Katie Dishman of the Marriott Corporation, Elioak Farm, The District Department of Transportation, Tom Buckley of WUSA-TV, The Dreibelbis Cousins and Tom Consoli of The University of Maryland all provided photographs.

Finally, thanks to my friend of over fifty years David Blackwell for his photos and graphic design.

DAYS OF INFAMY

For those whom former NBC news anchorman Tom Brokaw dubbed "The Greatest Generation," December 7th, 1941, was, as President Franklin Delano Roosevelt labeled it, "A day that will live in infamy." Years later, Aram Bakshian, a speechwriter for Presidents Nixon and Ford, revealed that the line was originally written as, "December 7th, 1941, a day that will live in world history." One of FDR's ghostwriters thought that "world history" was a neutral, flat concept and changed world history to infamy.

Most Americans alive on this date can remember exactly where they were when they heard the news of the bombing of Pearl Harbor. My father, Charles Henry Dreibelbis, aka "Dribby" because no one could pronounce "Dreibelbis," recalled the events of the day with each passing year and I never tired of hearing his recollection.

During the late 1930's, Dad and Uncle Jack had come to Washington, DC from the hamlet of Millersburg, PA, to seek their fortunes. The prospects for young men in Millersburg, located on the Susquehanna River, were limited to being a merchant, working in a shoe factory, or traveling miles to work in coal mines. During the post depression/prewar years, Washington, DC was booming with construction jobs and it offered employment opportunities for men throughout the mid Atlantic states. Dad and Uncle Jack would drive four hours from Millersburg to DC on a Sunday night, work Monday through Friday, return home for the weekend, then repeat the drive the following Sunday. The distance from Millersburg to DC was only 120 miles, but this was long before the Interstate Highway system. The tandem traveled through the historic towns of Gettysburg and Frederick, MD on their way to and from home. While working in DC, they lived in a boarding house a stone's throw from the Library of Congress where dinner was something of a Darwinian experience, as hungry construction workers fought for food served family style at a long dinner table.

The weekend of December 7th, they decided to stay in DC because they had been given tickets to a Washington Redskins football game vs. the Philadelphia Eagles at old Griffith Stadium. These Redskins were in their glory years as they made frequent trips to the NFL Championship game and featured future Hall of Fame quarterback Slingin' Sammy Baugh, the pride of Texas Christian University. Baugh was a triple threat player who was a pin-point passer, played defensive back, and often led the league in punting.

As Dad and Uncle Jack watched the game along with 27,000 plus fans, the P.A. announcer began making a series of announcements, "Would General _____ please report to his office. Would Admiral _____ please report to his office." The announcements for high ranking military officers to report to their respective offices continued throughout the game. Uncle Jack leaned over to Dad and said, "Charlie, something is up." Jack was prescient. No announcement was made during the game concerning Pearl Harbor because Redskins' owner George Preston Marshall did not want, "to distract fans from the game."

Indeed something was up. Newspaper boys, "Newsies," were outside Griffith Stadium following the game crying, "Extra, extra! Japan Bombs Pearl Harbor!" People relaxing at home after dinners of Maryland Fried Chicken or Virginia Smithfield Ham heard the news on radio stations WMAL, WRC, WJSV, and others. The news changed Washington, DC from a sleepy southern town, where the Nation's Capital just happened to be to a bustling and sometimes chaotic war town. As was the case for so many men and women the news changed my Dad's life as he joined the Army Air Corps and was stationed near London where he eventually became a bombardier flying missions over France and Germany.

Fast forward twenty-three years to November 22nd, 1963, the baby boomers' Day of Infamy. Our family had recently moved from The District to the suburb of Oxon Hill, MD, located about two miles outside the city. We still considered ourselves "Washingtonians" and were close enough to DC that our mail was post-marked "Washington, DC," and we could still see the Washington Monument in the distance from our subdivision.

It was Friday afternoon at Oxon Hill Elementary School, a school built in the early 20th century, which was surviving on fresh coats of paint and skillful patch work of contractors, plumbers, and handymen parents. It was not unusual to see fathers doing weekend patch up work and using U.S. Government vehicles. The afternoon of November 22nd, my fifth-grade class taught by Mrs. Sheen was busy creating Christmas decorations for the annual school bazaar. The decorations would be sold at the bazaar to raise money for some school need, such as a new film projector or landscaping the grounds.

My bright idea for a decoration was to attach holly from a large bush in our backyard and pinecones from a tree in our front yard to a ribbon which could be hung as a decoration anywhere in one's home. I decided that spraying the pinecones silver would be a nice touch so I "borrowed" a can of spray paint from my Dad's workshop as a finishing touch to my work of art. I showed Mrs. Sheen the elements of my decoration and she was less than thrilled with the idea of me using spray paint. She finally acquiesced and told me I could use the paint as long as I took everything outside, was careful, and used newspaper. I can't imagine a teacher letting a fifth grader loose today with a can of spray paint. The kid would have half the school "tagged" in a New York minute.

As instructed, I was careful with my aim, used newspaper, and completed my work just beyond the boundaries of the playground. I carefully attached the pinecones and holly to the ribbon, then moved my creation to a side door of the school with a sign that read, "DO NOT TOUCH! WET PAINT! PROPERTY OF G. DREIBELBIS! MERRY CHRISTMAS!"

When I returned to class I was met by a crying class and Mrs. Sheen trying to hold back tears and remain stoic. There was a large black and white TV on a cart with loud volume. "Gary, President Kennedy has been shot in Dallas and he may be dead. All we can do now is wait and pray." said Mrs. Sheen. All I could say was, "Why didn't somebody come outside and tell me?!?" It was the statement of a selfish fifth grader. Mrs. Sheen repeated in a warm voice as she attempted to hold back the tears, "Gary, will you please take your seat."

Shortly after I took my seat, CBS' Walter Cronkite, the most credible man in the nation, made the announcement, "From Dallas, Texas, the flash apparently official, President Kennedy died at 1 o'clock PM Central Standard Time, 2 o'clock Eastern Standard Time, some thirty minutes ago." Cronkite stared at the clock for a few seconds, fought back tears, and tried to continue his reporting. The tears and prayers intensified throughout the class. Mrs. Conway, our school principal, echoed the news we had just heard because not all classes had TVs. She also announced that teachers and classes without TV sets could move in an orderly manner to classes with TVs.

As for me, I wanted to cry with the others but could not. I didn't know the meaning of the word "surreal" but that is the way I felt. This could not be happening. This is the kind of thing that happens in other countries, those Godless Communist countries and third world countries. Not only was the President dead but this was an affront to my nation and hometown.

The details came in slowly from Dallas. Dan Rather, then a reporter for Dallas' CBS affiliate KRLD, was the "Go To" man giving first hand information as it was given to him. Rather recapped not only what was known about the assassination but moment by moment information concerning the alleged assassin Lee Harvey Oswald.

Sorrow soon turned to fear and the questions started to flow. Who was responsible for this? Was it a Communist plot? Was the Soviet Union or Cuba involved? Would Soviet MIGS be flying up the Potomac and bombing us to pieces? Many of us thought these were valid questions because of our vast storehouses of knowledge and the information we had gleaned from our parents' dinner table conversations. There was nothing worse than a group of snot-nosed fifth graders playing junior news analysts.

The confusion intensified because our school leaders did not know what to do. It was well past 2 o'clock and school dismissed at 3 PM so it was silly to dismiss classes for less than an hour; still, mothers with cars descended upon the school demanding to pick up their children. This added to the chaos and the principal decided to allow children to go home with their parents. Dad had our only car and Mom didn't drive so this was a moot point for me. I continued to feel numb as I watched the coverage until I heard my bus boarding announcement over the P.A. system.

It is amazing for me to consider this event today and how slowly the news came in because I am looking at it through 2017 lenses. In my college mass media classes I have shown a documentary produced by CBS, "Four Days in November," an excellent compilation of the events of November 22-25 presented in two hours. Watching the events unfold is the video equivalent of watching paint dry or grass grow. This is because there was no electronic news gathering equipment such as portable cameras, videotape, and satellite trucks. Events were recorded on film which took time to process. CBS was so desperate to get footage

4

on air that technicians ran partially developed film or "wet stock" where viewers could see the water marks on the film.

News coverage was also different for newspapers. When I arrived home at about 3:30, there was the usual bundle of newspapers by my front gate. I was a paperboy for the now defunct Washington Evening Star which for years had been the queen of Washington newspapers with outstanding reporters and columnists.

The Star covered the Metro scene with the typical issues and crime reports of any city newspaper as well as the national political scene. It was in many regards a national newspaper.

As I opened my bundle of papers, I noticed that there was no news of the assassination because the paper had gone to press before it occurred. The only story concerning President Kennedy was that he was in Dallas for a political trip. I dropped the papers in my wagon and began delivering to the sixty customers on my route. Many of them were waiting for me at their doors, hoping to read more details about the assassination and I had to explain that the papers were probably being loaded into delivery trucks at the time of the event. Most customers understood and continued to watch the coverage on TV. A few, mostly cranky senior citizens, complained, and some illogically blamed me for the lack of coverage. One older woman questioned my ancestry. She was holding a can of National Bohemian beer as the curses flew. I finished my route at twilight the kind of sky that was a precursor to Thanksgiving.

My father would soon be home from his job with General Services Administration and we would dine on the usual Friday fare of lima bean casserole. Dinner preparation was in progress as I checked in with Mom. Suddenly, I heard the familiar grind of the newspaper truck coming around the corner and heading to our house. The truck was orange and brown with the words "Evening Star" emblazoned on its sides in old English lettering. I ran to the truck driven by the route manager, Mr. Zollinhoffer, who explained in breathy tones that The Star had decided to run an extra because of the assassination. Extras were unheard of and were a thing of the past by the early 1960s. He explained that I was to offer the extra edition of the paper to my usual customers for ten cents, and if I had extra papers left I could sell them on the street.

Mr. Zollinhoffer went on to explain that he was finishing his regular deliveries when The Star radioed him telling him to return to Star headquarters to pick up the extra editions. He turned his truck around and headed back through DC's madhouse of rush hour traffic. It was pitch dark by the time I made my extra delivery.

The papers were loaded into my wagon and I began knocking on customers' doors to offer them the extras. Selling the papers was no problem as demand exceeded supply. Many customers wanted multiple copies of the paper to keep as grim souvenirs of the event. I told customers of the orders given to me that I was to sell only one paper to each customer. It was difficult for me to maintain my "Star Boy Ethics" because people were offering me $1 a paper. One customer offered me $10 for five papers. People approached me on the street and offered $1 or more per paper but I politely told them of The Star's policy. Almost every customer bought a paper with the exception being the elderly woman with the National Bohemian beer can. "No thanks," she snarled. "Besides, I voted for Nixon," and the door slammed. I assumed that she had consumed more than one can of Natty Boh.

After making my deliveries I had a bright idea and ran home. I called The Star's newsboy circulation department, identified myself and route number, and requested as many extra papers as The Star would provide. Within an hour I had 100 papers delivered to my front gate and began my second round of deliveries. People soon got the word that I was back on the streets, and I sold out the supply before the third street on my route. Most people paid $1 a paper so I made a healthy profit of over $150, not bad for 1963.

After counting my gain, I joined my parents and watched the CBS coverage on our 17-inch black and white RCA TV. Air Force One had landed at nearby Andrews Air Force base and Dad swore that the plane had flown over our house during its descent into Andrews.

Television crews had made their way to Andrews with their cumbersome video equipment. One of the first images was of the President's casket being manhandled off a delivery truck and transferred to a hearse.

Mrs. Kennedy was also on the truck and a serviceman assisted her by placing his hands under her armpits and unceremoniously lifting her off the rear of the truck. She was still wearing the pink dress she had worn in Dallas, refusing to change clothes, despite the fact that JFK's blood was splattered on her dress. "Let them see what they have done." she reportedly said.

The hearse would make its way to The White House during the late evening but I never saw that coverage. My parents ordered me to join my younger brother Doug who was already asleep in our bedroom. There was no TV in our room so radio was my companion as I turned the dial to WTOP to monitor events.

After the casket had been delivered to The White House there was little happening as DC and the rest of the nation fell into an uneasy sleep. Radio took TV's lead by playing somber classical music throughout the night. Both cancelled all programming and commercials for the entire weekend and Monday.

With the music turned low, the gravity of the situation hit me. Our President John F. Kennedy was dead. My selfishness had overcome me. I had been selfish at school when I chastised my classmates for not coming outside the school to tell me the news. Later, profit was my motive as I sold newspapers not thinking that I was capitalizing on our President's death. As I listened to the music in the darkness of my bedroom, I felt shame that I was a selfish kid. What intensified the feeling was that most kids seemed to like the Kennedy family and it made no difference whether the parents were Republicans or Democrats. Kids had a vague recollection of President Dwight Eisenhower. We knew through school that he was a great war hero but to us he seemed old and unenergetic. His wife Mamie seemed to be a nice person but to most of us she appeared to have the appearance of a well dressed grandmother.

The Kennedy clan oozed cool. JFK in contrast to President Eisenhower was much younger, had a full head of hair, a great smile, and appeared to be tan even on our black and white TVs. Jacqueline Kennedy was stylish and attractive. Young girls wanted to emulate her, and prepubescent boys simply stared at her with open mouths. Later, people would compare her to Mary Tyler Moore on The Dick Van Dyke Show. The Kennedys also had kids and we could see Caroline run around The White House and the Hyannis Port family compound. The average kid could relate to them. As I thought of the Kennedys, I experienced a delayed emotional reaction. I processed the finality of the situation: We would never see JFK smile or wave again.

Saturday, November 23rd was uneventful for the most part, as preparations were made for the JFK's funeral on Monday. More information was released concerning Kennedy's alleged assassin Lee Harvey Oswald. In an announcement which stunned many the National Football League decided to play its scheduled games on Sunday the 24th.

The Sunday November 24th coverage was interrupted in the afternoon with the startling shooting of Lee Harvey Oswald by Dallas nightclub owner Jack Ruby at Dallas police headquarters as he was being transferred to county facilities. Oswald died shortly thereafter. We saw the shooting and Oswald being lifted into an ambulance, his face ashen and body lifeless. My parents and I wondered what could happen next. Information trickled in concerning Jack Ruby: He was a Dallas nightclub owner, a glad hander, and one who knew the Dallas police. The event and motive seemed random and senseless to many.

Meanwhile, the President lay in state in the rotunda of the U.S. Capitol, as 250,000 mourners filed past to pay their last respects. At one point the line extended at least twenty blocks to DC Stadium, now RFK Stadium, and many were turned away by the time the viewing had concluded.

My father awakened me early the morning of the 25th. "We're going downtown." he said, and I wasn't sure what he meant. Then it dawned on me that he wanted to go downtown to see the JFK's funeral procession.

Following a quick breakfast, we headed to downtown DC as the sun rose over the Anacostia River. Dad navigated the back streets of Southwest DC which ran through some of the poorest neighborhoods in the District, and headed to his secret parking space near his work at the General Services Administration Building on 7th Street S.W.

As we walked through the biting cold, damp November air we could see the crowds forming on Pennsylvania Avenue, the route for the funeral procession. We were able to worm our way to the Old Post Office Building which is now a Donald Trump Luxury Hotel. Dad refused to follow the sheep. The crowd at street level was rows deep so we eventually climbed to the top stairs of the Old Post Office for a better view.

The procession eventually left the Capitol and proceeded down Pennsylvania Avenue. TV cameras were perched atop a building near where we were standing. Television crews had worked around the clock to haul cable and position cameras to cover the procession and burial at Arlington Cemetery.

The crowd tried to guess when we may see the procession reach our point of view. Some had transistor radios and monitored the procession's progress as it left the Capitol grounds. The true indicator of the precession's progress came from the haunting sound of the muffled drums in the distance. I had never heard anything like them. Gradually the drums became louder and we knew the procession was near.

Soon we saw the casket and caisson, then the riderless horse followed by a sea of humanity, dignitaries from all over the world who had come to pay their respects. French President Charles DeGaulle and Ethiopia's Emperor Haile Selassie were the most recognizable to us and in the first wave of dignitaries. The crowd was silent, and there were few snapping photographs. Dad did not bring a camera and he was much more concerned about us shuffling to gain a better vantage point.

The procession took several minutes to pass us, as it proceeded west towards the mall then to the Lincoln Memorial before crossing the Potomac River on its way to Arlington Cemetery. The crowd stood in silence for what seemed to be many minutes before dispersing to catch DC Transit buses, making their way to distant cars, or simply walking home. Aside from the crowd, DC was a ghost town with government offices and businesses closed.

Dad and I made our way to the car and then wound our way through the S.W. and S.E. streets to a Little Tavern Shopp where we might get hamburgers and hot chocolate. We found that the Little Tavern Shoppe on Pennsylvania Avenue near where we used to live in the Anacostia section of DC was open and full. We got burgers, coffee for him, and hot chocolate for me. We rode home and the radio was the only sound in Dad's 1956 Ford Customline.

Mom greeted us at the door but there was little communication. My brother Doug was six years old and had only limited appreciation of what had transpired. We watched TV and there were replays of the burial at Arlington. Members of the color guard folded the U.S. flag and presented it to Mrs. Kennedy as the band played the U.S. Navy Hymn, Eternal Father Strong to Save. In approximately 72 hours our President had been assassinated and buried. It was all difficult for my ten year old mind to comprehend.

School was in session the next day and people pretended to resume a normal lifestyle with businesses reopening and TV resuming regular programming and commercials. Pictures of the late President appeared in storefront windows. The nation slowly became accustomed to the words "President Lyndon Baines Johnson."

Somehow things began to return to normal, but not really. We knew that we no longer lived in a Leave it to Beaver, Father Knows Best world of '50's sitcoms. It is an overused term, but it was the end of an age of innocence. You didn't have to be a sociologist, historian, or political pundit to arrive at this conclusion. Even a ten year old kid could figure it out.

3305 D. STREET S.E.

I was born Gary Charles Dreibelbis, April 17th, 1953, at old Providence Hospital on the S.E. side of DC. Providence was a pre-Civil War Catholic hospital and it was never clear to me why my parents chose it. Perhaps it was the choice of Mom's doctor, Dr. Strawbridge. Years later Mom told me that Dr. Strawbridge often enjoyed more than a few drinks and that most women hoped to give birth before happy hour. Unfortunately, I did not coincide with the doctor's timetable and I was born at 1:35 AM. Mom reminded me of this each year as she awakened me at 1:35 AM each year in my respective time zone to sing happy birthday to me, a tradition for which I should have been grateful but became more annoying to me with each passing year. On April 17th, 1953, the New York Yankees great Mickey Mantle hit a 565-foot home run off the Washington Senators' Chuck Stobbs, which cleared the bleachers of Griffith Stadium and landed in a neighbor's yard across the street. Dad always said that Mantle knew I had arrived and he hit the homer to celebrate my birth.

3305 D. Street S.E. was where I spent my first six years. Dad always said that we lived in Anacostia but it was technically Greenway, home to working class families and retirees. It is now one of the poorest sections of DC Our apartment was a one bedroom affair but Dad was a handyman and able to enclose the back porch to create a second bedroom. The new bedroom featured a radio that Dad had embedded into one of the walls.

The living room was large and housed two of Dad's most prized possessions: a 17-inch black and white RCA TV, which had two closing doors and looked like a piece of furniture; the other, a curious piece of furniture called a shell table. The shell table resembled the shell of a giant clam and had a large surface suitable for holding a clock or other large objects. The table was purchased prior to Dad's marriage to Mom and I believe that Mom thought it was hideous. A comparison could be made between the shell table and the classic film A Christmas Story when the father won a woman's leg lamp as a "major award." The father cherished the lamp which the Mom despised, and she was secretly filled with joy when the lamp broke. Unfortunately, the shell table was a large durable piece of furniture that was a fixture in my parents' home until Dad died.

There was a small kitchen and dining area which completed the layout. It was enough room for a family with two small children and there was the bonus of a large backyard shared by the apartment's eight units. The downside was that the backyard was only partially fenced so the yard became a convenient "pooping station" for neighborhood dogs. This produced something of a canine produced minefield and we had to exercise caution during backyard activities. The mines were more visible when it snowed along with accompanying yellow snow.

3305 was a long block away from Minnesota Ave., a major thoroughfare linking much of S.E. DC. Kimball Elementary, my first school, was little more than a football field's distance from our apartment. Two blocks north of 3305 were the railroad tracks of the Baltimore and Ohio Railroad. I could walk to our front sidewalk and see the trains in the distance.

There was literally an "other side of the tracks" on D Street. "The other side" was an enclave for a number of black families living in homes that were a step above shanties. Years later I discovered that many of these families had migrated from the South and also from the S.W. section of DC. Those from S.W. had ancestors who had been members of alley communities. Over half of the dwellings in S.W. lacked bathrooms and over 70 percent lacked central heating. Outdoor spigots were the only plumbing for many of the dwellings which were only a few blocks away from the U.S. Capitol.

Whether or not it was official, DC was a segregated city during my childhood. It was in most ways a southern city a fact that I did not appreciate until I attended college in the Midwest. Blacks had their own neighborhoods, movie theatres, clubs, and restaurants. There were sections of DC which rivaled the richness of Harlem's culture. Many forget that DC is the birthplace of the great Duke Ellington and that he performed in DC before moving on to Harlem's brighter lights.

As for our side of the tracks, we didn't have a great deal in the way of post-war material possessions with the exception of the TV set and shell table. Dad paid $700 for the TV set, worth thousands by today's standards and who knows what for the shell table. If the table was at a

Goodwill or Thrift Store today it would not be labeled as an antique; instead, there would be a "Please Take" sign on it. It wouldn't even merit a "Best Offer."

My parents did not have a car when I was born. Dad walked a block to catch a green and white DC Transit bus to his office at GSA. When my Aunt Mary became ill with terminal cancer, Dad had to borrow a car for us to visit her in Harrisburg, PA. Our first family car was a used Studebaker which resembled something from an old Buck Rogers movie. Despite the fact it was used, the Studebaker was way ahead of its time with features such as push button transmission and a heater which warmed backseat riders. By 1956 Dad had graduated to a black and white Ford Customline. It was a handsome car with one drawback. My parents and I noticed that cars in front of us would slow down for no apparent reason. Family friends laughed when we told them this and they had a ready answer—we looked like a DC police car.

The Ford Customline far surpassed the TV and shell table as my Dad's pride and joy and his sentiment was shared by Mom. I can remember us driving to nearby Fort Dupont Park which was within walking distance of our apartment, grilling hamburgers, and my folks starring moon-eyed at the car with pride. We had the car for ten reliable years until a drunk driver crashed into it in front of our house. I think a small piece of my Dad's heart went with the Ford when he had to get rid of it.

Our apartment was not close to shopping so we drove about ¾ of a mile to the neighborhood dubbed Greenway, a major business area featuring a variety of businesses including clothing stores, a bowling alley, the Senate Theatre which had a large black clientele, and the king of grocery stores, Giant Food.

It may sound strange to wax poetic about a grocery store but Giant, a chain of stores in the DC/Baltimore area, was way ahead of its competition and was responsible for many of the grocery store features that we take for granted today. Giants were the first grocery stores to feature in-store bakeries and the baked goods were as good as any in the DC area. Giant bakeries were called Heidi Bakeries and featured customized cakes. I always demanded that my birthday cakes were Heidi Bakery cakes. Fresh seafood was another Giant feature with seafood freshly caught from the ocean and nearby Chesapeake Bay.

Fresh crabs, oysters and clams were only a couple of hours away from DC stores. As I grew older and my palate became more sophisticated I came to love blue crab and I maintain there is nothing quite like it as to shellfish fare.

Giants featured live lobsters with taped claws in tanks. If I became separated from my parents they never had to bother the store manager with having to make a "We have a lost child announcement" over the P.A. system. They knew that I would be observing the lobsters in their small watery domicile.

Giant also introduced unit pricing, something shoppers take for granted today, as well as appointing dietician Esther Petersen as an advisor for healthy eating. All these features plus excellent customer service made Giant a favorite with DC consumers. Eventually, Giant developed Super Giants, featuring food, clothing and other durable goods. Super Giants became the forerunner to K-Marts and Wal-Marts.

By 1959 Dad determined that we needed more living space reasoning that as Doug and I became older we would need more room and a poop free backyard. He found out that an elderly couple from our church had a row house for rent on Minnesota Ave. in the Anacostia section of town about two miles from our apartment. We made the move to the new residence in June of '59 on the hottest day of the year.

Today the Greenway section of DC is one of the poorest sections of the District, where drugs are plentiful and crack houses numerous. There are a couple of diamonds in the rough. Fort Dupont, a wooded area which was once a Civil War fort, is a recreational area for picnics, ice skating, and top rated summer concerts. The Washington Nationals have built a baseball academy for youngsters with state of the art baseball facilities behind Kimball Elementary School, a short walk from our old apartment. The academy offers baseball instruction as well as a healthy afternoon meal and academic tutoring after baseball activities. It is a prime example of what Major League Baseball teams can do for the community and the academy received a major thumbs-up from MLB Commissioner, Rob Manfred.

Such as it was, 3305 D Street was our first home, and one always remembers firsts. One can only hope for the best as to neighborhood improvements for the current residents of Greenway—a place so near but so far away from the U.S. Capitol building.

2304 MINNESOTA AVE

We made the move to the 2304 Minnesota Ave. following the school year. While I missed the apartment, and most kids don't like transitions, the move was an adventure. Our family friend Myrtle babysat Doug and me while four men from Anacostia Movers, who looked as though they could be defensive linemen from the Washington Redskins, moved our belongings.

"Aunt" Myrtle attended our church and was one of my family's best friends. Myrtle's house was within walking distance of our house and our family visited her on numerous occasions. She was considered a "special" family friend and years later I found out why. She had an alcoholic husband, Earl, who made daily stops at the liquor store about 100 feet from our house to pick up six packs of Ballentine or Carling Black Label beer. When we went to visit Myrtle and Earl, he would be drinking one brand of beer or the other while chain smoking Kent cigarettes. Earl's day job was working for AT&T and one of his responsibilities was running the phone lines from the press box to the bench for Washington Redskins' games.

Within a few days we were settled in our new home, but there were a few details which needed attention. During the first days of residing in the new home, we had to endure snowy TV signals because we had no roof antenna. After a few days Dad climbed on the roof to install an antenna while the rest of the family finished breakfast. Mom decided to serve me tomato juice instead of my usual apple and I complained loudly about the beverage change. She reasoned that you make the best of things following a move. My immediate response was "Yuk!" and I poured most of the juice in her coffee when she left the kitchen. Realizing what I had done and that there may be consequences I announced that I was going upstairs to see what Dad was doing on the roof. Five minutes later Mom joined us. Perhaps Momma Sherlock noticed that her half-filled coffee was suddenly full. Perhaps she noticed a certain thickness to her coffee as well as acidic taste. Perhaps she noticed my hasty retreat upstairs to "help" my Dad. In any event, I was busted. She marched me downstairs to the kitchen, made me drink a

15

full glass of tomato juice, and topped it off by putting red pepper on my tongue. This was her preferred method of punishment for dishonesty instead of washing my mouth out with soap. Believe me I would have preferred a bar of Dove any time to McCormick's red pepper.

On the plus side, things progressed well as to the TV antenna installation and arrangement of living room furniture. By Sunday night we had a clear TV signal and were able to watch our family favorite, Disneyland. The next morning, we discovered that our new residence was not trouble free. Mom came in to our bedroom and discovered a roach crawling across Doug's face. Mom was not a screamer but she did tell Dad that they would have to go to all-out war against the roaches. The problem was that they had no idea as to the scope of the war.

During the house walkthrough my folks had examined the basement and were satisfied that it was a large usable space in need of renovation. The former tenants were hoarders of the worse kind and had left behind piles of newspapers and magazines for no apparent reason. I swear that some of them must have dated back to the Coolidge administration. Lurking within these piles were scores of roaches. People have heard of roach motels but these piles served as high rise roach condos.

The first line of defense was use of a heavy insecticide that my Dad brought home from work (probably used as gas warfare during World War I) followed by removing the piles of paper. A brave family friend, who apparently received some form of hazardous duty pay from Dad, hauled the piles of paper to the dump. Next, Dad painted a substance called No Roach on all the cracks and where the walls met the floor. No Roach looked more like a pancake topping than an insecticide. It was effective but the downside was that you had to clean up piles of sticky roaches. Eventually my folks won the roach war.

Our new living arrangement was a curious one and years later when I describe it people think that I have been using some mind altering substance. We occupied the main floor consisting of a living room, two bedrooms, and a kitchen/dining area leading to the basement. There were French doors which separated the living room from the hallway and stairs. Upstairs was a small one bedroom apartment with a large bedroom and small kitchen. It was a glorified studio apartment. At the opposite end of the hallway was another bedroom. The units were rented to separate parties. In the middle of the hallway was a bathroom shared by our family and the upstairs tenants. This was the only bathroom in the building so morning preparation for work and school became something of a bathroom revolving door.

The occupants of the small apartment were a young woman named Velma, a single mother, and her baby daughter Irene. It was the first time I had known anything about a single parent family. The bedroom at the opposite end of the hallway was occupied by a government clerk named Mack who was probably in his '50's.

I had a schoolboy crush on Velma who was in her early 20's and very attractive. She worked for PEPCO, the Potomac Electric Power Company, and would always bring me treats after work. Velma taught me to appreciate rock music and two of the first songs I can remember were Lipstick on your Collar and Tequila blaring on radio station WEAM.

One late summer afternoon, Velma came home and ran upstairs. After a few moments I decided to run upstairs as well to see what was going on. When I got to her apartment the door was open so I ran through the kitchen into the living room. The living room opened into the bedroom and there was no door between the two. It was the first time I saw a nude woman and I liked what I saw. I believe at that very moment I arrived at puberty. Freud talks about a latent period but I believed I bypassed it going from zero to sixty at that point. I can never remember saying, "Yuk! It's a girl." Females became wonderful, mysterious creatures to me after I saw Velma.

Velma looked at me as I stared and softly said, "Gary, you don't belong here." This was great insight into the obvious so I retreated downstairs to watch Bozo the Clown on Channel Four. Bozo was not nearly as interesting as what I had seen upstairs.

One Sunday afternoon there was a knock at our door. My parents were taking their customary nap while I watched cartoons at low volume. I answered the door and there was a man whom I vaguely remembered in military dress. "Hi Gary! I'm your cousin Lynn. Are your folks at home?" Lynn was one of my North Carolina cousins from Mom's side of the family and I remembered him from Grandfather's funeral a couple of years earlier.

I invited him to come in and he sat in the living room while I awakened Mom and Dad. Mom thought that she was dreaming, but my parents eventually made it to the living room and greeted the smiling Lynn. He informed us that he had been stationed at Aberdeen Air force base some forty miles away and that he could see us on weekends when he got a pass. Mom was pleased and Dad was happy that she had a relative from "down home" that would come and visit on a regular basis. We had very little contact with the North Carolina relatives.

Mom invited Lynn for dinner even though we usually had our main meal after church consisting of either roast beef or ham. Sunday nights were traditionally for homemade ice cream made with an old fashioned, hand cranked ice cream maker. The ice cream maker had been obtained with Top Value stamps, similar to Green Stamps which were given to customers based upon how much you purchased from a local store. You pasted stamps into stamp books and redeemed the stamps for a variety of items listed in a catalog. Mom improvised dinner for Lynn consisting of left over roast beef, snacks, and all the homemade ice cream he could eat. He seemed very satisfied and it had to be a couple of steps up from the usual chow hall grub.

Making homemade ice cream was a fun process for the entire family. Mom would whip up the concoction which included cream with the flavor du jour and poured it into a aluminum canister. The canister was placed inside the outer container with a hand crank. Ice was poured around the canister and rock salt was poured on which assisted in the freezing process. Dad, Doug, and I took turns cranking the canister, each person cranking until his arms were tired. The process took about thirty minutes as you cranked and added more ice and salt about every five to ten minutes. The result was a soft, flavorful, 2 gallons of pure joy.

Mom's specialty was teaberry ice cream. Teaberries were small, round red candy-type berries we obtained from our Pennsylvania relatives. Teaberry ice cream was a Pennsylvania Dutch specialty and little known in the DC area. Years later the Clark Chewing Gum Company scored when it made teaberry chewing gum. Clark featured teaberry gum on TV commercials where people danced "The Teaberry Shuffle."

The Sunday tradition in our household was for my folks to nap in the afternoon following dinner while Doug and I quietly watched cartoons, start ice cream at 4PM, enjoy ice cream at 4:30, attend the Sunday evening church service at 5:30 (the Southern Baptist were big on Sunday evening church services). 5:30 may seem like an unusual

18

time start a church service but our pastor, Rev. Charles Holland, was a master of demographic research. The service was originally held at 7PM; however, after talking to parishioners he realized that he was up against Disney and The Ed Sullivan Show, tough competition even when you are promoting God. He moved the service to 5:30 to avoid TV competition and attendance soon doubled. This allowed everyone to return home by 7PM in time for Disney, with Ed Sullivan at 8PM. This also allowed our family time to eat more ice cream following church.

Lynn enjoyed our company and the food when he came, but after a few weeks he was enjoying something else—Velma. He noticed her comings and goings when he came to visit and soon started asking questions about her. It wasn't long until the two were dating. At first I was jealous but then came to my senses, knowing that Velma deserved an older man; besides, how can you compete with a man in a uniform?

Lynn and Velma were a cute couple but cuteness could only go so far. For some reason after dates they started smooching in the bathroom, the only bathroom in the house. This became a major problem because after having my usual Saturday night treat of pop corn and Royal Crown Cola I needed to use the facility. I would climb to the top of the stairs and watch Lynn and Velma engage in long smoochfests. When it seemed as if I was about to burst with everything under my belt disengaging from the rest of my body I would start whistling. "Oh Gary. Would you like to use the bathroom? We're sorry." The smoochfest moved to the hallway while I used the bathroom as quickly as I could.

Lynn and Velma married within a few months before a small group at our church. My parents arranged to have their reception in our now clean, roach-free basement, complete with wedding cake and punch made from a frozen cylinder that you melted by pouring ginger ale over it. It was a low-budget but satisfactory affair.

Speaking of the clean, roach-free basement, it became the bedroom for Doug and me shortly after the wedding. To many today it may have seemed primitive but it became our 'Little Man's Den." Dad ripped out the shelves which had held the papers for the roach condo to make more space. He painted the floor fire engine red with paint that he had obtained from work. Stand-alone closets and a bureau were placed in the middle of the basement cutting it in half so half the basement was our bedroom while the other half a play area.

The basement opened into a large narrow backyard, and once again Dad used his special spatial skills to divide the yard into garden and play areas. Home grown tomatoes were Dad's specialty and there was nothing like a burger with a slice of tomato with lemonade on a hot August evening.

Our world outside the rowhouse was entirely different from the apartment on D Street. D Street offered little noise. There was the sound of trains passing in the distance and some noise from street football games. There was so little traffic that players never had to worry about being hit by cars.

The Anacostia and Minnesota Avenues of those days bustled with activity. It was also one of the most diverse areas of DC. If one turned left from our front lawn and walked north they would see a Chinese laundry operating out of a rowhouse eight doors from our house. Continue on for a few feet and there was Katz' Market complete with hand crafted sandwiches and household basics. Mr. Katz was the kids' friend because we could redeem soda bottles found on neighborhood streets for two cents apiece. He was also like Sesame Street's shop owner Mr. Hooper in that he knew all the neighborhood kids and would let you buy on credit because he knew where you lived. Walk a few more steps and there was a bakery with wonderful smells and a display window chocked full of cakes and other goodies. Sorry, Heidi Bakery. I had my first cinnamon roll there at Stevanson's Bakery. Various baked goods were placed into black and white checkered boxes.

Soon you reached the corner of Minnesota and Pennsylvania Ave. the same Pennsylvania Ave. as is home to the White House only four miles away. Our perception then was that it was in a different world 400 miles away. In reality it was about a fifteen minute drive, if the traffic was moving and you hit all the traffic lights at the right intervals.

On the corner of Penn and Minnesota was Bretler's Drug Store where my folks got our prescriptions. It was distinguished by its large neon sign with a giant pestle and mortar and by the fact that Old Man Bretler believed that Coca Cola syrup was the best remedy for curing a stomach ache. I faked more than one stomach ache to get a couple of table spoons of the sweet elixir.

When you crossed Penn Ave. you hit L'Enfant Plaza named for the Frenchman who designed DC Pierre L'Enfant. It was a nondescript park with a bus stop, some park benches, and dozens of squirrels. Today it is home to drug deals and homeless people. DC's designer deserves better. Facing the park was Morton's Department store where many neighborhood families purchased there back-to-school clothes. Doug and I got some clothes from Morton's but most came from hand me downs from our older cousins.

Turning left from Morton's and heading west on Penn Ave. you passed liquor stores and bars frequented by working class government workers before hitting the John Phillip Sousa Bridge, named for The March King, which spans the Anacostia River. The Anacostia was always the poor stepchild to the Potomac because it was so polluted and muddy. Today, some boaters sail on the Anacostia while other brave souls go fishing. There have been recent attempts by conservationists to clean up and revive the river. Beneath the bridge is Anacostia Park the setting for crime novelist George P. Pelecanos' book Down By the River where the Dead Men Go. My friends and I would play in the park during safer times.

Crossing the Sousa bridge you reached Barney Circle the launch point for streetcars connecting Anacostia and downtown. You could walk or ride a bus to the circle, pay twenty-five cents and travel to a new world of Capitol Hill, The Mall and The Smithsonian Buildings, Downtown, and if you were really adventurous, travel all the way to Georgetown.

Across from Barney Circle was Congressional Cemetery, the final resting place for American heroes such as Henry Clay, Daniel Webster, and John Phillip Sousa. During my childhood it was little more than a weed patch and those at rest there certainly deserved better. In recent years, preservationists have cleaned up the cemetery and it is now a more fitting final home to some of America's greats. In 2013, "Eco Goats" were used to clear the brush and poison ivy from the cemetery. The "Eco Goats" drew world-wide publicity for their efforts. Congressional Cemetery is also the final resting place for FBI Head J. Edgar Hoover. A cemetery caretaker told me that one of the few problems that occur at the cemetery is that people leave pink high heels shoes on Hoover's grave. I will leave this to the reader's imagination and research as to why this is the case.

Re-crossing Sousa Bridge and heading east, there was another small world of businesses. Before Domino's and Pizza Hut there were relatively few pizza places in DC. One of the first was near the corner of Penn and Minnesota Aves., Mario's which opened in the late '30's. I had my first slice of pizza there, purchased with allowance and bottle return money. Mom wouldn't go there because she thought she wouldn't like pizza. Pizza was one of several of her culinary dislikes which I never understood. She didn't like brownies, chicken, or turkey. She would order a small ham for herself and prepare turkey for everyone else at Thanksgiving. It was up to Dad to make the dressing and turkey gravy.

As for pizza and me it was love at first bite. My first slice was pepperoni, sausage, and mushroom. I ordered this combo because the high school kid and his girlfriend in front of me in line ordered it and I didn't want to appear to be a novice. I continue to order this combo today. Later, I would discover that DC pizza was similar to the New York "slice" with crust that would fold over.

Before 7-11s there were High's Dairy Stores in the DC area where you could purchase dairy products and other basics. Moving up the avenue was a strip mall with Tucker's Restaurant where I had my first restaurant dining experience. Tucker's was known to the locals as Tommy Tucker's, although the owner Mr. Tucker's real name was Fred. Tucker's had killer Salisbury steak and hot fudge sundaes. People's Drug Store, a chain that ruled the Washington-Baltimore drug store market for years, was sandwiched between Tucker's and the Highland Theatre, one of two theatres serving our neighborhood. Heading back home and turning right from our house was the liquor store where Earl bought his daily stash and a DGS, District Grocery Store. DGSs were small independently owned grocery stores scattered throughout the city. An alley next to the DGS led to our church, and we were able to walk from our house to church in five minutes. One walking down the alley today would find that it is a bustling business area. Unfortunately, the business is dealing crack cocaine.

Near our church was a huge mansion, The Frederick Douglass House. It was on a large parcel of land, which seemed out of place in the midst of the surrounding row houses. There was a large hill in front of the mansion which was ideal for sledding when the snows came. Parents would dress kids in layers of clothes to the point where we looked like an army of Michelin Men. It wasn't until later in school history classes we learned that we were sledding in the front yard of the great abolitionist Frederick Douglass. We learned that Douglass fought for equal rights for all and was famous for the quotation, "I would unite with anybody to do right, with nobody to do wrong." It is one of my favorite quotations from any orator. The Douglass Mansion is opened to the public today.

On the subject of snow in DC, it was a matter of whether you were you pleased or frightened. If you were a kid you were pleased, because if it snowed more than an inch in the DC area it meant no school. If you were an adult it was an entirely different story. The problem was that DC drivers are terrible snow drivers, and I don't think that the situation has improved over the years. Drivers make excuses that DC has a "different kind of snow" and claim that it is wetter and more hazardous than snow in other parts of the country. Part of the problem is that many DC residents were/are transplants from other parts of the U.S. and have never driven in snow. This means that numerous rookie snow drivers were menaces on city streets. Another problem is that the city can be difficult to navigate in normal weather due to its circles, squares, and other geometric shapes that dot its city streets.

The other panic attack regarding snow in the DC area is that people hit grocery stores as if it were the Normandy Invasion loading up on milk, bread, and other essentials. People who don't even drink milk buy enough milk to last until a spring thaw. Liquor stores do their fair share of business with people figuring that a little nectar of the gods will make cabin fever bearable.

Backtracking down Minnesota Ave. and heading east, one would encounter more brick row houses until coming to the Good Hope Road/Nichols Ave. Nichols is now Martin Luther King Avenue and features parades celebrating Dr. King's birthday. One of the most famous businesses on the avenue was Curtis Brother's Furniture, featuring the World's Largest Chair in the parking lot. Curtis Brothers is long gone but the chair remains as a landmark. The sad aspect of today's Anacostia neighborhood is that unless you consider Popeye's Chicken or Mc Donald's sit-down restaurants there were no sit-down restaurants in Anacostia as of this writing. In November, 2011, The Uniontown Bar and Grill, an establishment rivaling those on Dupont Circle or Georgetown, was closed by law officials because it was a front for cocaine trafficking.

Back at home, I believed that our family pioneered the concept of the "Staycation" during our time in Anacostia. We didn't have the funds to travel to Disneyland or other premiere vacation spots so Dad would take off a week of work and we would take day trips never traveling more than sixty miles from home. We had our favorite , familiar destinations that we visited each year, and we seemed to thrive on the familiarity. It got to the point that if it was Monday we knew we would be headed to point A.

One of our favorite attractions was The Enchanted Forest, located in Ellicott City near Baltimore, a fairy tale theme park similar to those built in the suburbs of large cities across the country. The Enchanted Forest was a far cry from Disneyland or Knotts Berry Farm. Admission was $1 for adults and fifty cents for kids.

You were greeted by a large white castle with orange spires which would never pass for Disney's Cinderella's Castle. Inside, some of the features included a motorized Mother Goose, and you could ride in goose train cars, Little Tug, a working tug boat that you could ride on a lake, as well as a trip through "Shoe" of The Old Woman who had so many children she didn't know what to do. Perhaps birth control was not an option in her time. The park eventually closed and the attractions were moved to a nearby farm where people can still visit. There is no trespassing at the original site with a dragon figure and sign warning people to stay away.

For amusement parks, we had Glen Echo and Marshall Hall. Glen Echo was the bigger and more popular of the two and you could take a street car to get there. It was on the other side of us in Montgomery County, MD, and for some reason Dad refused to go there. Glen Echo had a huge swimming pool, ideal for the oppressive DC summers, but the management refused to allow blacks to swim in the pool. Dad never said anything but I believe it was a reason why we didn't visit Glen Echo.

Marshall Hall was the family choice for an amusement park. It was situated in southern Maryland on the banks of the Potomac and across the river from George Washington's Mount Vernon. Marshall Hall featured all the traditional amusement park rides, headlined by one of the best wooden roller coasters on the east coast, along with The Mad Mouse where you rode in a mouse car and always felt as if you were going to fall off the elevated tracks.

A special trip to Marshall Hall was on the S.S. Mount Vernon cruise boat. The S.S. Mount Vernon was docked at Maine St. and sailed south on the Potomac to Marshall Hall and Mount Vernon. You could debark at either location, spend a few hours there, and then catch the boat back to DC. The first time I visited Mount Vernon was sailing there on the S.S. Mount Vernon. My first impression was that I was shocked to see that the mansion appeared smaller to me than the images on post cards but I was still impressed by its beauty and significance. The surrounding buildings such as the smoke and ice houses were also impressive and I learned The Father of Our Country was a master of many things. It wasn't until later that I learned he was a master of slaves as well.

Another favorite historical destination was Harper's Ferry, WV. Harper's Ferry was the site of John Brown's attack on the federal arsenal in order to secure guns and ammunition to free slaves. Brown, his family and friends were unsuccessful with the raid, and Brown was hanged for treason. It is ironic that Robert E. Lee led the Federal troops in the capture of Brown and his party. Harper's Ferry featured the natural beauty of the confluence of the Potomac and Shenandoah Rivers. Thomas Jefferson once hiked on a hillside and saw the view of the river and proclaimed that it was one of the most beautiful sights that he had ever seen. Doug and I loved hiking up to Jefferson Rock and watching the trains emerge from a tunnel cut through a nearby hillside. Another attraction was the marker for where three states, West Virginia, Virginia, and Maryland meet. We would straddle the marker so we could be in three states at the same time.

Perhaps my favorite place to visit was Great Falls, VA, with its natural beauty and historical significance. Great Falls is a series of waterfalls that do not rival Niagara but are still impressive with their force as the whitewater cuts through the granite formations. Today, daring kayakers paddle at the base of the falls narrowly missing deathly whirlpools.

Today Great Falls is part of the National Park System and is a quiet place with the sound of the falls and other sounds of nature. There is also an excellent visitors' center showing the historical significance of the area. During the late 1700's Great Falls was a thriving river town featuring a canal built by George Washington. Washington and others envisioned a water route that would ship goods from Georgetown/DC to Ohio via the Potomac and other rivers. The waterfalls stood in the way of the route so Washington built a canal to circumvent the falls. One can still see evidence of the canal throughout the park including the entrance to the canal near river level.

Years ago when we visited Great Falls there was no visitors' center but there were two tourist attractions—The Pavilion and a merry go round. The Pavilion included a snack bar, souvenir stand, tables and chairs, and an area for bands and dancing on Friday and Saturday nights. The merry go round was one of the best I have ever seen. It was within eyesight of the falls and the horses and other creatures had been transported from Austria where they were hand carved. There was the traditional brass ring where if you grabbed it you got a free ride. On one trip, Mom noticed that horses' tails had become somewhat ragged and volunteered to make new ones. She produced several dozen new tails for the steeds and as a result Doug and I were allowed to ride for free.

Great Falls was always an opportunity for a family picnic. Dad insisted on a wood instead of charcoal fire and maintained that food cooked over a wood fire tasted better. Picnic fare was always burgers, baked beans, Mom's killer mustard potato salad, and lemonade poured from a plaid Thermos jug. Sometimes Mom would mix things up by surprising us with ham salad sandwiches.

Despite the fact that families took trips to Ocean City, MD, Virginia Beach, VA, and New York City, we always looked forward to our "staycations." Years later I knew that Dad was trying to entertain us with limited funds. We never seemed to mind. It was similar to the Mastercard commercials," Family trip to New York City, $1500; Family trip to Virginia Beach, $1,200; Family trip to Ocean City, $1,000; a Dreibelbis Staycation, PRICELESS.

ANOTHER CHRISTMAS STORY

Jean Sheppard's film Christmas Story has become a classic viewed by millions with some TV cable stations showing it wall to wall on Christmas day. I believe the success of the film is due to its universality, and that almost everyone can identify with some aspect of the film. This is certainly true when I recall Christmas in and around DC.

A DC Christmas was always special, and it was made more so by my parents again doing more with less. One of the first Christmases I remember was when we moved to Minnesota Ave. I believe that Dad received a raise right before Christmas, because the Christmas of 1959 seemed to have a few more frills than other ones I can remember. One of the pre-Christmas traditions at our house was for Santa to deliver the tree untrimmed a few days before Christmas. This was done while we were in school and we would come home to find the tree in a large bucket of water in the backyard. My parents always swore that Santa had made the delivery but they had not seen him. Santa would return Christmas Eve to decorate the tree. This seemed to make sense to Doug and me and we thought that Santa was smart to get the tree delivery out of the way because that left him more room to transport presents.

The Christmas of 1959 provided a gift which cost nothing but continued to give me pleasure for sixteen years. The entire Christmas season I kept mentioning that I wanted Santa to bring me a dog. Christmas morning was filled with a variety of presents but no dog. My folks could tell that I was disappointed but I said nothing. After a few minutes I thought I heard a puppy whining, so I opened the door to see if there was a dog outside on the porch. My Dad teased me and said, "You've got dog on the brain." I turned back to the living room and saw a black figure run behind the TV set. "I did see a dog! I did see a dog!" I cried. I ran to retrieve the puppy from behind the TV and finally pried it from its hiding place. Unfortunately for me the puppy in its excitement greeted me by pooping on my pajama top.

After I changed to different pajamas the puppy and I got acquainted. It was a black chow/poodle mix which I dubbed a "choodle" and named her Pom Pom after a dog in a children's story. Pom Pom came courtesy of one of my Dad's coworkers, who was trying to unload puppies. After decorating the tree and assisting Mom with putting out the presents he spent the night sleeping with Pom Pom and trying to keep the whimpering dog quiet. The revealing of Pom Pom as the last and most special present was a similar family tradition to the film, A Christmas Story, when Ralphie receives his Daisy Red Rider BB gun after all his other gifts.

The Christmas of 1960 revealed a new item—a metallic Christmas tree with a revolving color wheel. These were the type of trees in vogue during the late '50's and '60's and eventually went the way of the lava lamp. Doug and I gave a big thumbs down to the metallic tree and Santa brought a real tree the following Christmas. Other than the metallic tree it was a bountiful Christmas.

One of the highlights was a Texaco tanker truck which Dad acquired by saving Texaco gas coupons and redeeming them for the truck. Dad was an Amoco man but he broke down and filled up with Texaco for a few months prior to Christmas. Other gifts included a puppet stage with a variety of puppets, and a toy farm that appeared in the Sears (formerly Sears and Roebuck) Christmas catalog "Wish Book." The "Wish Book" was one of the dominant sources for presents during the Boomer Era. This was an era when Sears, and I always wondered what happened to Roebuck, ruled as to chain department stores, along with J.C. Penney's and Montgomery Ward's. The Sears on Alabama Ave. S.E. was our "go to place" for almost any type of durable goods.

The presents were great, but the highlight was a Lionel Train set. Part of the magic of the set is that my parents assembled the layout in the basement where Doug and I slept without waking us. We were only about ten feet away from the layout complete with train and a Plasticville village.

During the 50's and '60's Lionel Trains were popular Christmas gifts, and during the Christmas season Lionel would air half hour shows, which could be classified as infomercials on local TV stations. The infomercials featured the latest train engines and action cars. Lionel's O gauge trains were the hit before smaller HO gauge trains surpassed them. HO was popular because of its smaller size and the fact that one could have a larger layout with more trains and scenery in less space.

Lionel's action cars were a major attraction because these were actual working cars. Our layout included several: a hobo car where a plastic man was on top of the car and would duck obstructions when the car reached a certain part of the track, a giraffe car which operated on the same principle in a Bronx Zoo box car, and a helicopter car which shot a helicopter from the car at a strategic time. The helicopter didn't really fly and it was catapulted from the car whirling end over end like a kicked football. You never knew where the 'copter was going to land and later it was a great attraction for the family cat.

Another Christmas tradition similar to A Christmas Story was for families to go to Downtown DC to see the decorated Christmas windows and to visit Santa Claus. The major department stores competed to see who could outdo one another for the best window. The Hecht Company usually had some type of theme such as "A Country Christmas" with mechanical humans and animals enjoying Christmas on a farm. Woodward and Lothrop often scored "A Disney Christmas" while Lansburg's always had train layouts. After we got our Lionel layout, it became a tradition for us to go to Lansburg's on Christmas Eve afternoons when they were already having clearance sales on trains and scenery. Dad would always buy a new train car to add to our layout as long as the item was on sale.

A visit with Santa was always next after window viewing. It was amazing that there were not more kids in line to visit Santa on Christmas Eve, but there could have been reasons for this. Kids and parents probably thought that Santa had taken care of all the kids' wishes by now; also, many people who were visiting relatives for Christmas were on the road. My folks probably had figured this out and thought it was the best to avoid Santa's line.

I noticed that some Santas had a distinct smell on their breaths indicating that perhaps they had enjoyed a little too much "Christmas cheer." My belief in Santa was strong even though there were Santas in every department store and others ringing bells by Salvation Army kettles. Mom explained that Santa could not appear at every store or kettle and that he arranged "helpers" to be everywhere to visit with children. This seemed logical to me. Judging from the number of Santas I saw in the DC area Santa must have been running a very successful employment agency.

29

I did find the song "Santa Claus is Coming to Town" a little creepy and confusing. The lyric, "He sees you when you're sleeping, he knows when you're awake..." made Santa seem like a stalker. As for the toys he was bringing, it always sounded as if they were saying "elephant boats" and I always wondered what an "elephant boat" was as well as "rooty toot toots and rummy tum tums." This too sounded bizarre.

My doubts about Santa began in second grade when I went for a visit and Santa asked me, "What's your name little boy?" I had been to see Santa enough times and if Santa knew everything I figured that he should know my name. "Don't you know me, Santa?" I responded. Santa mumbled something under his breath and we continued with the visit.

The event which really broke my belief in Santa Claus occurred in January, 1961. Our next door neighbors had a grandson, David, who was my friend and we walked together to school. David's mom was a single parent working for the government and the two lived in the nearby Hillcrest Heights, MD. His mom would drop him off at the neighbor's house before going to work and pick him up in the evening.

The first day back to school after Christmas break I went next door to pick up David for the walk to school. There was a photo of David on top of the TV set in which he was kneeling beneath a Christmas tree, smiling next to a toy train layout. I looked to compare my layout to his and they looked stunningly similar. I didn't say anything about the photo as we walked to school except to invite David to come to my house to see my new train layout. For some reason he declined. That night at dinner I mentioned to my parents that I saw a photo and his train layout and that our layout looked just like his. Their faces went ashen. I think Dad managed an "Oh." as a response.

The next morning I was eating my usual cold weather breakfast of Quaker Oats and apple juice. Mom had long since given up on giving me tomato juice. I finished breakfast and prepared to brush my teeth but I was interrupted by Mom. "Gary, I have something to tell you." she said in that tone of voice where I was wondering if I was pleased on frightened. "Gary, the train set Santa brought you was David's. David and his Mom had to move out of their house into an apartment and there was no room for his train. His mom offered to sell it to Dad and he bought it for you and Doug. Gary, THERE IS NO SANTA CLAUS."

Deep down I anticipated this. It was getting to the point where Santa Claus, along with the Easter Bunny and Tooth Fairy, seemed too good to be true. David and I walked to school on that cloudy January day saying little. He was a smart kid and I think he knew what was up; after all, he was in second grade reading Dick and Jane, and I was in first grade still reading Alice and Jerry, so he had to be smarter.

When we returned home I invited him to the basement to be a junior engineer. He was a pro at operating the train, starting slowly at first, and then picking up speed as would be the case with a real train. He knew exactly how to guide the train to the proper spot to fire the helicopter from its box car and how to slow the train to maximize the effect of the hobo or giraffe ducking to avoid decapitation. He operated the train to my amusement until his mother picked him up to go home. I never asked him for the controls. He never said anything about it being his train.

David and I continued to be junior engineers guiding the New York Central steam locomotive, one where you could put tiny pellets in the smoke stack to make it smoke, for the next few weeks. Dad eventually retired the train to the attic until the next Christmas season. During the weeks we operated the train David was the chief engineer and I never had a problem with this. He never said anything about it being "his old train." In many ways the spirit of Santa Claus was still alive. While it may sound corny to many, I still have a deep appreciation for Frank Church's "Yes Virginia, There is a Santa Claus" editorial written by Frank Church in the New York Sun in the late 1800's. Santa's spirit was alive back in 1961 and, for me, it remains so today.

A GREAT PARADE IN THE SNOW

The winter of 1961 was one of the coldest on record for DC The post-Christmas season produced a new kind of excitement for Washingtonians and the nation— the inauguration of John F. Kennedy. Inauguration eve the weather had been clear but that night well over a foot of snow fell over the DC area.

I've mentioned before that the DC area residents do not deal with snow the same way as New Yorkers, Bostonians, or Chicagoans, and the collective I.Q.'s of DC residents falls to the level of a gerbil. The panic buying of essentials has been mentioned and this became more evident during the winter of 1961 as people were convinced that they were on the verge of an East Coast version of the Donner Party. Giant, Safeway, and A&P grocery stores were jammed and cashiers with old NCR cash registers and no scanners punched register keys until their fingers were bloody. I once witnessed a near fistfight at our neighborhood DGS store over a cartoon of Lucky Strike cigarettes. The liquor store across the street did a non-stop business when it snowed as people hauled out cases of Ballentine, National Bohemian, Gunther, Pabst, and Schlitz. The harder stuff also made its way off the shelves as customers thought that after a few belts or brews they could care less about the snow.

As for the Kennedy Inauguration, school and government offices were closed anyway as an official holiday had been declared. Doug and I were awake early to see how much snow had been dumped on DC and were waiting to watch The Ranger Hal Show on WTOP-TV. A young Sam Donaldson was doing the news before Ranger Hal and reporting the latest news concerning the blizzard. The immediate concern was would the inauguration and parade still be on. Donaldson assured viewers that everything was still a go. Local snow removing crews assisted by The National Guard and other military had cleared the snow on the Capitol grounds as well as the parade route down Pennsylvania Ave.

Dad wanted to see the parade which was figuratively in our backyard. After a hurried breakfast, he put snow chains on the car. The initial plan was to drive to Barney's Circle just past the Sousa Bridge and catch a streetcar downtown. I'm not sure if the streetcars were jammed or not running but we drove to the GSA office building and parked. We walked up Penn Ave. towards the Capitol and found a spot on a street corner giving us a clear view of the parade. A number of people had transistor radios and were listening to JFK speak after being sworn in as President. Others had Kodak box cameras to record the parade.

By law, the President must be sworn in by 12 AM so we were there well before the parade. I didn't hear the President's famous speech and the line "Ask not what your country can do for you, ask what you can do for your country." until we saw the replay of it on the news at home. Eventually in the distance, we heard the drums of the first of many marching bands representing every state.

It continued to be cold and the familiar DC food trucks, or "roach coaches," seen outside the museums and around the mall were doing a booming business selling coffee and hot chocolate. Dad bought two hot chocolates and they may have been the best I ever tasted due to the chill. It seemed as if there were nonstop bands before we saw the President and Mrs. Kennedy, along with Vice-President and Mrs. Johnson, but they eventually passed us, waving, smiling, and braving the cold. They seemed oblivious to the cold and they might as well have been participating in the Cherry Blossom Parade.

After the President's party passed by we watched a few more bands and floats then headed for the car to beat the cold and traffic. We drove through the dismal streets of Southwest DC, streets lined with slum housing only a few blocks from the U.S. Capitol. The rhythm of the snow chains could be heard in the background as we listened to the parade coverage on the radio. I asked Dad if he had voted for Kennedy and he said "No." "Why not?" I asked. "People who live in DC can't vote for President." he responded. I didn't understand this and wondered how it could be that The Nation's Capital, perhaps the most important city in the world, could not vote for the President of the United States. Dad tried to explain it to me, but his civics lesson was unsuccessful.

The next day we were in our second grade class with our teacher Miss Flagg pledging allegiance to the flag after which was a prayer. These were the days before school prayer was abolished, and the abolishing of school prayer in DC schools was a big deal because of the large Catholic and Baptist populations.

Following prayer, I shot up my hand and before Miss Flagg called on me I blurted out, "Why is it that people in DC can't vote for who they want for President of the United States?" Miss Flagg shot me a look that could have melted what was left of the snow outside, "Gary, we will talk about this during our social studies lesson so just be patient," she responded. There was an edge in her voice, but I continued with my questioning. "It just doesn't seem fair! Why can't we vote?" Miss Flagg didn't care for me and the feeling was mutual. I also knew that I was on the verge of being sent to the principal's office. This was before the age of protests and years before critical thinking was taught in schools.

Social studies time arrived, and Miss Flagg gave a long convoluted explanation as to the fact that Washington, DC, was not really a state but a district and that the "DC" stood for the District of Columbia. She continued her lecture by telling us that DC came from land donated by Maryland and Virginia. "Well since we came from two states why can't we vote? Why can't we call ourselves Washington, Maryland, Virginia?" I asked. Had I been more clever I would have labeled us "Washmarginia." "How can we change this? This just isn't fair! Aren't we Americans?" I could tell that Miss Flagg was not amused and I was on the verge of being sent to the office, so I shut my piehole. Miss Flagg made an awkward segue to crafts or something that had nothing to do with what I considered to be an important issue. Perhaps Miss Flagg should have been a politician and not a teacher.

Later I discovered that The District of Columbia was run by a commissioner and a bunch of Tom, Dick, and Harry congressmen (with the emphasis on "Dick") who were trying to protect their phony baloney jobs and could care less about the people of DC. Out of the mouths of babes, the issue I raised was an important one. It wasn't until the 1970s that Washington, DC, received home rule and was allowed to vote for a mayor. It had been given the right to vote for President before that. Eventually, DC was tossed a bone by being allowed a non-voting representative to the House of Representatives—Whoopee! Today there is a large banner outside of RFK Stadium which reads "Taxation Without Representation" because DC residents pay federal and local taxes the same as everyone else, with no representation in Congress.

In other socio-political news, people could notice a change in DC, which was more than political. Slowly, DC was coming to life during "The Age of Camelot." Downtown stores seemed to be open longer.

Restaurants thrived and there were more night spots. The lights seemed brighter, and while they did not rival New York's "Great White Way," there was still a noticeable difference, as the city didn't roll up its sidewalks at 6PM. DC was becoming a real city.

The weather remained cold into February and a few weeks after the Inauguration, I noticed slight pains in my chest but they came and went. I felt fine and continued to go to school in proper winter clothes. By early March there was a comparative heat wave in DC, with the temperatures reaching the balmy 50s. Kids began shedding their coats on their walks home from school and I was one of the sheep. On a Sunday night in mid-March, I wasn't feeling quite right as we returned home from church. It was mid evening and were watching The Ed Sullivan Show. It was the first time I had seen the great Louis Armstrong. He had his trumpet and trademark handkerchief and was sweating profusely.

Gradually, I began sweating as well as if to empathize with Mr. Armstrong. I began feeling light headed so I excused myself and attempted to navigate the basement steps and head to bed. The stairs began taking on the sensation of the merry-go-round at Great Falls. When I reached the foot of the stairs, a mere few feet from my bed, I lost the day's contents of my stomach: roast beef, mashed potatoes, homemade ice cream, et al. Hearing my heaves, my parents came running. They cleaned me up, brought me back upstairs, propped me up on the couch, and covered me with blankets. I didn't move for the rest of the night.

The next day there was no way that I was going to school, and Mom called on my behalf. For some reason my parents thought that potato soup was good relief and nourishment for an upset stomach. I sampled three spoonsful because I had missed breakfast. HURLLLLL! Bye-bye potato soup. Mom became more concerned as I lay immobile on the couch watching game shows and Bozo. When Dad came home, they called the family doctor, Dr. Summerfield. Doctors were not making house calls in the early 60s but Dr. Summerfield knew that I was a healthy kid and that I must have one foot in the grave and another foot on a banana peel for my folks to call. After he finished tending his office patients, he arrived at our house with his doctor's bag.

36

I was lying flat on the couch when he tried to prop me up by lifting me under my arms. The pain felt like daggers piercing my sides and I let out a scream as tears streamed down my face. "This boy has pneumonia." said Dr. Summerfield. Listening to my chest with his stethoscope confirmed this. Next was a shot of penicillin which hurt but not nearly as much as the pains in my sides. He prescribed some pills and said it was OK for me to have Coca Cola syrup or flat ginger ale to calm my stomach. This was far more preferable to me than potato soup.

Within a week I was fully recovered. By Thursday I was having my usual peanut butter sandwich with vegetable soup or grilled cheese with Campbell's tomato soup. I attended church on Sunday and few knew that I had been sick. Monday I attended school with the promise that I would wear my coat both to and from school. I had no trouble keeping this promise because I did not want a repeat performance of the previous week. Miss Flagg gave me make-up homework and seemed happy to see me. Maybe she missed the aggravation which I provided.

My parents said that the pneumonia came from having been out in the cold for the Inauguration parade and had been brewing for weeks. Perhaps so, but I wouldn't have traded the experience for anything.

SCHOOL DAZE

My first almost three years of school were in DC public schools. I say almost three years because my parents pulled me out of Eugene Orr school when we moved to Oxon Hill, MD in April of 1961. Kimball school, a long block from our apartment, was my first school, as I entered kindergarten in September of 1959. Mrs. West was my first teacher, and she was a balance between being firm and affirming. Years later I realized that she was a dead ringer for actress Lena Horne with longer hair. We learned the basics such as memorizing our home address in case we got lost, The Pledge of Allegiance to the Flag, and not to run with scissors. Social skills were a major part of the curriculum. We had the obligatory nap time along with graham crackers and milk even though kindergarten was a half day.

My first day of school almost ended in disaster. Mom walked me to school and expected me to find my way home. When the bell rang ending our day I ran to Minnesota Ave. and attempted to cross in the middle of the block instead of the crosswalk. I was attempting to cross a major thoroughfare in noon traffic. As I stepped off the curb, I felt a strong arm grab my arm and pull me back onto the sidewalk. "You're jaywalking!" she said and I had no idea as to what she meant. She led me to the crosswalk where I crossed safely with the other children. Had she not rescued me my tombstone might have read Gary Charles Dreibelbis 1953-1959.

Later that afternoon, the phone rang and Mom answered. It was the principal calling about my jaywalking attempt. Mom hung up and said, "Daddy will be home soon." She said this in a very gentle voice and not the ominous "Wait until your father gets home!" voice. When Dad came home, Mom gave him the news of my mistake. He changed clothes and told me to come to the kitchen table while Mom finished preparing dinner. He took out a piece of paper and drew two streets, an intersection, and four crosswalks. The instruction was that I should only cross at corner crosswalks when it was safe to do so. There was also instruction concerning "WALK" and "DON'T WALK" signs.

There were a couple of crises for me during my early schools days; at least they seemed like crises to a five-year-old. DC elementary schools were incubators for every type of germ and virus imaginable. When one kid came down with the malady of the week every kid came down with it. I swear that I saw one kid break out with measles right before my eyes. Measles and Chicken Pox were running rampant in my class but somehow I escaped the first wave. My folks thought I was lucky and so did I. Then one morning I awakened to find spots on my arms. I ran to the bathroom and found more spots on my face than an FAO Schwartz plush leopard. Mom called school, and I guess she got a "Join the Club" response from the school secretary. She began reading Dr. Benjamin Spock's Baby and Childcare book which was the health Bible for baby boomer moms. She also tried to recall some down-home North Carolina wisdom and home remedies.

I gave measles to Doug and there was an immediate concern because he was two years old, and it was reported that measles could cause blindness in very young children. Our bedroom became a cave, and I forget what I did to pass the time. It was one of the most depressing times of my childhood. TV was verboten because the conventional wisdom was that TV could cause blindness for children with measles. One of my favorite shows was Sam and Friends, a local show featuring Jim Henson's Muppets. The show aired for five minutes following the local news Monday through Friday. My parents allowed me to watch the five minute show then immediately shut the TV's cabinet door when the show was over.

The double whammy hit a few days later when I discovered small bumps on my face and body—Chicken Pox. Now I was really depressed because the end of measles seemed to be in sight. As I recall, I was never deathly ill, just lonely and depressed. My only company was a comatose Doug and the radio.

The major side effect occurred one afternoon when Mom was on the phone and I got a nosebleed. I'm sure that there was less blood in the shower scene of Hitchcock's Psycho than came pouring out of my nostrils and I tried not to disturb Mom. The blood kept coming as I tried to hold my head over the bathroom sink and panic set in. Soon, the bathroom resembled a chain saw massacre with blood on the sink, walls, and bathtub. I cried out to Mom and she hung up the phone. She was greeted by a bloody mess and somehow she was able to stop the

40

bleeding by tilting my head back and stuffing cotton up my nose. After changing out of bloody clothes, I retired exhausted to the bedroom and I was probably a quart low. Time heals all wounds and after a few days which seemed like an eternity, I was back in school.

Upon my return, a second crises arose. I found out from the other kids that Mrs. West had been out of school for over a week. "Did she have the chicken pox or measles?" I asked. I was afraid that I had given her both. No one knew the reason for her absence. A parade of substitutes held forth and tried to maintain order but chaos reigned; however, as Nietzsche wrote, "Out of chaos comes order." I've never read Nietzsche, I just remember the line from Mel Brooks' Blazing Saddles and it sounds profound.

I don't know if we cheered when Mrs. West returned but we were a happy bunch of kindergarteners. Mrs. West gave us information about her absence without telling us too much. She told us that her husband had come home and found her unconscious in the bathroom. He called the ambulance and she was rushed to the hospital. She didn't tell us how long she stayed but my guess was about a month. Her reappearance coincided with early April, which was a magical time for me with diminishing March winds, rising temperatures, Cherry Blossoms at the Tidal Basin, baseball, and my birthday on the horizon. Mrs. West was back with us and all seemed right with the world.

The other item of note I can recall is one day when a black student who lived on the other side of the tracks asked me a question out of the blue, "Would you ever call me a black nigger?" I had heard the word on the street but had never been confronted with it one-on-one. He did not ask the question in a confrontational manner, he just asked it. "No," I said because it had never occurred to me to call a black person that term.

It wasn't as if I deserved a Junior Nobel Peace Prize or was a juvenile civil rights activist it's just that I had never thought to use the word. Later, I found out that "The N Word" was used quite liberally by whites throughout the DC area. June came and classmates said goodbye. I would never see these kids again because we made to the move to Minnesota Ave.

The summer of 1959 was one of discovery and I have mentioned many of the features of our row house. Late August arrived and it was time to enroll me in Eugene Orr School. Orr was a stark brick building in comparison to the friendly exterior of Kimball. The other difference was that there was virtually no playground equipment. There was a set of monkey bars, blacktop, and that was it. There was no protective surface such as is the case with today's playgrounds, and kids were constantly falling from the bars on to the blacktop. There were times when the school nurse's office resembled a M*A*S*H unit.

There were some redeeming qualities to Orr. To the left of Orr's front entrance was a small general store operated out of someone's home. The store was on the main floor and the owners lived on the second floor. This was a very sad excuse for a general store. I believe the sole reason for the store was to sell candy and soda to school kids; those items were about 90% of the store's inventory. There were scattered odds and ends of other merchandise, such as Ajax cleanser, a few cans of SPAM and some Heinz Baked Beans, but that was about the extent of the grocery choices.

If a kid walked back to Minnesota Ave., one could have a great sandwich and soda at Mike's Delicatessen, with its distinctive round Coca Cola sign at the entrance. Across the street was Flynn's Music Store where, and I hate to admit it, I took accordion lessons. I could eventually play a mean Lady of Spain.

The day following Labor Day was the first day of school. Mrs. Singletary, a woman who was probably in her 50s was our first grade teacher. Her classroom contained some of the items of our kindergarten class but now we were down to serious business. Mrs. Singletary was a serious reader, so we were reading the ad-ventures not only of Dick and Jane but we were also reading the adventures of Alice and Jerry. My parents had prepped me for reading since I was three by having me identify letters of the alphabet on building blocks, as well as reading captions from TV commercials. It wasn't exactly Sesame Street, but it seemed to work, because I was one of the best readers in the class.

Mrs. Singletary demanded that each child have a neat desk and work area, so she asked parents to supply us with cigar boxes in which to place our school supplies. The manager of the nearby liquor store was puzzled when there was a run on empty cigar boxes from parents. Some of the kids decorated their cigar boxes. Mom created what I considered to be the "blue ribbon" box. She painted my name on my box along with a picture of Disney's Bambi.

Besides reading, math and art were part of the curriculum. Mrs. Singletary taught basic addition and subtraction by using building blocks and adding or subtracting blocks in a row. With art she urged kids to draw or paint items from their own experiences. My specialty was barns and farm scenes that I saw in the Maryland countryside when we went to visit our relatives in Pennsylvania.

First grade went well and I ended up with all "As". Summertime was spent exploring the neighborhood, collecting soda bottles and going on our "staycation." Labor Day and second grade came before I knew it.

As was previously mentioned, Miss Flagg was my second grade teacher and for some reason she didn't appreciate my critical thinking skills or much else that I did. Once she sent me to the office for tapping my foot too loudly when we were listening to music. The principal called Mom, and there was an acid-tongue meeting of the minds over my musical enthusiasm.

My critical thinking skills got me in trouble again when I questioned Civil Defense bomb drills. The drills occurred during the cold war with the Soviet Union when there was major distrust between the two countries as to who would first flick "The Big Bic" wiping the other off the globe. Walter Cronkite, then dubbed the most credible man in the country, narrated a film we saw concerning the Soviet threat. We figured that if Uncle Walter was telling us this news it had to be true. Some people in the DC area began building bomb shelters hoping to escape radiation following a bomb drop. Shelters had all the creature comforts of home including cans of SPAM, canned vegetables, and drinking water. Dad actually brought home instructions as to how to build a fallout shelter but I don't think he ever seriously thought about building one. The instructions were provided to all government employees.

There were mass fallout shelters scattered throughout the DC area in the basements of government buildings and other underground enclaves. The circular red, white, and blue Civil Defense sign seemed to be everywhere. Public service announcements told us that in case of emergency we were to tune our radios to either 640 or 1240 on the radio dial.

The bomb attack drills joined fire drills as a regular occurrence in DC public schools. Air raid sirens sounded on a given day and we were supposed to react to them by calmly making a line and proceeding in an orderly manner to exit the school building. We were to stay in place until the all clear command was given.

The bomb drills made absolutely no sense to me. If planes were coming to drop bombs why should we go outside? Wouldn't this be like shooting fish in a barrel? One night when Dad was watching the news the reporter said that if a hydrogen bomb was dropped on the DC mall, it would destroy everything from DC to Baltimore some forty miles away. After hearing this, I reported the news to Miss Flagg and questioned the reason for bomb drills. I received my customary pass to the office. Mom was summoned to the office and appeared in less than a half hour. "He does have a point," Mom said. The principal said that I could return to class but not to raise the issue again because it would scare the other children.

Drill instructions did change in the coming weeks but they were only slightly better than what we had been doing. The instructions included closing windows (Gee, we didn't want any fallout to get in), closing shades (We didn't want to see the white mushroom cloud and fiery afterglow), and ducking under our "sturdy" desks.

Years later when I was a teenager, there was a mock Civil Defense poster with similar instructions, except for the final one which was to bend over as far as you could and "kiss your ass goodbye." I guess I had the same sentiment years before the poster in a slightly different way. My prayer life increased dramatically over this time with my sentiment being, "Lord, don't let the Commies blow my butt to kingdom come."

Not long after my bout with pneumonia, we moved to Oxon Hill, MD, during the spring of 1961. Even though Oxon Hill was only a little over a mile from the DC line, I felt we had moved to the sticks. The road leading to our subdivision Southlawn was dirt when we made the move. Southlawn was a Maryland version of Levittown with 600 cookie-cutter type houses.

My new school was Oxon Hill Elementary, and I was entering it near the end of the school year. Mrs. Campbell, a stern, fair, and competent woman, was my new second grade teacher. My first day of class began with a brief welcome and the other kids could have cared less about me. They were used to the kids from military families coming and going so it was a fluid situation.

We began my first day by singing America the Beautiful, pledging allegiance to the flag, followed by prayer. Then Mrs. Campbell surprised me by saying, "Now children, let's welcome Gary by showing him how we sing Maryland, My Maryland." The class starting singing with bright voices and I thought, "Wait a minute! This is the same tune as Christmas Tree, Oh Christmas Tree." You may have heard the song if you watched the Preakness Stakes horse race. Maryland, My Maryland brings up images of Christmas trees, snow, and jingle bells but does not stir one's emotions the way the singing of My Old Kentucky Home does before the Kentucky Derby. I decided that as the new kid on the block I would not bring up the similarity between Maryland, My Maryland and Christmas Tree, Oh Christmas Tree; besides, I think the other kids already knew this.

The last few weeks of second grade were eventful. Besides being a nuclear threat the Soviet Union was kicking our butts in the space race. The Soviets had already put a man into orbit, while the U.S. was still at the starting gate. Perhaps one of the most inspiring speeches given by a U.S. political figure was JFK's "Man on the Moon by the End of the Decade Speech." The speech inspired hope and the concept that the U.S. could do anything if there was focused energy.

When Alan Shepard became the first American in space, our class watched and cheered. Walter Cronkite called the action, and he seemed as excited as our class. Mrs. Campbell brought in a bulky black and white "portable" TV set which was about the size of a foot locker so we could watch the event. She was the best at getting to school early and nabbing the best TV set for us to watch important events. We kids watched Shepard's flight and breathed a collective sigh of relief when we knew he was safe.

There was another highlight besides the space race. I developed a crush on a girl named Laura. Velma had been my first crush but, being the older woman, she was way out of my league. Velma was major league and I was class A Peoria. Laura was my age with long blonde hair and blue eyes. She usually wore jumpers and was one of the more stylish of the second grade girls.

The topper was that she read Winnie the Pooh to us after recess. This followed lunch and games of kickball on the playground. Hearing her read the latest adventures of Pooh was a good way to settle down and transition into the afternoon. Years later at our 35th high school reunion, I reminded her of reading Pooh to our class. She was surprised by my memory but she had no recollection of her performance. "I remember reading Pooh to my kids but I don't remember reading it in class. I do remember Mrs. Campbell sending me to stand in the coatroom as punishment." I wish Mrs. Campbell had sent me there too to keep Laura company.

The last few weeks of second grade gave way to balmy weather and summer vacation. Something had happened to me since moving to Oxon Hill. It was as if someone had thrown a switch in my back and I became baseball crazy. Baseball had been somewhat interesting to me when we lived in DC. Dad would watch the games when we visited Myrtle and Earl (Earl would usually pass out by the seventh inning stretch) and I remember listening to the distinctive voice of Washington Senators announcer Bob Wolff as he called the play-by-play. Wolff's mantra was it wasn't how you called the game but how you sold the beer. He brought the games to life which was no small feat considering the fact that the Senators were perennial cellar dwellers. The saying was, "Washington. First in war, first in peace, and last in the American League." Wolff eventually went to New York's Madison Square Garden to become the announcer of The Westminster Dog Show. I guess he traded one dog show for another.

It seemed as if all the kids in the neighborhood were on fire about baseball as there were nonstop wiffleball games in the streets. One kid, Tommy Shelton, had the biggest backyard in the neighborhood, a corner lot surrounded by a wooden fence. We turned it into our own ballpark, with distance signs on the fence and a white batter's box on a bare spot in the yard. Mrs. Shelton thought that our work was creative until she discovered that we used her Ajax cleanser to mark the batter's box. Anything hit to left field bounced off the back of Tommy's house similar to "The Green Monster" wall of Boston's Fenway Park. One had to hit it on the roof or "upper deck" for a home run. Right field was a shorter distance, and two kids who batted left handed had us beat as to home runs.

There was good reason to be excited about baseball during the summer of '61. The New York Yankees' Roger Maris and Mickey Mantle were putting on a slugging show as they pursued Babe Ruth's record of 61 home runs for a season. Newspapers carried daily tallies as to how many home runs the tandem had compared to Ruth on the same date.

Along with the Maris and Ruth excitement, Washington had a new expansion team, "The New Senators." The "old" Senators owner Calvin Griffith pulled up stakes and moved the team to Minneapolis-St. Paul and was reported to have said that blacks in DC would not go to baseball games but that they could make a lot of noise during a "rassling" match. He also said that he was pleased to have a team playing in front of the hard working white citizens of the Twin Cities. Washington was given the expansion team because the powers of Major League Baseball felt that the Nation's Capital should not be without the national pastime. The Los Angeles Angels were added as the other expansion team. The new Senators were a band of has-beens and never-weres but it was still exciting to have a new team.

The baseball summer gave way to third grade and a new teacher, Mrs. Robinson. She was a forty-something red head and was a student's kind of teacher. Mrs. Robinson was a wonderful artist and could draw almost any cartoon character on the blackboard with colored chalk; for instance, she would draw a character such as Top Cat with a cartoon balloon coming from his mouth saying, "Hey Kids, here's today's lesson."

Mrs. Robinson was innovative in numerous ways. During a poetry unit, she had us choose and memorize a poem. I chose Robert Lewis Stevenson's "Where Go the Boats." She had us recite the poem to that class while audio taping our performances. We heard the playback of the performances, and for some kids, it was the first time they had heard their recorded voices. Mrs. Robinson made the experience a little more interesting by having a contest as to who had the best performance and offering a prize of a finger painting set. After the kids heard the playback, I was voted as the best performance and won the finger paints. Mom had coached me the night before.

The celebration of my poetry reading was short lived. The lead story in October of 1962 was that the Soviet Union was building missile silos on the island of Cuba. Satellite photos proved the fact that this was being done some 90 miles from the Florida Keys. The clarity of the photos, which appeared during press conferences and nightly newscasts, was astounding considering the 1962 technology.

The bomb drills of second grade now seemed worthless to us. President Kennedy hit the airwaves with an ultimatum to the Soviet Union that there would be a blockade of U.S. naval ships surrounding Cuba. If the Soviet ships delivering missiles refused to turn back there would be a confrontation at sea.

Up to this point, kids had always been aware of the possibility of a Soviet attack, but the fear had faded somewhat because no attack ever materialized. I believe that our parents felt some skepticism, and this trickled down to the kids. It was almost as if the government had cried "wolf" once too often; then, the Cuban Missile Crisis came and kids didn't know how to feel. We didn't know the meaning of the word "surreal," but I think that is how we felt. We were certainly aware of what was going on because of newscasts and press conferences but the general feeling was that this can't be happening, and certainly not in our own backyard. There was also a feeling that the Soviet Union was a bunch of bullies and that we refused to be bullied. Perhaps that is the way kids think when they feel invincible.

My thought was that President Kennedy was going to pull a military rabbit out of his hat and that this would soon be over. People in the DC area tried to adhere to their normal routines. Government workers went to work, stores and businesses were open, and school was in session. Teachers acknowledged the crisis but they didn't dwell on it. It was similar to what one saw concerning the British during World War II, "keeping a stiff upper lip" in the face of adversity.

Kennedy's blockade worked and the Russians blinked. Their warships carrying missiles turn back towards home and the country and most of the world breathed a collective sigh of relief. Our third grade activities continued with more relaxed teachers and we returned home to more relaxed parents in the evening. Evening news programs moved on to issues such as Civil Rights. JFK continued to be my hero, and he was right up there with Washington Redskins running back Bobby Mitchell, The Redskins' first black player.

It was probably a third of the way through the school year when we arrived at class one morning to see the cartoon image of Top Cat on the blackboard with a dialogue balloon coming from his mouth with the message, "Please welcome your new teacher Mrs. Keiger. Do good work for her as you did for me—Mrs. Robinson." Our reaction to this news was disappointment and disbelief. Mrs. Robinson might as well have written a P.S. with her message, "Oh and by the way, the government has decided to cancel Halloween this year."

Today's kids might be more accepting of change but we didn't like it. Teachers were considered royalty then even if they weren't paid very much. A good teacher walked on water. If you happened to see your teacher at the store you stopped, open mouthed, and stared. You thought, "Wow, my teacher is a regular person."

Mrs. Keiger turned out to be a kinder, gentler version of Miss Flagg. She was by the book and she lacked Mrs. Robinson's creativity and experience. Mrs. Keiger would have fit in well with today's "No child left behind, teach to the test" crap of today (sorry to get political here). I'm pretty sure she came off the Frostburg State Teachers College assembly line COD.

There were some redeeming aspects as to Mrs. Keiger. She had bright blue eyes and a Mona Lisa type smile. She was also the first person I had ever met who wore contact lenses, a rarity in the early '60s. One morning in an attempt to lighten things up she asked the class, "Do you know that I wear glasses?" One bright soul said that she probably wore glasses when she was grading papers. She proceeded to pop out her contacts and explain that they were contact lenses. For most of the kids it was a trick akin to pulling a rabbit out of a hat. The other redeeming factor was that she could play the flute and was quite good. Folk songs were her specialty and she could take us to far-away lands with her music.

A highlight of the year besides winning the poetry contest was meeting a kid named David Blackwell. David was part class clown, part intellectual, and part, "It's David Blackwell's Anything Can Happen Day." David was the straw that stirred the drink. He was the first to expose the class to Mad magazine and his philosophy of life was similar to Mad's cover boy Alfred E. Newman's "What, me worry?" He was a ball of energy and creativity.

One day Mrs. Keiger assigned a project where we had to create a display concerning some aspect of the state of Maryland. This was similar to a science fair display. Since I loved trains I created a display "Railroads in Maryland," complete with Baltimore and Ohio box cars delivering goods to a Maryland town. David decided on "Maryland's Oysters." Oysters from the Chesapeake Bay were one of Maryland's major exports.

He brought in an aquarium with mud and oyster shells along with some fake seaweed. His plan was that once he brought the aquarium to class he would fill it with water and create an underwater oyster bed. Upon filling the aquarium with water the whole project became a muddy mess and the shells were invisible. The entire class laughed and one member, a brainiac, laughed the hardest. I think his project was "Atoms for Peace in Maryland" or something like that.

David asked Mrs. Keiger if he could dump the water and fix his project for the next day. She took pity on him and gave him a second chance. The next day he returned with the aquarium and it looked pretty much the same. He poured water into the aquarium and we expected the same result. Insanity has been defined as doing the same thing over and over and expecting different results. David was not insane. He had cut a piece of plastic to fit over the dirt and shells. He added water and it could not reach the shells and dirt. Voila, a miniature oyster bed. I believe he received a superior on the project.

One day each week, and I think it was Fridays, Mrs. Keiger allowed us to bring in records, and she would play them at random for the half hour after lunch and recess. Some kids brought in kids Golden Records with songs such as "Smoky the Bear." Other kids brought in their parents' records with hits like Patti Page's "How Much is That Doggie in the Window" or Mitch Miller and His Sing Along Gang Records—Yuk! No rock allowed.

David decided to mix things up a little by bringing in a small 33 RPM record produced by Mad magazine with the title "It's a Gas, Alfred E Newman Vocalizes." Our DJ Mrs. Keiger decided to play it and I knew by the title that this was going to be like listening to a slow train wreck coming out of Union Station. The song started out innocently enough with a jazzy organ solo supplying most of the melody. After a few riffs the melody reached a crescendo –Dah, dah, dah, dah, ——BELCH! It was the kind of burp that could only be produced by someone who had guzzled a six pack of Coke in less than three minutes—I think it rattled the windows. The melody repeated with the same crescendo and burp. The class reaction went from smiles and giggles to gut busting laughter. It was the same as trying not to laugh in church.

Mrs. Keiger gave David a stern reprimand and I guess it offended her musical sensitivity. In defense of the record, I thought that the sax was good. At the end of the day I said, "Hey David, it could have been worse. It could have been a fart." I don't think that even David would have pushed the envelope that far.

David and I were in classes all the way through high school. After school I would go over to his house and do who knows what. His mother was a kind but quiet person and there was something a little bit different about her. She seemed to be a little older than other moms. Years later I found out that David was adopted but the story doesn't stop there.

I reconnected with him at high school reunions. It was like old times as two friends with photographic memories compared stories while enjoying several bottles of nectar of the gods. David had become a photographer and one of his specialties was photographing fashion models around the DC area. He had also been a tour guide on a DC tour bus and his love of DC rivals mine. After a few brews, David revealed to me that he had discovered the identity of his biological mother.

After much research through various public records he found out that his biological mother was a woman named Valerie Solanas. She had given David up for adoption when he was very young, and he had a vague recollection of her giving him to a couple on Atlantic Ave. S.E. and saying, "Goodbye little fella." Valerie Solanas achieved notoriety as the woman who shot artist Andy Warhol. She had done some work for Warhol and apparently, there was a major disagreement with him. Evidently, she wanted Warhol to produce her play, Up Your Ass, and later accused him of losing or stealing the play. She walked into his office at what he dubbed The Factory and shot him point blank, missing with the first two shots and hitting him with the third. Warhol survived. Solanas turned herself in to the police and was charged with attempted murder, assault, and illegal possession of a gun. She was diagnosed with schizophrenia and pleaded guilty to "reckless assault and intent to harm." She spent three years in prison.

Solanas also wrote a book, The Scum Manifesto, which urged women to overthrow the government, eliminate the money system, and eliminate the male sex. She was an extreme feminist and that could be considered a British understatement. In comparison to his biological mother, David's creativity seems harmless.

The typical arrangement of students' desks in our third grade class was groups of four which were placed evenly throughout the classroom. Within each cluster of desks, two students faced one another. Mrs. Robinson instructed David Blackwell to move his desk separately next to her desk which was located at the front of the class. Every morning, after students recited The Pledge of Allegiance, Mrs. Robinson would read to the class from The Farmer's Almanac. She would announce to the class that now David will read from the Mad Almanac. David was a Mad monthly subscriber and had a stack of Mad Magazines inside his desk. Mrs. Robinson let it be known she was a fan of Mad Magazine, especially when she drew a large colorful portrait of Alfred E. Neuman which was displayed on the wall next to the blackboard. Just imagine how politically incorrect this would be in today's elementary school class!

As for the rest of third grade, Mrs. Robinson returned to teach our class. No explanation was given but her return was greeted with the enthusiasm usually given to returning war heroes. We were greeted by her artwork on the blackboard, a book cover of Henry Huggins and Ribsy the dog that we had been reading before she left. The caption on the side of the artwork read, "Today we will continue the adventures of Henry and Ribsy—-Mrs. Robinson." We thought we were dreaming. Mrs. Robinson greeted us and of course we wondered what had happened to Mrs. Keiger. We were told that she was doing fine and, "taking a little time off." No one questioned this and we were glad to have Mrs. Robinson back at the helm.

Things were much as they had been that fall until one day Mrs. Robinson passed out permission slips for a field trip that would be signed by our parents. The field trip was catching the train at Union Station in DC and taking it to Alexandria, VA, a couple of miles outside the city. The round trip couldn't have been more than ten miles, but you would have thought that we were on a rail trip to the moon. It was the first time many of the kids had been on a train, me included.

As we left Union Station we traveled through a series of tunnels before we emerged to see the sights of DC as we took the southwest route. It seemed like mere minutes as we pulled into the station with a large block sign "ALEXANDRIA." There on the platform waving to us was a smiling Mrs. Keiger. We waved back and at the same time wondered what is she doing here? We met her on the station's platform for just a few minutes and long enough to say, "Hi" then we were back on the train to Union Station. Some of the more observant of us noticed that she was not wearing one of her tailored dresses or suits but a loose-fitting blouse. The more worldly among us who had graduated to Birds and Bees 101 whispered that Mrs. Keiger was going to have a baby. The "P" word was not used and no one talked about her condition when we returned to school. Mrs. Robinson guided us through the spring and into summer vacation. It was a good spring and Dad took me to my first baseball game, the Senators vs. the Cleveland Indians. The experience was similar to when Dorothy lands in Oz and the film goes from black and white to color. As I entered the stadium, I was amazed at the bright green field and the colors of the uniforms, this after watching games on TV in black and white. I noticed that on the Senators schedule there would be a double header against the New York Yankees on August 1st. Mickey Mantle, Roger Maris, Yogi Berra and the rest of the Bronx Bombers were coming to town for two games. Dad said that he would get us tickets if I bought my own snacks. It was a deal between us that lasted throughout my childhood. The Yanks won both games, of course, as 48,000 jammed DC Stadium, a record that still stands for DC baseball attendance.

The summer of '62 was pretty much a rerun of '61, without the Maris/Mantle home run chase. There was more and more wiffleball which gave way to football games played on the field of Oxon Hill High School just a few blocks away. We thought that playing on the high school field was big time.

Most of the same cast of characters from Mrs. Robinson's class made their way from the front to rear hallway for Mrs. Gering's fourth grade class. She was another students' kind of teacher who could make learning fun no matter the subject. "What is the chief export of Maine?" she would ask. "Potatoes!" we yelled in unison. "What is the chief export of Pennsylvania? "Coal!" "What are the chief exports of Louisiana? "Sugar and Rice!" most kids yelled. I yelled out "Pelicans" because I had heard that Louisiana was called "The Pelican State." We each chose a state for a class project and created a display which would be displayed on Parents' Night. I chose North Carolina because Mom was a Tar Heel State native and I thought that I could get some insider information from her.

Within a few weeks of the new school year we were learning French. I think now that our class was guinea pigs for an innovative program combining instructional video with live instruction. This was long before distance learning came into vogue. Twice a week we watched a television program, Parlons Francais, featuring a female French instructor, actors, and puppets. We learned French words, phrases, and eventually entire conversations. It aired on WETA Channel 26 the educational channel for Washington, DC.

Our live instruction came from Madame Smith who had come from France after marrying an American serviceman. Madame Smith was energetic and the instruction was rapid paced. She would point to kid after kid and hold up objects that we would attempt to identify using the French word for the object. We moved on to simple French phrases and eventually to two-person dialogues.

After a couple of months, Mrs. Gering announced that we were going to be the main event for a parents' night presentation. We would be on the stage of the multi-purpose room singing French songs and performing skits. Some of the kids freaked out at this but I thought that this was my chance to be a French star. For some reason I was chosen to be the lead in most of our school productions. I was never an elf or reindeer but Santa Claus in the Christmas show nor was I a "fifth" carrot in the Easter Show. I was the Easter Bunny hippity, hopping all the way. This was when you could actually have shows called "Christmas" and "Easter" in public schools.

I think the reason I was chosen for leads was because I had a loud voice and could project to the rear of the auditorium; also, I had no stage fright and it was a totally foreign concept for me. Finally, the acting skill of Spencer Tracy was not a requirement. Years earlier Tracy had said that the key to acting was to "Memorize your lines and don't bump into the furniture." This is pretty much what I did on stage.

A girl named Margie was paired with me for one of the dialogue skits. Margie portrayed a patient visiting a doctor, moi, with various ailments which she would tell in French. My remedy was to give her a large pill, about the size of a golf ball, which was supposed to cure her ailments. After I gave her the pill she was supposed to moan in pain until I punched her in the stomach and she spit out the pill. The trick was that she was to hold the pill in her mouth and pretend to swallow it then

54

moan and wait for my fake punch to spit it out. She would then spit the pill past my head.

The night of the show everything went well as we sang French songs and performed our skits. Madame Smith and Mrs. Gering beamed from the stage wings as if they were proud stage parents. Margie and I were on near the end of the program. The skit went well until its climax. We had memorized our lines and were getting good laughs from the audience. I gave Margie the pill, there was the moan, then punch. Instead of spitting the past my head she spit and the pill hit me on the chin and bounced to the stage floor. BIG, BIG LAUGHS!

I didn't respond with the next line because the laughs were too big. With excellent comedic timing I stayed silent for about ten seconds, then broke into my best Curly of the Three Stooges WHOO, WHOO,WHOO,WHOO,WHOO. This was totally unscripted. This brought down the house. We sang our final French song, curtains close, curtain calls for all, Fini.

Our parents came to the classroom to pick us up, and Mrs. Conway, the school principal, came to offer her congratulations. The experience was a success and French was added to the school curriculum for the remainder of our school years.

Things were different during the summer of '63. Besides the usual baseball and football games, I becoming a young businessman with my new paper route. I inherited the route from a high school kid named Glenn who had outgrown the route and wanted to pursue other interests such as the school's art club and young women. I had been subbing for him on Wednesday's when he was painting his landscapes in art club and wooing the club's female members.

The paper route cut into my sports activities but this was OK because the summer heat was unbearable by 3PM. Walking the paper route was mild in comparison to playing in the heat. It got to the point where I could hit pockets of shade for relief and customers began offering me water or soda on extremely hot days.

I discussed my fifth grade teacher in Chapter One. She wasn't that bad of a teacher but I always thought she had higher aspirations than teaching a bunch of fifth graders. One of the features of fifth grade was something called SRA Science. The whole concept was performing different science experiments and attempting to predict the outcomes.

One unit dealt with weather and you could make your own barometer and other forecasting equipment from items found around the house. I eventually had my own primitive weather station in the backyard and had about the same batting average in predicting the weather as the weather guys on TV. A barometer made from a milk bottle, popped balloon, and drinking straw was my chief indicator.

Another highlight was that the school received funding for more entertainment such as educational films.

One of our favorites was Disney's Donald Duck in Mathmagic Land. Many of the kids could empathize with Donald and his difficulty in learning math. We also had live entertainment. There was a police sergeant, who would give assemblies concerning traffic safety, and a magician named Dick Gray who traveled the elementary school circuit performing shows. Mr. Gray was good, and I think that he had appeared on national TV. U.S. military bands were also a favorite. The Air Force had an excellent band, The Men of Note, while The U.S. Marine Band, The President's Own, also performed school concerts.

It seemed like an eternity for kids for things to return to normal after the Kennedy assassination, but things would change for the better in early 1964 as The Beatles came to the U.S. The Boys from Liverpool debuted on The Ed Sullivan Show to one of the highest ratings in Ed's history. Their first public concert was in DC at the old Washington Coliseum. The concert turned out to be one of the biggest missed opportunities of my life, or at least my first eleven years on earth.

HOW I ALMOST SAW THE BEATLES, OR P.S. I LOVE YOU

Most pop culture fans know that The Beatles made their U.S. debut on The Ed Sullivan Show. If you saw the broadcast or video of it you remember a wooden Ed Sullivan swinging his arm and introducing The Beatles, the crowd going bananas as they sang "She Loves You," and the captions as they showed close ups with each Beatle, and the caption with Paul Mc Cartney's close up, "Paul—Be careful girls. He's married."

D.J.s at radio stations around the country, such as the legendary Murray the K in New York, couldn't play enough music of The Boys from Liverpool. The Mop Tops hit DC hard as well and WPGC and WEAM played them every hour. The girls in Mrs. Sheen's class asked if they could bring Beatles records for us to play at our Valentine's party. Her response was that they could bring the records as long as there were no screaming, yelling, or suggestive movements. I don't think we even knew what constituted a "suggestive movement." If you can recall Eve Arden as the high school principal in the movie Grease, you can visualize Mrs. Sheen.

What I did not tell the girls or anyone else in Mrs. Sheen's class was that I was harboring a deep secret concerning The Beatles, who had played their first public concert in DC on February 11th, mere hours before our Valentine's Day Party.

Our Valentine's party had its traditional exchange of cheap Valentines created by even cheaper artist with second grade humor. An example would be a talking head of lettuce with the caption, "Lettuce Be Valentines." Girls thought this was cute while guys had two fingers in their throats gagging. The pink cupcakes were good as usual and no one got sick from eating too many which was always a bonus. Mrs. Sheen was playing some kind of Muzak, perhaps it was Percy Faith. After three cupcakes I couldn't decide if I wanted to jump over the school building or take a nap once the buzz wore off. If I chose the latter my hope was that everyone including Mrs. Sheen would let me doze while visions of pink cupcakes with those silly message hearts (Hot Stuff) danced through my head.

Just when it looked as if the second option might come true, the girls delivered what seemed to be a dozen Beatles records. Things were starting to look up. I didn't think that The Beatles had recorded that many, so there must have been some duplicates.

The Beatles record which was getting the most play in DC, besides I Want to Hold Your Hand, was P.S. I Love You. As long as it wasn't played too often in class, that would be OK with me. I liked the song well enough but I heard it constantly coming from the Willis' house across the street. I should have been more patient with the Willis household, because they were brave enough to house six kids in a three bedroom, one bath house. There must have been a lot of "P.S. I Love You" going on over there during the past years.

Mrs. Sheen collected the records along with 45RPM adapters. A few months ago one of my Facebook friends posted a photo of a 45RPM adapter and posed the question, "What is this?" as a quiz. The responses from the younger set were amazing. The music began with Mrs. Sheen serving as D.J. and in control of the class. The girls were happy, wiggling, and trying not to break out in dance. The boys were content with this and tried not to gorge themselves on cupcakes and other snacks.

After about fifteen minutes, Mrs. Sheen played "She Loves You." The girls displayed tremendous restraint but they were like ticking timebombs ready to explode. Suddenly, one of the boys in a mock display of Beatlemania which he had witnessed on TV started mimicking the screaming girls he had seen on The Ed Sullivan Show. It was a joke in his mind but all the motivation the girls needed to start screaming and wailing in earnest. Soon the entire class was screaming and wailing, some in genuine enthusiasm and others mocking the true Beatles' fans.

Mrs. Sheen, the ultimate control freak had lost all semblance of control. In desperation she ripped the cord of the phonograph out of the wall with such force that the wall could come down like the walls of Jericho. To make matters worse, our principal, Mrs. Conway came to the door thinking that some disaster such as an over consumption of sugar had befallen the class. A red-faced Mrs. Sheen tried to hold it together as she explained the situation through clenched teeth. Mrs.

Conway was a woman of carefully chosen words and she did much more with nonverbal communication than other educators did with lengthy threats. She looked at Mrs. Sheen for a few seconds and said, "Don't let it happen again." It was obvious that Mrs. Sheen was not going to win the teacher-of-the-month award.

Everyone relaxed because Mrs. Conway had not blown her stack all the way to Baltimore and also because it was almost three o'clock and time to go home. Mrs. Sheen handed back the records as we prepared to board our buses. She probably wanted to break them over our heads.

The secret concerning The Beatles that I did not share with anyone was that I had a chance to see them in concert a couple of nights earlier at The Washington Coliseum. I didn't share the secret because I felt some embarrassment and also because I thought that no one would believe me.

The Fabulous Four played at The Washington Coliseum, formerly Uline Arena, the night of February 11th 1964 less than twenty-four hours after they had appeared on The Ed Sullivan Show. They took the train from New York to DC's Union Station a few blocks from The Coliseum. The Washington Coliseum was famous for ice shows, Ringling Brothers' Circus, and sporting events.

The Marquee of The Coliseum read "THE BEATLES" and did not mention the opening acts of The Chiffons, The Caravelles, and Tommy Roe. Tommy Roe would later say that it was all about The Beatles and that he played his couple of songs and got off the stage as soon as he could. The SRO crowd of over 8,000 paid between $2-$4 a ticket for the concert. In comparison, The Washington Redskins charged $6 a seat.

A few days before the concert, two young women in my neighborhood, Pat and Sally, announced that they had tickets to the concert and that they had purchased some extras. Pat and Sally became the most popular tandem from the DC city line to Baltimore. They were sixteen-years-old and everyone referred to them as "The Twins" but I could never figure out why. They had different last names, plus Pat had raven hair and Sally was blonde. I eventually discovered that they were stepsisters because their parents had divorced and remarried.

59

At first there were lots of takers for the tickets but the interest suddenly waned. Even though the tickets were $2-$4, there were other factors involved. The concert was right before Valentine's Day dances for the older high school kids so dance tickets and corsages had to be purchased. There was the pre-dance dinner at Hot Shoppes and filling your car up with 29 cents-a-gallon gas at the corner Esso station to consider as well. In short, the older kids didn't have a good cash flow at this time

I, on the other hand, didn't have this problem. I was too young to go to a Valentine's Day dance so I didn't have all those costs. I was a young man of independent means, with my paper route and Christmas tip money from my customers. In today's terms I had what could be called "baller money."

The twins were able to get rid of most of their tickets but it came down to the last few days before the concert and there were a couple left. The day before the concert I was returning home from my paper route and I summoned up the courage to stop by the twins' house to see if there were any stray tickets. Mind you, I was two months away from my eleventh birthday. The raven haired Pat answered the door with curlers in her hair. She must have known it was a ten-year-old at the door and not some stud. "Hi Gary, what's up?" Pat knew me from the street football games and my paper route. Trying to be cool and putting on my best paperboy businesslike air I asked, "Hi, do you still have tickets left for the concert?" Pat looked surprised but was kind.

If I had been seven years older I would have asked her to the concert. "I have one ticket left and I called my cousin in Waldorf but she hasn't called back. If I don't hear from her I'll let you know." "Thanks Pat!!!"

All I could do was hope that Cousin Waldorf wouldn't call back.

Suddenly it dawned on me that I didn't have a way to get to the concert. I went back to the door and Pat answered once again. "Hey Pat, if I get to go can you give me a ride. I'll pay for parking!" She laughed and said that it was a deal and that I could squeeze in their car. I went home and waited. We had dinner and then watched the local news. The Beatles had arrived at DC's Union Station, and the concert was already SRO. The concert was only twenty-four hours away but there was no call from Pat.

60

The evening passed and I think we were watching The Andy Griffith Show when the phone rang. It was Pat. "Hi Gary. My cousin hasn't called back so I guess you can have the ticket. Can you come by after your paper route and pick up the ticket?" I managed to squeak, "Yes," but in my enthusiasm I told her I could come to her house right now with money and pay for the ticket. I ran out the front door and went four doors to her house. She gave me the ticket and I now had a seat for the hottest event to hit Washington since the British invaded in 1812.

I was back in time for the last few minutes of Andy Griffith, and I could barely contain myself. I waited until the Sanka commercial at the end of the show to announce, "I'm going to The Beatles concert tomorrow night." My parents looked at me as if I was a child who had just emerged from a cornfield. 'What?!" said Mom. "I'm going to The Beatles concert." Pause, pause, pause..."Oh no you're not! Mom responded. Dad was silent. I think he wanted to keep the peace and he knew there was no reasoning with Mom at this point.

I left our house and returned to Pat's. She was surprised to see me again and I muttered, "I can't go." I wanted to give her some lofty explanation, such as President Johnson had invited me to The White House to attend a state dinner but I was so disappointed that my creative juices had vanished. "Sorry Gary, but I'm sure someone will take it or I'll sell it outside the Coliseum." I wanted to say, "Sell MY ticket outside the Coliseum!" but I held my tongue, thanked her, and said goodbye.

Back at home I went to my room without stopping to say good night to my parents. I turned the radio to WPGC and an Eddie Leonard's Sandwich Shop commercial was running..."No matter where you are, you know you're never far from an Eddie Leonard's Sandwich Shop." The jingle always sounded upbeat but I was sad. I wondered how many couples would be going to an Eddie Leonard's Sandwich Shop after the concert.

The morning of the concert I was silent at breakfast. Mom said nothing. When there was conflict in the household little or nothing was said. School was a fog; fortunately, it was quiet and there was lots of individual work including SRA science projects, individualized reading, and more individualized reading. The concert was mentioned at lunch and recess but I said nothing about my near miss as to attending. The Beatles came and went from DC. Beatles music flooded the airwaves in the weeks to come as they smoked the Billboard Top 100 Charts. Spring, summer, and open windows filled our physical airwaves.

In the years to come The Washington Coliseum would host The Rolling Stones, Patsy Cline, and Bob Dylan. Malcolm X spoke there to a sellout audience and boxer Joe Frazier wrestled there before he became a heavyweight champion boxer. The Coliseum eventually became a relic, when the larger Capital Center was built in the Maryland suburbs, and eventually became a church, then an indoor trash collection building, and later an indoor parking lot.

The Magic of The Beatles was recaptured fifty years later in February, 2014. Only 3,500 of the original seats remained in the old building and there were holes in the ceiling but the group Beatlemania presented a re-enactment of the original concert. The group even started at 8:31 PM, which was the starting time for the concert. The prices to see the re-enactment were slightly higher than the original Beatles concert: $45 for standing room and $100 a seat.

As George Harrison wrote, "All Things Must Pass." Today, The Washington Coliseum is an REI flagship store offering virtually anything one would want as to outdoor gear including bikes, ski, and snowboard shops, along with programs to outdoor areas near DC. Some of the tours include Monuments by Night, sunset kayaking tours, backpacking in the Shenandoah National Park, and rock climbing at Carderock.

As for me, my tonsils came out in March of '64 and I received a new bike as a reward for being a good patient. Maybe there was a little residual guilt there. Baseball season came, and President Johnson threw out the first ball at the Washington Senators' opening day, the first of many openers I would attend.

In late spring Mom went to the hospital and the household was in turmoil. My concern for her was comforted by The Beatles and the Washington Senators: one sublime, the other ridiculous.

Decades later and a couple of years short of The Beatles DC concert, my wife Eileen found an unopened DVD of The Beatles' DC concert at Rasputin's Music Store. Rasputin's is a chain of music stores in the San Francisco Bay Area that is a music lover's dream. Why the owners decided to name the store after the Russian Mad Monk is a mystery to me. Shortly after Eileen's find, I found a poster of the DC concert at a collectibles store in Southern California. I gave it to my daughter-in-law Sara who shares our love of The Fab Four.

One night, accompanied by a bowl of popcorn, Eileen and I watched the DVD of the 1964 concert. There was footage of John, Paul, George, and Ringo talking and joking on the train to DC before pulling into Union Station. The Coliseum concert features the group on a manual revolving arena-type stage, so the entire audience could be up close and personal. The audience response was similar to The Ed Sullivan Show, only now you had over 8,000 fans instead of the few hundred that were in the audience for his show. DC police were there to maintain order. Maybe Mom was right. She worried for my safety.

I do wish I had been there. Video diminishes dynamism, and the DVD was in "living black and white," but my mood soon switched to gratitude. As I looked at a smiling Eileen who loves The Beatles, I looked at her and thought, but did not say, "P.S. I Love You."

MORE SCHOOL DAZE

For some reason it seemed as if the older we got the more agitated we became. Perhaps the seeds were being planted for puberty. I'm pretty sure I had reached puberty by second grade. In any event, Mrs. Sheen was ready to pull out her hair by the time summer vacation arrived.

There were bigger events than ballgames and paper deliveries during the Summer of '64. People were getting used to President Johnson and Civil Rights was becoming a major issue. Dr. Martin Luther King spoke to thousands on the DC mall that summer and the country was becoming more aware of the civil rights issue. At summer's end, Labor Day had become a mega-holiday for us. This had been our thinking for the past several years as we tried to squeeze in as much fun as we could before returning to school.

We started activities earlier than usual on Labor Day because we wanted to experience every second of daylight to the fullest. It was a long time until the winter solstice but we knew that the days were getting shorter. Labor Day was an excuse for neighborhood Olympics. Not only was there wiffleball but bike and roller skating races along with our own version of The Soap Box derby with various makeshift racing contraptions. Lunch was consumed at breakneck speed so we could return to activities. Dinner was a family bar-b-que followed by street football. There were light poles spread roughly 70 yards apart which served as our touchdown markers. Pass patterns consisted of running down and out to a neighbor's 1961 Buick. The streetlights came on at 8PM, so we had night football and played until 10PM when our parents yelled out their front doors in a curfew chorus which signaled that it was the end of summer.

I am a firm believer that public schools should not start until after Labor Day. I can't figure out why schools start in August in sweltering heat and why there are so many "in-service' days for teachers. There is also a great deal of time wasted with showing videos which have nothing to do with the curriculum. Start school after Labor Day, end in early June, and stop wasting time.

Mr. Kincaid, our sixth grade teacher, was the first male teacher most of the kids had experienced. He was a snappy dresser with neat black hair, glasses, and he always looked as if he had just taken a shower. Mr. Kincaid was serious about his job but he had a dry sense of humor. One of his redeeming qualities was that he was a baseball fan.

The girls were maturing fast but the guys were not too far behind. A major problem for the guys is that the girls were already making eyes at the junior high school boys but this was all for naught because their parents wouldn't allow them to date. Things are different today.

Oxon Hill Elementary was always experimenting with new curriculum ideas and I remember that instead of assigned reading we began receiving book kits which came each week with a variety of fiction and non-fiction books. The kit came in a large case secured by straps and Mr. Kincaid opened it as if he were opening a treasure chest. We referred to the kit as our "Reading Care Package."

The concept was great because you could pick what you wanted to read and complete a one-page book report. Everything was fine for me until Mr. Kincaid discovered that I was reading only sports books. On my week-four book report he wrote, "You must read something other than sports books." I turned to another love, U.S. History, and that satisfied him for a few weeks.

One of my favorite sports authors was Joe Archibald, who wrote a series of sports books for kids. Archibald's books were sports books equivalent to Horatio Alger books: If you worked hard and played fair you could succeed in life. One of Joe Archibald's books dealt with a young high school football player, and there was a reference of "the fifty-one yard line." As an avid reader and fan I thought it was my duty to alert him to this error and I wrote him a letter. To my surprise he responded with a letter thanking me for my interest in his books. There was no reference to me pointing out the mistake of the fifty-one yard line. I figured that this was a standard form letter he sent with his signature.

Sixth grade seemed to accelerate faster than the other grades and it may have been because kids had more outside interests. Spring had just arrived when one morning we were greeted by Mrs. Conway who told us that Mr. Kincaid had been in a serious car accident and was not expected to return to class for the remainder of the school year.

Margie, my co-star in the pill-spitting French skit, began to cry. Mrs. Conway responded with, "Now Margie, crying is not going to help Mr. Kincaid." Perhaps she was right but maybe this was the response one gave before psychologists told us that crying was a way of getting in touch with one's feelings. We were informed that Mrs. Kough, the school librarian, would be our substitute for the remainder of the school year. Mrs. Kough was a kind, business-like person, but this was another one of those disruptions that kids didn't like.

Mrs. Kough followed the lesson plans of Mr. Kincaid and tried to maintain an everything-is-normal approach to the classroom. One day the book kit came and there was a copy of John F. Kennedy's Profiles in Courage. The book was a Pulitzer Prize winner recording the stories of Americans who stood their ground in the face of adversity. I decided that I would try to impress Mrs. Kough by reading it for my book report. Unfortunately, I was suffering from spring fever, baseball was in the air, the Good Humor truck was in the neighborhood, and the girls were looking better than ever. I read maybe three or four chapters and skipped through the rest of the book. I wrote my book report and gave the impression I had read the entire volume.

When the book reports were returned there was a comment written across the top, "Please see me." With my sixth grade reasoning I thought, "Oh, Mrs. Kough wants to see me because I have written such a wonderful review of this book." WRONG! When I went to see her she questioned me in a manner such as Congress questions political Presidential appointees. "Gary, what about the chapter on so and so? Gary, what about the chapter on the next so and so?" The questioning continued and it became obvious that I had not read the entire book and I felt as if I were sitting there in my underwear.

The questioning finally ended and then came the blow. "Gary, this was not a good effort, and this is not typical of your work. Do you think that President Kennedy would have been pleased with your work?" Now I felt three inches tall and still in my underwear. I left in silence. She had brought President Kennedy, my hero, into the picture and it was the ultimate guilt trip that a teacher could lay on a kid. My youthful pride was at stake here. I read the entire book and revised the report. She did not expect me to revise it. A couple of days later she returned the report with the comment, "Now that's more like it." Today in my home office there is a framed photo of JFK that my wife Eileen purchased for me at a thrift store. It is a close up of him looking off into the distance with his quotation, "Every person can make a difference and every person should try." I've often thought of that book report when gazing up at JFK.

Mrs. Conway returned to class not long after the book report incident. She was like the E.F. Hutton of Oxon Hill Elementary: When she talked, everybody listened. "I want you to know that I visited Mr. Kincaid at his home last night, and I want you to know that he is doing much better; in fact, he was watching the ballgame. He asked how everyone was doing and I said, 'fine.' He thanked everyone for the present." Margie had collected money from the class and bought him a pen and pencil set from G.C. Murphy's, a variety store similar to Woolworth's.

We unceremoniously graduated from Oxon Hill Elementary School in June of '65. Today there are fancy graduations from elementary schools complete with diplomas, balloons, gifts, and dinners, or at least a pizza party. We got none of the above—I don't think that we even went to Mc Donald's. Elementary school graduations go along with my distaste of bumper stickers which read, "My Child is an Honor Student at _____ School." My response, "Big Deal!" My favorite bumper sticker was, "My Pit Bull Can Eat Your Honor Student." Now that's a bumper sticker I can get into.

All sixth graders anticipated the entry to John Hanson Junior High School. Maryland, unlike many states, referred to the middle grades of 7th-9th grades as "junior high school." John Hanson Junior High School was named, obviously enough, for John Hanson. "Who is he you might ask?" If you want to win a bar bet ask someone who was the first President of the United States? The person will probably look at you as if you have had your fill, think that you may want to call a cab for home, and respond with "George Washington." John Hanson was the first President of the United States under Continental Congress. Make sure you have plenty of documentation with you before you make this bet. The sign as you come to the intersection at Livingston and Oxon Hill Roads is a Maryland Historical marker proclaiming that John Hanson was The First President of the United States Under Continental Congress. As you read further, the sign suggests that President Hanson was our first President. Check with your friendly neighborhood historian or go on-line and decide for yourself.

President Hanson had some nice digs about a mile from John Hanson Junior High School. It is a large mansion, now called Oxon Hill Manor, overlooking the Potomac and was later owned by FDR's Under Secretary of State Sumner Wells. Today it is used for weddings and receptions as well as other high-class affairs. The local story is that Hanson or someone looked from the site over the Potomac and proclaimed that it was like "Oxford on the Hill," hence the name "Oxon" instead of "Oxen." This person may have been subject to too much hyperbole or too much ale.

Even though we were on the verge of being teenagers we still took our sports seriously during the summer before John Hanson. We did increase our attendance to movies because that was where the girls went to escape the heat. The guys would sit several rows behind the girls and tried to blend in with the seats. Labor Day brought out the usual burst of energy but the next day as we entered school we became "big kids." As an aside, whoever came up with the term "Tweeners" should be sent to their room with no dinner. It's another example of one of those bogus "We're living life in speed up" terms.

Opening day of classes at John Hanson saw us herded into the multipurpose room like cattle where we sat at long tables used for lunch. The principal, Mr. Little, who was six feet four inches tall, introduced himself and told us what was happening next. He told us to listen for our names as to which teacher we would be assigned to for our home rooms. It was a little bit like draft day on ESPN. Next, we were to follow our teachers to our rooms and receive our schedules. As it turned out, my group was all guys and we had P.E. as our homeroom and first period. We were greeted by our coaches and told that our gym uniforms were provided but that we needed to purchase a Masterlock for our lockers. The coaches went on with a variety of logistics which a number of the kids quickly forgot.

We received our schedules and it was a whole new ballgame for us as to classes and periods. The bell rang for the change of classes and mass hysteria reigned as 400 kids who could not find their butts with both hands attempted to find their second period classes. It was as if we were sheep without a cause.

Things were better third period and even those who were directionally challenged could find the lunch room after third period. A class called CORE occupied my afternoon. CORE was a class developed by the state board of education and it comprised everything except for math, science, music, French, P.E. and shop.

Miss Hanlon was the teacher, and many of the kids from my subdivision, Southlawn, were in the class. Miss Hanlon was in the same class as Velma, a beautiful older woman who made me wish that I was fifteen years older. I could get to like this class!

About three weeks later a guidance counselor came to the door and announced that I was in the wrong section of CORE and that I was being transferred to another class. No offense to guidance counselors reading this but I enjoyed my contact with them about as much as getting root canal or standing in line at the department of motor vehicles. With guidance counselors I always thought, "So this is the solution to what problem?" They were also trying to get me to take their homely daughters to the next school dance. They also gave us the dreaded Cooter Preference Test. To take the test they gave you a needle-like object which would never pass through Homeland Security at the airport and you punched holes into an answer sheet as to which item you would most like to do. Playing baseball, girl watching, and sleeping were not included. The whole exercise was supposed to give you insight as to your future vocation. My results showed that I would be good at being a forest ranger or cowboy (look out Smokey Bear and Roy Rogers). Years later I read that the great NBA coach Phil Jackson took a similar test and the results were that he would be good as a lawyer, homemaker, or trail hand. Wow, Phil Jackson as a trail hand with no Michael Jackson or Kobe Bryant!

The guidance counselor took me to my new class, and there were some kids from Southlawn as well as other communities such as Birchwood City and Forest Heights. Good news—David Blackwell was in my class. The trade off in teachers was Miss Hanlon for Mr. Pennington, which was like trading off Taylor Swift for Joe Pesci; however, looks can be deceiving.

David Pennington wore short sleeve white shirts with ties that were tied about the length of Fred Flintstone's, and you could tell what he had eaten for lunch because part of it was on his shirt. He had a pronounced gut and he looked as if he had just rolled out of bed before coming to class. Despite his lack of Style, David Pennington was one of the best teachers I had at any level Kindergarten-College. When I communicate with former classmates today on Facebook or other social media they all remember Mr. Pennington.

With Mr. Pennington we learned mundane things such as diagramming sentences, along with having to learn every single preposition. He also told us that ending a sentence with a preposition was forbidden. One of his favorite statements was, "Prepositions are something you should never end a sentence with...Jerk!" Mr. Pennington was ahead of the curve in many areas. He did units on The Republic of China and The Soviet Union because he thought we should know more about these world powers. He had copies of the magazine Soviet Life on a reading table in the back of the classroom. Some of the school officials thought he was a subversive. He contributed mightily to my love of Russian History. He taught us about comparison religions such as Buddhism, Hinduism, and Muslims. His class was like a living National Geographic Magazine, and he would show any film he could get his hands on about other countries.

Political correctness was not part of Mr. Pennington's style. There was a girl in class who had attended Catholic elementary school and he referred to it as a "fish school." Mr. Pennington was a Southern Baptist and proud of it. He nicknamed one confused girl in class "Maxwell" after Maxwell Smart of the popular TV show of the time Get Smart. Our French teacher was an attractive woman who had attended The University of West Virginia. When it came time for French class Mr. P. would say, "Let's go across the hall and see that good lookin' West Virginia gal." He wouldn't last five minutes in today's schools but he was a great teacher despite his lack of political correctness.

There were two non-academic jewels in his crown. He was the coach of the school's baseball team and the sponsor of Teen Club. He had played baseball at Marshall University and despite his gut he was a good all-around athlete. He was friends with Marshall great Hal Greer who went on to stardom with Wilt Chamberlain and the Philadelphia '76ers. John Hanson's baseball teams excelled, and that was in large part due to Mr. P.

Every kid in school knew of Mr. P. because of Teen Club. Teen Club happened on Friday nights in the school auditorium and you paid a 50 cent admission fee. Mr. P. knew the kids who couldn't afford the fee and he let them in for free without any embarrassment. Teen Club featured dancing to some local garage band, games such as ping pong and billiards, Cokes for a dime, and an excellent viewing of members of the opposite gender. The bands played hits by groups such as The Buckinghams, Herman's Hermits, and the Beach Boys.

For most kids it was their first exposure to slow dancing. As soon as the familiar chords of The Animals' The House of the Rising Sun Began you could have mopped the floor with the oozing hormones. There were always a few awkward seconds before boys asked girls to dance but most guys had been sizing up their potential dance partners since the opening of the auditorium doors. The whole ritual went something like this: First chords of the song for about ten seconds then:

*"There is a house in New Orleans they call the
Rising Sun...
It's been the ruin of many a poor boy and lord I
know I'm one."*

By this time matches had been made, and if you got the right partner you experienced four minutes and eight seconds of adolescent heaven and I know that it is four minutes and eight seconds because I still have the 45RPM. As for those not lucky enough to find a partner, they stayed in the back of the auditorium shooting pool or playing ping pong.

Junior High teachers were not quite as memorable as elementary teachers because you had so many of them. Miss Hall, the French teacher, was memorable not only because she was attractive, but also because she cast me in the Christmas play. Evidently she had some thespian experience at the University of West Virginia. It may not have been the drama department at Princeton or UCLA but it was good enough for John Hanson.

Another distinctive teacher was our shop teacher Mr. Elmer Melson (Don't call me Nelson! It's Melson with an "M".) He was referred to as ELMO which stood for "Everlasting Mouth Odor." He had the breath that could start a windmill on an old Dutch painting. One Christmas two of the crueler kids left a Christmas package on his desk and it turned out to be a bottle of Listerine.

Mr. Melson dressed in a shirt and tie along with a weird kind of trench coat which made him look like a wannabe flasher. He wore glasses and looked as if he had a little too much Vitalis in his hair. I was a miserable failure at shop and soon discovered that I could not fix or build anything. Dad and Doug were great as handymen but I had none of their skills. This led Dad to give me the advice that I had better get a good education or else I would starve because I had no practical skills.

One of the most memorable features of John Hanson was "The Bridge." Kids would pass Oxon Hill Senior High School and walk through a brief patch of woods. At the end of the woods was The Bridge which crossed a small stream. The Bridge was peaceful in the morning but in the afternoon it could become a narrow boxing ring. During the school day if someone got into an argument with another student the challenge of "Meet me at The Bridge" was issued. For the most part the usual suspects were fighting at The Bridge and the rest of us were left alone.

The two times I was issued "The Bridge Challenge" I was a towering mountain of Jell-O. The first time I responded by saying, "I'm not a coward, but my feet don't like standing around and seeing my body getting abused." The challenger didn't know how to take this and thinking I was a mental case simply walked away.

The next challenge I accepted but circumvented The Bridge by taking the long way home. The next day my challenger asked, "Where were you?" I told him I got lost but could I take a raincheck. Again, this challenger thought that I was a candidate for St. Elizabeth's Mental Hospital in DC and left me alone.

Not far from The Bridge was a group of winos who would hang out at the rear of Al's Market or Safeway. They were known as "The Unofficial City Council of Oxon Hill," and you would run into them if you were avoiding The Bridge. They were captured for prosperity by my friend and photographer David Blackwell in a photo he entitled, "Bad Financial Advice."

There were two major fashion statements at John Hanson: The Blocks and The Collegiates. The Blocks would be called Greasers in any other part of the country and I have no idea who came up with the name "Blocks." Blocks looked as if they had missed the casting call for the community theatre production of Grease. You get the picture: black leather jackets, black Converse tennis shoes (no Joe Lapchick shoes allowed) slick hair and Banlon shirts. Don't ask me why Banlon shirts. Girls dressed basically the same way with the exception of Banlon shirts. Their blouses could be classified as "Early Goodwill."

Collegiates thought they had some sense of style with button down shirts, comfortable slacks and no jeans, and stylish shoes such as penny loafers complete with a penny stuffed in the top groove. The girls wore neat blouses and skirts and for a time Go-Go boots were the rage. These were short white boots that came up about calf high. There was no economic reason for anyone to be in one group or the other. I found out later that there were Blocks who became doctors and lawyers and Collegiates who became societal rejects. That is part of the fun of going to your high school reunion.

My first date was in the winter of 1968, The Snowball, with a girl named Diane. Diane was a dead ringer for the actress who would play Winnie on the TV show The Wonder Years. Mr. Pennington hired a really good band, Lawrence and the Arabians. Lawrence and the Arabians could play virtually any rock song at that time and if you compared them to the typical Teen Club garage bands, it would be like comparing a Corvette to a Ford Falcon. Evidently Mr. Pennington saved up some Teen Club money to get these guys because it was rumored that they got $1,000 a gig.

Prior to dating Diane, I went to dances solo or "Stag." Going Stag was not that bad if you were patient. You waited guys out until they got tired of their dates and left them to go hang out with their friends. You would then swoop in and rescue the abandoned party. This was good because you could often have several dances with the abandoned one and not have to pay for her corsage or dinner.

There was an advantage to having a date and a steady dance partner but transportation was not one of them. I wasn't sixteen so I couldn't drive. Dad furnished the transportation in a used pink Chevy Impala he had purchased. The pink was the same shade as a Mary Kay salesperson's pink Cadillac. Dad made sure that the car was washed but the embarrassing thing besides the pink color was that he purchased one of those pine tree air fresheners. Another source of embarrassment was that Dad insisted on having the radio tuned to some station with Muzak instead of to WPGC, WEAM, or one of the Top 40 stations. Diane and I listened to elevator music to and from the dance.

Things went well at the dance and Diane and I would walk together in the school hallway between classes. In a few weeks posters went up in the school hallways for the Spring Fling dance. Church softball and the Major League Baseball season were starting. This along with algebra put a lot on my plate. I kept putting off asking Diane to the dance assuming that we would go together.

One day we were walking in the school hallway and I was giving her a play-by-play of the previous evening's church softball game. Following this account I popped the question as to taking her to the dance.

"Oh, I'm sorry Gary. Glenn C. asked me to go with him and I thought you might be busy so I said yes." This was my first lesson in not taking women for granted. Stag was the option for me for Spring Fling. Softball, baseball, and dealing with algebra continued throughout the spring of '68, and I got over not taking Diane to the Spring Fling. All these things were the candy store of life, considering what the country and DC was going through in 1968.

'68 WAS NOT GREAT

1968 is considered by many historians to be one of the worst years of the twentieth century for Americans. It hit those of us in the DC area especially hard. The U.S. was mired in Viet Nam, and there appeared to be no way out. We watched the evening newscasts, and CBS and Walter Cronkite in particular became more critical of how President Johnson was handling the war. The President announced early that spring that he would not seek the Democratic nomination for President of the United States.

Just a few years earlier there seemed to be signs for hope for the U.S. We were making progress in the space race against the Soviet Union, and The Rev. Dr. Martin Luther King had spoken before a crowd of over 250,000 on the Washington Mall on August 28th 1963. My perception of DC was that it was still a segregated city and there are numerous historians who will back this perception.

I remember that we did not go to The Mall to hear Dr. King's speech and we heard it on T.V. This was not a parade so I think Dad was afraid of the mass of humanity and what might happen at the event. My recollection was that there was ambient fear in the DC area, and the government and many businesses in the city were closed. Dr. King's speech, dubbed the "I Have a Dream Speech," became one of the best know in American oratorical history and has been studied by people ranging from school kids to scholars of oratory. The speech, given at the Lincoln Memorial, came at the end of the "March on Washington," a movement to end school segregation and discrimination in the workplace. King's speech is credited with easing the passage of the 1964 Civil Rights Act and the 1965 voting rights act. It is a sermonic speech in content and tone and oratorical critics write that the speech resonates with individuals more deeply than any other modern speech.

Four years later in April of '68, King embarked on a Poor People's campaign. As part of the campaign he traveled to Memphis, TN, intending to lead a march supporting striking garbage collectors. On April 3rd he delivered a speech, and while it is lesser known than his "I Have a Dream Speech," it is truly significant in the life of Dr. King. His final words acknowledged that the evening of April 3rd, 1968, could be his last: "...And I've seen the promise land. I may not get there with you. But I want you to know tonight, that we as a people will get to the promise land. And, I'm happy tonight. I'm not worried about anything. I'm not fearing any man. Mine eyes have seen the glory of the coming of the Lord." The next day he was assassinated by James Earl Ray while standing on the balcony of Memphis' Lorraine Hotel.

I have tried to compare my perceptions of the night of April 4th with video footage I have recently viewed of how the death of Dr. King was reported. My perceptions of the past are pretty accurate when I look at the video through 2017 eyes. Walter Cronkite was again the deliverer of horrible news to the American public. My recollection was that there was not nearly the amount coverage of the King assassination as there was with JFK's assassination, and that we received details much more slowly.

It wasn't long after the news broke that rioting began in over 110 U.S. cities, and Washington, DC was one that was hit the hardest. As word of King's murder by Ray hit the streets, crowds began to gather at 14th and U Street N.W., which was the center of black commerce. Stokely Carmichael led members of the Student Nonviolent Coordinating Committee (SNCC) to stores in the 14th and U corridor and demanded that they close out of respect for Dr. King. The crowd was peaceful at first, but someone threw a rock breaking a store window and all hell broke loose. The story goes that the rock which ignited the violence was thrown through the window of a People's Drug Store at 14th and U. By midnight, April 4th, there was widespread looting of stores with people carrying away as much merchandise as they could handle. The local news began covering the violence, and we learned that DC was a city in trouble.

News organizations faced similar problems of covering the riots as they had faced covering JFK's. assassination. They were still using film instead of videotape, and the film had to be processed; however, the other problem was that unlike the Kennedy assassination, the reporters and film crews were operating in a war zone. The next morning Walter Washington, the government appointed Mayor-Commissioner of DC, ordered that the damage be cleaned up. Many DC residents were still angry and Carmichael addressed a group at Howard University warning of violence. Following the rally crowds walking down 7th Street N.W. and H Street N.E. got into violent confrontations with police by throwing rocks and bottles. Fires were set to numerous buildings, and violent crowds prevented firefighters from extinguishing many of them. At one point the rioting came within two blocks of the White House, and both local and national news reports showed smoke hovering over the White House. There was also rioting in parts of my old neighborhood in Anacostia.

By this time we could see and smell smoke at our house less than five miles from the worst rioting. Dad began to pack belongings into the trunk of our car preparing for an escape in case the rioting came closer. It was a prevalent feeling among those in Oxon Hill that the rioting could spill over the DC line and hit the suburbs. Dad was pretty much ready for us to "head for the hills."

Local TV stations had what seemed to be non-stop coverage of the rioting. One of my recollections was James Brown, The Godfather of Soul, coming on one station and pleading with people not to riot. Brown had been scheduled to play a concert in DC and he had recently played a concert in Boston which many say saved the city. Brown's concert in Boston was the night of Dr. King's assassination and Boston authorities, fearing violence wanted to cancel it. Brown and authorities decided to go on with the concert without a crowd. The concert was televised and Brown appealed to viewers to be nonviolent. As a result there was very little violence in Boston.

Indianapolis was another city which escaped violence. Many credit Senator Robert F. Kennedy, who was campaigning for President, for calming the crowd with a speech given to a predominantly black audience. Senator Kennedy drew comparisons of Dr. King's assassination to his brother's assassination. The brief speech is one of the hidden gems of American oratory. Kennedy was the only white public official to address a black audience. I have shown the video of his speech numerous times to my public speaking classes.

Meanwhile in DC, the violence continued on Saturday, April 7th, although it had subsided somewhat and many give James Brown credit for calming numerous angry rioters. If one looks at the numbers, they are staggering. The rioting crowds outnumbered the DC police force by almost seven to one. President Johnson dispatched over 13,000 federal troops which included 1,700 National Guard troops. TV images showed Marines mounting machine guns on the steps of the Capitol, and Army troops from the 3rd Infantry guarded the White House. Some black shop owners were able to escape the burning and looting by tagging their stores with the words "Soul Brother" on the stores' exteriors. A curfew was imposed, and gun and alcohol sales were banned in the city. By the time most of the city was quiet on April 8th, over 1,000 buildings had been burned with almost 90% of them being businesses.

Several days later the Washington Senators played the traditional Presidential Opening Game against the Minnesota Twins in front of 32,000, the smallest crowd for an opener in seven years, due to the fear of civil unrest in the city. My parents did not allow me to attend the game and it was the first opener I had missed in six years. Senators' shortstop Eddie Brinkman had been called to duty as a National Guardsman and roamed the stands of DC Stadium in his military uniform to preserve the peace.

It is not an understatement to say that the riots nearly killed DC's economy. I can remember that many suburban whites refused to go into the city unless they worked there and that many would not shop in the city preferring to shop at newly constructed suburban stores. Years later when I came home from college and ventured to drive in the riot torn areas rubble still remained; in some cases, it remained until near the turn of the century. Eventually the 14th and U corridor recovered and is now a hot spot for trendy restaurants, night clubs, and stores. It took a long time coming.

Two months after Dr. King' death, tragedy struck again. By early June, New York Senator Robert F. Kennedy appeared to be headed for the Democratic Party's nomination for President. He had campaigned hard in delegate-rich California and had defeated Eugene McCarthy in the state's primary. Shortly after midnight on June 4th, RFK came down from his campaign suite at Los Angeles' Ambassador Hotel to address the crowd with his victory speech. Following the speech he attempted to avoid the crowd by exiting through the hotel's kitchen and was shot in the head by Sirhan Sirhan. He was taken to Good Samaritan Hospital where he fought for his life. Because of the time difference with the West Coast we did not hear of the shooting until breakfast. We knew RFK was still alive but the situation was very grave. Teachers did their best to comfort us but they too were obviously shaken. Kids liked RFK because of his youthful energy and because he was part of the Kennedy clan. It also seemed unbelievable to us that there could be two assassinations of such prominent national figures in two months. Many of us thought, "What's next?" We went through the school days and both students and teachers were in a zombie-like state. RFK fought for his life for two days but died at 1:44AM on June 6th. In a few weeks, DC Stadium, home of the Senators and Washington Redskins, was renamed Robert F. Kennedy Memorial Stadium.

Whenever I return to DC, I try to make a sojourn to Arlington Cemetery the final resting place for John F. Kennedy and the man I will always refer to as Bobby Kennedy. I pay respects to both men but there is something about Bobby's gravesite that is special to me. Facing his gravesite is a monument with excerpts of some of his best speeches. As many times as I have read them, I am still inspired every time I visit the site. One of my favorite RFK quotations is, "Some see things as they are, and ask why. I see things that never were, and ask why not."

Summer came and we tried to blot out the events of the first half of the years with our usual activities, but it was difficult to do. The Viet Nam war was getting worse, and the news media, especially CBS, was turning popular opinion against the war. The other consideration was that we were fifteen-years-old and military service was now a perceptible thing with many guys joining Oxon Hill High's ROTC. As the year progressed I tried to adopt Mad Magazine's Alfred E. Newman's attitude of, "What, me worry?" It became increasingly more difficult to do.

FIELD TRIPS

Many East Coast kids had to travel for miles for field trips that were in our own backyard, and that we took for granted. One time our school bus was parked in front of the Smithsonian's Museum of Natural History and we saw a row of tour buses with kids disembarking. "Who are those kids?" I asked. The teacher responded, "Oh they're probably kids from New York City." "Why can't we go to New York City?" I asked. "Look at what you have here." she responded. She had a point. She was also being diplomatic. Many of the students at the schools I attended were from lower middle class or middle class families. Dads had low level government jobs and there were many military families who were not making a lot of money. We also had a number of blue collar families. Working Moms were a rarity, and many stayed at home and tended the home fires until their kids got older. It would have been a stretch for many families to afford a field trip to New York and I knew that it wouldn't happen with my family.

We didn't take field trips when I was in the DC school system. Our big adventure when I went to Orr Elementary was taking a sack lunch to Anacostia Park on the shores of the Anacostia River a few blocks from school for our end of the year school picnic. The school provided chips, snacks, and Kool Aid, and we thought this was a big deal. School kids picnicking there today may encounter more than a couple of drug deals.

Field trips were much better at Oxon Hill Elementary. A few weeks after entering Mrs. Campbell's second grade class we hopped on the school bus and traveled to the Smithsonian's Museum of Natural History where we were greeted by the huge elephant shot by Teddy Roosevelt. We always called the museum the "Museum of Stones and Bones" because it housed rare gems such as The Hope Diamond along with numerous fossils. School buses took on a new aroma when traveling on field trips. For one, field trips were more than the usual mile we traveled between home and school which meant you were exposed to the variety of elements which comprised the school bus stench for a longer period of time. I once told my fellow classmates that they could

83

blindfold me, drive me around DC three times, have me eat an onion sandwich, and carry me on to a school bus and I would know exactly where I was. Several factors contributed to this. There were some kids who had showered last Thursday——August 3rd, 1961. The current date could have been October 3rd, 1961. The morning trip was somewhat bearable because we left school after DC's rush hour so it was a pretty quick trip. The afternoon ride home could be murder because kids walked around and acquired more B.O. and we could get stuck in heavier afternoon traffic.

For a regular school day very few kids brought sack lunches. A hot lunch at Oxon Hill Elementary cost a grand total of a quarter and this included milk. You couldn't pack a lunch for that price, and if you did, who would want to eat it? If you wanted a Dixie Cup of ice cream you had to pop a dime. For field trips, everyone had to pack a sack lunch, and who knows what was in some of those sacks. In the morning sun, hard boiled eggs became hard toiled eggs. Mystery meat sandwiches smelled like the alley behind a butcher shop on a ninety-degree day, and tuna fish sandwiches took on the odor of some large dead marine beast that had washed up on the shores of the Potomac.

Some kids took off their shoes, shoes that they hadn't taken off for days and had probably worn to bed. They were the kind of shoes that you wanted to throw out the bus window when the kid wasn't looking.

Then there were the flatulence festivals among the guys who were usually riding in the middle of the bus, so everyone was exposed to their output. The girls were much more discrete but I could swear that they were launching "silent but deadlies." In some ways this was more annoying because you could prepare for the guys "flutterblast." The girls were sneak attackers.

Mrs. Campbell's Smithsonian field trip had a major bonus. After visiting the museum for a couple of hours and enjoying the "stones and bones," we had lunch picnic style on The Mall. At one point the guys were having their version of a food fight when Mrs. Campbell told us to hurry up and finish eating because she had a surprise for us. What could it be? Fudgesicles? Dreamsicles? She started walking, and we followed her two by two in a human DC version of Noah's ark, with name tags hanging around our necks. Tourists looked at us smiled and were probably thinking, "What a bunch of little DC dorks." In turn we looked at some of the tourist wearing shorts, knee socks, and ten gallon hats and thought, "Look at those big dorks. They must be from someplace like Truth or Consequences, New Mexico."

We followed Mrs. Campbell to Penn Ave. and saw throngs of people lining the streets as if they were waiting for a parade. After a few minutes we heard a roar in the distance. Soon, we saw a convertible in sight. Riding in the convertible was a smiling, waving Alan Shepard, the first Mercury astronaut. There were flatbed trucks with TV cameras behind the car covering the motorcade. Mrs. Campbell knew about the motorcade in advance and had timed our visit beautifully so we could see it.

Following the motorcade it was time to return home in a bus that smelled slightly better because it was sans lunches. We could brag to our parents that we saw the man who was the first American to travel in space.

Many locals maintain that it could take up to six months to tour all the Smithsonian buildings and tour them properly. The trip to The Museum of Natural History whetted my appetite for visits to the other Smithsonian buildings as well as to revisit The Museum of Natural History. The Smithsonian Institute was founded by a British citizen James Smithson. Apparently he thought so much of the American people that he donated funds for the building of a proper museum (Thank you Mr. Smithson). Smithson never set foot in the United States to see the creation bearing his name.

The various Smithsonian buildings allowed our teachers to plan excellent field trips. We could cover about one building a day if we toured them at a rapid pace. There was no time for lingering around and gawking at the Hope Diamond or other items of interests. Teachers followed Mrs. Campbell's example of timing, and field trips were timed with the precision of a Swiss watch or train schedule. We got to school at nine, did the Pledge of Allegiance, sang Maryland My Maryland, and BOOM it was out the door to the el stinko school bus. If we had good traffic karma, and none of us knew what karma was back then, we could hit our destination by 10AM.

The major obstacle was the then-new Woodrow Wilson Bridge. In my mind, Woodrow Wilson was a great American President who guided us through World War I and tried to get the U.S. to join the

League of Nations, forerunner to the United Nations. Wilson embarked on a train whistle-stop by whistle-stop cross country trip in an attempt to persuade the American public that we should join the League. Wilson suffered a stroke during the trip, a fact that was kept from the U.S. public. His wife, Edith Bolling Gaut, ran the country until the end of Wilson's term. One could make an argument that she was the first woman President in U.S. history.

With all that said, Wilson may have been a great President, but thousands of DC commuters have cursed him due to the bridge which bears his name. The bridge was dedicated in 1961 and became the link between Maryland and Alexandria, VA. Before the "Woody Wilson," drivers had to take a circuitous route through DC to reach Alexandria. At first the bridge was hailed as a godsend but it wasn't long until people realized that this drawbridge could cause hellacious traffic jams. To this day traffic can be backed up for miles if the drawbridge is open. Perhaps things are better today with all the technological toys drivers have at their disposal. Then, the only entertainment was to listen to the traffic report on WMAL to hear when the bridge was going back down and you could restart your engine.

Meanwhile back to the bus, drivers would listen to WMAL as we left school hoping that they could win the game of "Beat the Bridge." Drivers would put the pedal to the metal on Indian Head Highway for the short distance on the Capital Beltway before hitting the bridge. If the driver beat the bridge,you could hear his/her sigh of relief throughout the bus; if not, groans and probably a few inaudible curses.

Kids didn't care whether or not the bridge was up. We would look out our windows to see ships passing beneath the bridge. It was the Forest Gump of maritime travel; you never knew what you were going to get. You could see a large merchant ship pulled by tug boats, tankers, or military ships. The only drawback was that you had to experience bus stench for a longer period of time.

Assuming the bridge was down we could hit The Mall by 10AM. Another early Smithsonian field trip was to the main building known as "The Castle." Back in the 1960's, The Smithsonian was called "The Nation's Attic." The label was accurate. The Castle housed many randomly organized items which have since been distributed to other buildings. Many items that are now in the popular Air and Space Museum were in The Castle. We were studying aviation history in third grade and there suspended above us in The Castle was Wilbur and Orville Wright's plane, The Kitty Hawk. Walk a few feet and there was Charles Lindberg's Spirit of St. Louis.

We were good for about an hour and half of touring so it was time for our sack lunches. Mom always chose the safe bet of peanut butter and jelly. Jif and jelly were a pretty good bet. After more touring and seeing some of our early attempts at space travel it was time to head to the bus and play "Beat the Bridge" going in the opposite direction.

Another memorable field trip was to the Nike Missile Range. Somehow, I think it was through one of the Kids' parents that we got permission to tour the site. In my first attempt at photography, I took along a Brownie Box camera to chronicle the event. I went through the site innocently pulling my camera out of my jacket and taking photos along the way. The photos were developed within a few days, and I brought them to school to display during show and tell. The teacher was flabbergasted. "How did you get these?" That's supposed to be a classified area!" "What's a classified area?" I asked innocently. "Well, you know, top secret." Once again critical thinking got the best of me and I asked, "So what's a bunch of third graders doing there?" BANG! To the office I went. Sometimes when I consider how much time I spent in school offices I calculate that it could have been a good semester's worth of time. Off to the office I went but I was allowed to keep the photos. Fortunately, neither the FBI nor CIA came knocking on our door.

My love of classical music is a result of field trips to concerts given by the National and Baltimore Symphony Orchestras. The concerts were held in large high school gymnasiums and kids were bussed in from all over the county to attend. It was not unusual for 2,000 students to see a concert. This was in the wake of Leonard Bernstein and The New York Symphony's Young People's Concerts which aired on CBS-TV. The symphonies performed music that was kid friendly such as Tchaikovsky's 1812 Overture. I remember sitting near the front of the auditorium for a performance of Hector Berlioz' Symphonie Fantastique. The conductor told us of the man who had vivid dreams only to meet his demise at a guillotine. He told us various parts of the story and what to listen for at various times during the selection. The music came alive for us. Years later when I was in college, I marveled at the Chicago Symphony's rendition of Berlioz's work featuring what might be the best brass section of any symphony orchestra in the world.

Field trips were unusual in junior high and high school. I did have a solo field trip in high school. Mrs. Trohanis, a young, lively high school algebra teacher, came to me after class one morning to ask a favor.

Considering the fact that I was treading water with a "C" at the time, I had no idea as to what I could offer.

The Maryland State Board of Education was going to do its five-year review of Oxon Hill High School, and Mrs. Trohanis had volunteered to put together a presentation for the team. She told me that she wanted to do something special for the team by putting together a slide-tape presentation of the school. "Okay, why are you telling me this?" I thought. "Gary, I want you to do the voiceover for the presentation." she said. I didn't get it. You were staking the credibility of Oxon Hill High School on a "C" student plus if it's slide presentation why do you need me? Shouldn't the principal be doing this?

I thought of every objection I could. In the back of my racing mind I thought what if the Maryland State board of Education didn't like the presentation and voted to close the school? Visions of 1,500 students, their parents, and dozens of faculty and staff beating down my parents' door seemed very real.

Before I responded concerning my doubts and fears, Mrs. Trohanis went on to say that the slides would be synchronized to an audiotape that I would narrate. I would have the script in advance and could practice before the production. Her trump card was that her husband was an instructional technology major at The University of Maryland and that he would be doing the production work. All the production work would be done at the University and I would be excused from a day of school. I would have a nice lunch and be able to have all the ice cream I could eat from the University's School of Agriculture. This was becoming more interesting by the minute. The other positive factor was that if I did this, I might be able to solidify my "C" in algebra. "Sure!" I said with confidence.

Mrs. Trohanis, Mrs. Duncan, my journalism teacher, and I drove to College Park, home of the University of Maryland Terrapins (Terrapins has to be one of the worst nicknames for any college team rivaled by

The University of Richmond Spiders.) Maryland's new slogan "Fear the Turtle" just doesn't do it for me. Despite its proximity to my home I had never set foot on the University campus.

The taping went off with few hitches and everyone one seemed pleased with the final product. The payoff came with lunch in the faculty dining room followed by Ag School ice cream. The real payoff came when the principal decided to play the production in front of the entire student body. Following the debut, I had my fifteen minutes of fame as students and faculty congratulated me. Oxon Hill High went on to get an "A" rating from The State Board of Education. My fifteen minutes of fame may have expanded to a hot sixteen.

The other high school field trip of note came after the 1970 football season. I had played JV ball, but it became obvious that varsity football was not in the cards for me. Money was becoming a factor and if I had hopes of going to college I would have to start earning and saving it. I kept my paper route, and junior year I started working at G.C. Murphy's variety store.

My love of football led me to become the P.A. announcer for the team. As a result of working P.A., I was considered a sort of ancillary member of the team. Oxon Hill won the county football championship, and following the season we were invited to attend a session of The U.S. Supreme Court. Someone from the school, and I don't know who, had some tie to the court and arranged the trip. Coach Vic Savoca told us that we would be sitting in a session of the court and that coats and ties were mandatory.

The big day came and we hopped a spanking clean tour bus to The Supreme Court Building near the U.S. Capitol and after clearance we were led to the rear of the court's chamber. We weren't briefed, but we were seeing the making of the law of the land. After a few minutes, the proceedings may have been about as exciting as someone reading from the DC phone book but we still had an appreciation of what we were seeing, and fifty-five players, coaches, and staff sat in silence.

Following the proceedings, we were ushered into a small chamber room off the main chamber. We were told that we would meet Justice Byron "Whizzer" White, a Supreme Court justice who had played for the Pittsburgh Steelers back in the 1930's. Justice White spoke about the value of football and other sports while balancing academics. I remember him saying that one could benefit from the other as long as you kept both in perspective. He had the look of a Supreme Court Justice who had just come from Central Casting. Balding and bespectacled, he spoke in a strong steady voice appropriate for a person of his rank. Following his talk he fielded lots of questions and we had a team photo taken with him.

When we returned home from the trip, I remembered that I had a book at home, The Game, a history book of the National Football League and its teams. There, in the chapter on the Pittsburgh Steelers, was a full page photo of Byron "Whizzer" White in his Supreme Court robe.

Looking back at our field trip experiences, we never made it to New York City and I would not visit The Big Apple until my college years; however, I must admit that my classmates and I had some experiences that other schools never experienced. With the exception of the verboten Nike missile photos, I don't think I took many photos on our trips. Dad always talked about "mental snapshots" and that one should take a step back and appreciate what one was seeing. In our age of smart phones and other tech toys his words ring true. Unless my mind deteriorates to cream of mushroom soup no one or natural disaster can take those memories away from me.

A SICK MOM

Family situation comedies were the undoing of numerous American women—-point and period. You may say, "Whoa, Dude! Where do you get off making that statement?" It's a statement I've made numerous times when teaching my college mass media classes. Family situation comedies fed us a steady diet of what was supposed to be the ideal American family. Sitcoms told us how to dress, the ideal places to live, and what to buy.

TV sponsors ruled the roost in determining program content, and product placement was common in many programs. When Kodak was the primary sponsor of a sitcom there were more outdoor episodes with families taking photos. When the program switched from Kodak to Whirlpool appliances as the primary sponsor there were more episodes shot in the kitchen with Whirlpool Appliances in the background. In her book The Way We Never Were: American Families and the Nostalgia Trap, author Stephanie Coontz writes concerning the influence of family sitcoms such as Ozzie and Harriet, Leave it to Beaver, and Father Knows Best, as to shaping family values during the 1950's and early '60's. In many cases these shows led us to unrealistic expectations. When I was doing research for the book, Watching What We Watch: Primetime Television Through the Lens of Faith, I discovered a photo of a scene from the popular sitcom, Father Knows Best. The scene was of the Anderson family at the kitchen table with a plate piled high with hamburgers and with their heads bowed in prayer. Norman Rockwell could not have painted it any better.

The values and various trimmings were too much for most American women to achieve. Being a June Cleaver or Harriet Nelson, keeping a sparkling home, raising near perfect children, and looking like they had stepped out of the women's section of Macy's catalog placed the bar too high.

So what's a mother to do? Mom either works harder and drives herself to distraction, resorts to better parenting through chemistry, or gives up like a tortured rat in a B.F. Skinner psychology experiment. My Mom resorted to all three.

Alilee "Lee" Smith married Dad in 1952. I believe that her first years of parenting were fairly simple. I came along in 1953 and Doug in 1957. Mom said that in her early days of parenting she had to look for something to do. This was without state of the art appliances—she had an "Easy" brand wringer washer. Things got more complicated as we got older. Doug experienced health problems with his knees and he had multiple operations in his early years. This was coupled with the fact that Mom developed an inner drive to where she knew no limits as to work. Sewing became her thing and she was a non-stop seamstress. One Christmas she made Dad a sport coat and it was Brooks Brothers' quality. Dad opened the package and upon seeing the coat said, "Babe, you shouldn't have paid so much." Mom responded that she had made the coat and I piped up, "She did make it! I saw her." Dad looked inside the coat for the label and there was none.

She continued to sew and work harder with each year. She supplemented the family income with sewing and ironing for people. By 1960 things started going south for her. She was a victim of quacks and bad medical luck. She had her tonsils removed without full anesthesia. Another doctor diagnosed her with an ulcer and she was bedridden. A change in diet corrected the situation but she eventually refused to abide by the diet and returned to spending hours in bed. Migraine headaches were common as well and no doctor seemed to be able to treat them.

Within a couple of years, mood changes became evident. She changed from being mild mannered to angry and passive aggressive. When I was six she was working on a project and I was goofing around nearby and holding a Coke. I accidentally spilled Coke on part of the project. She became so angry that she slapped me several times. Dad saw this and slapped her once in return. She left the room in silence and Dad returned to working on his project. Mom went upstairs and began dressing as if she was going to church. Timidly, I asked her what was she doing. "I'm leaving." she said in a quiet but angry voice. She had no suitcase, just the clothes on her back and a purse. I thought that if I had attempted to run away from home I would at least take a small duffle bag with me.

I panicked as she went out the door. She crossed the street to the DC Transit bus stop in front of the liquor store. I didn't know the Sunday bus schedule and I was convinced that a bus would come by any second and whisk her away to who knows where. I ran to get Dad to tell him what was happening. A bus came past the stop without Mom getting on. Mom and Dad talked at the bus stop and it seemed as if they were having a calm, normal conversation. After what seemed to be many minutes but was probably five Mom and Dad came back home. I was relieved but had no idea what had happened. The situation had been scary when Mom left but it was scary in a different sense because of the manner in which it was handled when they came home. There was no screaming or yelling, no explanation as to what had happened, and no resolution to the conflict. It was as if nothing had happened at all. We continued the Sunday afternoon/evening routine of making ice cream, attending church, then watching Disney and Ed Sullivan.

Instead of being relieved that things had returned to normal I became uneasy and scared. It was as if Mom had turned off a switch and everything was OK: total Jekyll and Hyde. The next day was Labor Day and we went to Marshall Hall Amusement Park for an unplanned trip. We were a typical "Leave it to Beaver" family.

Mom's "leaving" became a pattern. Whenever she felt stress she threatened to leave. Dad would gently convince her to come home and everything was normal—for awhile. Relatively small things could set her off but she could weather major problems. She took on the responsibility at our church for being a Vacation Bible School teacher and did a great job. While other kids were making crafts out of popsicle sticks we were painting apple made from Plaster of Paris molds. She had our class learn a Roy Rogers and Dale Evans song, "How Do I know, The Bible Tells Me So." All the other teachers thought that we couldn't learn it but we did. We were the hit of the parents' assembly.

Crafts and sewing continued but Mom was taking more pills. At first it was for her stomach, then for her thyroid, then for some other ailment. The pill bottles increased and it appeared that there were one or two new ones each month. Mom was also beginning to gain weight. A few years ago I spoke with my doctor about Mom's situation and she nodded with a half smile. "Your mom was part of trend of the times. Male doctors often chalked up a woman's problems as 'female problems' or 'a lack of energy.' The solution was to give them a pill. It could be 'Momma's Little Helpers' or 'Momma's Dozy Downers,' whatever seemed to work. When the pills lost effectiveness the solution was to give her another pill. Doctors never seemed to get to the root of the problem that many women did not have a feeling of self worth."

The doctor's assessment made sense to me. I did have to suppress a smile because my warped mind went to a spoof commercial on Saturday Night Live featuring a hyper dog that was given "Doggie Downers" and a lethargic dog that was given "Puppy Uppers." The same principle seemed to apply with overmedicating women in the '50's and 60's. I compared notes with Eileen and discovered that her Mom was part of this trend.

As more pills were prescribed there was the problem of women self medicating. Many doctors rarely monitored the amount of medication their patients were taking. This resulted in a witch doctor tandem of doctor and patient. Many doctors were content with a woman being a functioning zombie as long as she was not throwing plates at family members.

Mom's use of punishment would probably be considered child abuse today. It was common for parents of the day to spank or take a belt to a child for a few licks. In many cases the spanking was deserved. In Mom's case it went over the top. Belt whipping wouldn't stop at ten but continue until her arms were tired. She also utilized switches taken from bushes in our yard which left welts. A few minutes later she would administer Johnson's Baby Magic to the welts.

The situation improved a bit when we moved to Oxon Hill. There was the excitement of the new house and a new convenience of a Kenmore dish washer. She never used it, preferring to wash the dishes by hand. The dishwasher served as a storage bin. She decided to supplement the family income by taking in ironing and sewing. She assisted in paying for my music lessons by sewing and making Christmas presents for my music teacher. When Dad decided to enclose the back porch to create more living space, Mom was at his side hammering nails in ninety degree heat. The porch turned into a dining room with a small room at the end which served as Dad's workshop. It was great handiwork by my parents, and a contractor could not have done a better job.

All of this showed progress for Mom but she had the problem of trying to deliver unrealistic expectations. She was trying to be a "Supermom" years before the term came into vogue. If someone brought her laundry and ironing with a request to have it done by Friday she would volunteer, "Oh, I can have that done by Wednesday." The same was true for sewing deadlines. If a room mother at school called and ask if she could bake a dozen cookies for a school party she would volunteer to bake four dozen. She operated on the hamster wheel of heightened expectations and her work was a version of the old TV show Name That Tune. If Bob said, "I can name that tune in four notes," Mom would have said, "Bob, I can name that tune in two notes."

By 1963 migraine headaches set in. Many people suffer from the intense pain and side effects of migraines, but Mom's were genuine headbusters. She could not stand light so her room was pitch dark even at high noon. Sound was also a problem so it was best if Doug and I went to a neighbor's house if we wanted to watch TV. Severe nausea came along with the headaches and so did plates of potato soup to calm the stomach. Doctors were not making house calls during the early 1960's but our doctor made an exception when Mom couldn't get to the front door let alone manage a car ride to the doctor's office. The doctor administered shots which gave her some relief.

An issue that cropped up in late 1963 and throughout 1964 was that Mom decided that she did not like the house. This came out of the blue and blindsided Dad. There was no rational reason for her to dislike the house other than the forty-five degree angle of the hill in our backyard. Dad made good use of the hill by planting a rock garden and growing killer tomatoes. There were times when we were traveling to the store and out of the blue she would voice her displeasure of the house and we would wonder why was she thinking this way.

A reason why she may have resented the house was that she felt isolated in comparison to our dwellings in DC. Minnesota Ave. provided everything we needed within walking distance: groceries, prescriptions, church, the dentist, and two neighborhood movie theatres. The bus provided transportation to Downtown, and you could hop a trolley car as well. The house in Southlawn was smack in the middle of the subdivision, and the closest shopping option was a 7-11 a half mile away. Eventually, a strip mall, Oxon Hill Plaza, was built in 1965. Mom couldn't drive and I can remember her feeling anxious when Dad was trying to give her driving lessons. She never got the concept of gentle braking and driving lessons were comparable to a thrill ride at Marshall

Hall Amusement Park. Dad was a gentle, affirming teacher, much kinder than the football coaches at Oxon Hill High, who also taught drivers' education. She simply could not get the hang of driving and she remained a non driver for the rest of her life.

In early 1964, Doug and I had tonsillectomies. This was not major surgery. Doug and I were eating hamburgers a week after but Mom experienced major stress. Maybe she was thinking about her own tonsillectomy and generalizing her experience to us. She had been steadfast during our minor surgeries but she must have experienced a delayed reaction shortly thereafter.

It was during spring break, and Doug and I were home from school and eating breakfast. We were told that if we did anything "bad" she was leaving. We took her seriously and we walked on pins and needles all day; however, boys will be boys. It was late afternoon when Doug and I were goofing around and broke an Easter egg he made as a first grade project. He started to cry and I tried to do everything possible to avoid Mom's wrath. She asked what happened and seeing the broken egg she asked no further questions. She put on her church clothes, walked out the door, and headed to the bus stop around the corner.

The first thing I could think of was to call Dad at work. Dad had warned me that Mom had not been "feeling well" and to call him if there was trouble at home. There was no dial tone. Mom may have sabotaged the phone so that we couldn't call out. I ran across the street to use the neighbor's phone, but there was no answer at Dad's desk. This was long before voice mail so I thought that maybe he was away from his desk so I kept dialing. At that point I thought that the only thing I could do was to run to the bus stop and plead with Mom to come home. Once again she had left without a suitcase.

I ran to the corner within sight of the bus stop and saw Mom but then a miracle happened. Dad had sensed that it was going to be a difficult day on the home front, so he left work early. He pulled up to the bus stop, opened the passenger side door, and urged Mom to come in. She did, and they made a U-Turn and drove off. About an hour later they returned home in time for Mom to start dinner; again, nothing was said by either party.

Following dinner it was pretty much the evening routine as usual. Mom washed the dishes then joined Dad to watch the evening news.

We all watched TV until about 9PM, then Doug and I went to bed. There was no TV in my room and the radio was becoming my friend. Next morning everything was fine. When Doug and I came home it was a question of whether we would be pleased or frightened. It was all quiet on the Oxon Hill front and we breathed a sigh of relief. The blow-ups with nothing said afterwards continued to be a mystery.

A few weeks later Mom had agreed to make cupcakes for our class Spring Party. The party was held, but there was no sign of Mom delivering cupcakes. There were plenty of cupcakes but none of them appeared to be Mom's. When I got home there was a strange woman making dinner for us in the kitchen. "Hi Gary. I'm Mrs. B., Debbie B.'s mother. Your Mom wasn't feeling well and had to go to the hospital. I told her not to worry and that I would come over and make sure that you and Doug were OK."

I had never met Mrs. B., but I knew that Debbie was one of the cutest girls in the class. In my selfish fifth grade thinking all I could think of was that Mrs. B. was doing something that Mom should be doing and how embarrassed I was that she was going to be telling Debbie. I was through thinking selfish thoughts when the phone rang and it was Dad. He said that Mom was in the hospital and that he would be home later that evening. Mrs. B. fed us an early dinner then returned home to feed her family. Dad had arranged for a neighbor to take over Mrs. B.'s shift.

Dad arrived home later that evening and told us that Mom had "a bad day" and called the doctor. She was told that she should go to the mental ward of Washington Hospital Center as soon as possible. Dad came home as soon as he could and took her to the hospital. She was resting comfortably, but she had no idea as to how long she was going to be there.

The next morning Dad went to work, and Doug and I got ready for school. The same neighbor fed us breakfast and made sure that we got off to school. We went to school and several kids asked if my Mom was OK. I said that I thought so and that was the best answer I could muster. I certainly didn't want to tell them that she had gone to the mental ward of Washington Hospital Center.

School seemed to be a blur that day as I had no idea of what to expect when we came home. Our neighbor was there to greet us, and she had everything under control. Dad returned from work at his usual time and he had taken off from work early to visit Mom. He had no new news except to tell us that there would be a new person watching us tomorrow. He didn't go into detail but our new "guardian" was a single mom named Donna with a baby. She was a friend of one of Dad's co-workers and needed a place to stay after she and her husband split. I believe that Donna was in her late twenties and she became something of a big sister to us. She stayed with us for a couple of weeks until Mom came home.

The two weeks had seemed like months. Dad told us that Mom might seem a little different but not to worry. Dad was right—she did seem different. Her eyes were wide and her speech slow. Doug and I were told that she had undergone something called electro shock therapy where her brain had been shocked so she would forget bad things and remember the good. This seemed to be an OK solution to me so we waited.

Over the next few days things did not go well as she was not able to cope with basic stress. The doctor recommended more shock treatments and she returned to the hospital. Dad scrambled to find a new keeper for us because Donna had taken a new job and was moving away.

We had met Dad's co-worker Lister and his wife Marilyn several times before, and they were just what the doctor ordered. Lister was tall with black hair and hailed from Alabama. He was a southern version of Dean Martin. In contrast, Marilyn was short and hailed from New York State. They were the odd couple but you could tell that they were very much in love. For some reason, Lister referred to me as "Jose" and Doug as "Greco." Lister went to work with Dad while Marilyn held forth at the house.

A couple days after Mom returned to the hospital Dad told me that I could come visit her. Doug was not allowed to come because he was too young. When we arrived at the hospital I found out that I was too young to visit patients. I was eleven-years-old but an exception had been made in this case for a special reason.

The mental wards of over fifty years ago were much different from today's wards. Alcoholics and drug addicts were in the same ward as others with mental disorders. The common room was large with individual rooms surrounding it. One room appeared to be a cell with the sign "Bad" written on the door. Apparently this was a place for problem patients.

In the common room there was a large long table with about twenty men sitting around it making crafts. Other patients were watching TV or reading, while others stared off into space or walked the ward with no apparent destination in mind. I maintained my composure but thought the place was creepy and I wanted to run off to the hospital cafeteria.

The reason I was there was because immediately after a shock treatment Mom forgot almost everything. She would stare at Dad and ask, "You're my husband, aren't you?" Later she would ask, "Don't I have two boys?" The plan was that I would be brought into the room by a nurse and she would remind Mom, "Lee, this is your son Gary." The first time I saw her it was the same glassy stare I had seen at home. The nurse introduced me and after a few seconds she seemed to recognize me. Mom smiled weakly as I walked to her bedside and said, "Hi Mom." "Hi Gary," as she remembered me, and I smiled in approval. "How are you doing?" I asked and she responded with, "Oh, I'm a little tired." I was allowed to stay for only a few minutes and then I was ushered out of the room by a nurse. Dad remained with Mom.

The nurse took me to the corner of the common room where patients were watching TV. I was told that I could watch TV with them. The patients were watching or pretending to watch a soap opera. The craft table where the men were sitting seemed to be much more interesting than the soap opera so I decided to take a look.

The men were joking, laughing, and smoking like chimneys. They seemed pretty normal to me. There were various crafts scattered around the table, leather, beadwork, ceramic tiles, etc. One guy had a pile of crafts in front of him. As I got closer to the table one guy asked, "Hey partner, what are you doing here?" It wasn't a threatening question, just a curious one. I told him about Mom. He responded, "Oh, she just got the lightening rod. Didn't help me much. I still wanted to drink. Welcome to the Alkie Table partner. My name is Fred and the rest of these bums can introduce themselves if they want to." The other men waved in acknowledgement.

Fred was the one with the most crafts in front of him. "Wow! You have a whole lot of stuff here.' I said. He laughed, "Yeah, I guess I'm going to have to open a store when I get out of here." Fred was a jovial type as well as the rest of the group. I had some vague notion about alcoholism. I knew that Myrtle's husband Earl was one because my parents said so and I could notice his strange behavior and mood swings. I overheard Mom and Dad saying that Earl would turn from "Joe Six Pack" weekdays to being a beast on weekends because he drank the hard stuff. He physically and verbally abused Myrtle and one time slapped her with such force that she fell down the stairs.

The "Alkies" seemed happy and mild. They were as if you had discovered a new group of uncles. When I came to visit they welcomed me, talked about baseball and how I was doing in school. It was preferable to watching soap operas with the zombies.

Mom spent the rest of the summer in the hospital. Marilyn and Lister spent the summer with us and I think that they had almost most as much fun as Doug and I. They were childless and Marilyn couldn't have children. Dad told us this but he never went into detail. The couple adopted us and considered us to be their kids. Even serious situations were made humorous. One night Doug complained of having a loose tooth so Lister tried to practice his dentistry skills on my brother. He tied one end of a string to Doug's tooth and the other end to a door knob. The conventional wisdom was that by slamming the door the tooth would come out. Numerous times of door slams failed so Lister tried to pull the string himself. I was in the corner practicing the accordion and seeing the struggle I started playing the dirge, The Volga Boatmen. Marilyn and Lister started laughing while Doug was in pain and trying not to cry. The tooth came out on the third pull and I think that Doug got a buck that night from The Tooth Fairy.

Mom came home a couple of weeks before school and she had not finished all her treatments. She actually felt one of the treatments and refused to take the rest of the scheduled ones. She seemed a little better but was a little spacey and she seemed to be operating in slow motion. There was a neighbor down the street who had been through shock therapy a few years earlier, and Mom bonded with her as they took long walks to the shopping center.

The years following the treatments were touch and go for Mom. There were extended good periods punctuated by periods of depression. The medications increased, and everyone thought that it was OK because the doctor was prescribing the meds. Eventually Mom isolated herself and my parents didn't attend my sporting events or other school functions. They also stopped attending church although Dad drove Doug and me to church each Sunday.

The only way I can explain what happened with Mom was that she was a victim of the times. She was also the victim of an unloving mother who made her drop out of school in the eighth grade even though she was making straight "A's." From all the information I've gathered, I can find no good reason why her mother made her drop out of school. When I was older and came home from college I urged her to walk the couple of blocks to nearby Oxon Hill High and take the nighttime GED classes. I know that she would have been a model student, and she passed with flying colors. I believe that if she had received a diploma it would have given her a sense of self worth and would have decreased the depression. For some reason she never took my advice.

Mom came from a family of eight who resided near the North Carolina town of Statesville. Her sister Blanche was the closest to her in age being six years older. One of her sisters had a baby before Mom was born so people laughed that she became an aunt before birth. Mom was an unwanted pregnancy. Her mother, Carrie Clanton, was a widow and dated a man, Thomas Smith. She became pregnant and they married. Carrie Clanton was forty years old when Mom was born. One does not need to be a mental health professional to see that Mom would have a less than perfect childhood.

I can remember seeing my grandmother three times and I was never close to her. The times I saw her were on a farm outside of Statesville. During her early years, Mom's family lived in Statesville then moved to the farm outside of town. My grandfather, Tom Smith, worked the farm and various other jobs during The Great Depression. One of his jobs was a truck driver and when Mom was old enough she accompanied him to far-away places such as Gettysburg, PA. She was my grandfather's jewel and for some reason he called her "Sis." On the other hand, I believe her mother was resentful and I can never remember Mom and grandmother showing any signs of affection such as hugging.

I learned that my grandmother was involved with the occult, voodoo, you name it, and she spent a good portion of the family budget visiting fortune tellers and other quacks. In turn she kept a tight rein on Tom's money, and she once took a knife to him when she discovered a couple of dollars in his shirt pocket. The childhood events and the trends of the times in the 50's and 60's contributed to Mom's mental state.

Due to many circumstances beyond her control, Mom never achieved her potential. The great football coach Vince Lombardi said "It is great to have potential, but people die with potential." In July 2003, my mother Alilee "Lee" Dreibelbis died at seventy-five, and with potential.

STAR BOY

Being a paperboy was one of the best learning experiences of my life. I mentioned in the first chapter some of my paperboy experiences. I delivered papers in an era when you could still get stuff delivered to your doorstep. Not only newspapers, but milk, doughnuts, cookies, and potato chips, as well as other goods could come straight to your door. Door to door salespeople were valued by some and detested by others. Fuller Brush men were everywhere and vacuum cleaner salesmen competed with one another by offering charm similar to a grown up Eddie Haskell.

When I took the paper route from Glenn, the art loving high school Don Juan, it was a new experience in being a young businessman. As I mentioned, The Washington Star sold you the papers at wholesale, then I became the retailer by charging the customer the face value of the paper collecting the money door to door each month. This was in an era when paperboys could collect money and not fear being mugged. Some customers weren't home so I left them a note that I had been by to collect. Many times they would leave money in their mailboxes with a note. Other customers were deadbeats and it was next to impossible to collect money from them. There was one customer who never had money but I would see him unloading six packs of Rolling Rock Beer from his car. "I don't have it today kid. Come back tomorrow." was always his response. Tomorrow was always the richest day in the year but tomorrow never came. At least this was in an era when you didn't have to worry about being greeted by someone at the door with an AK 47.

Delivering papers was pretty simple but one still had to be responsible. When I was in school, the papers were usually curbside by my house when I got home. During the summer I could time it where I was done with my sports activity in time to greet by route manager with his delivery. With papers piled high in my wagon I was on my way and the streets on my route are still etched in my memory: Carson, Furness, Shelby, Leyte, Sherwood, and Roanne. Roanne was the end of my route so I celebrated by riding down the hill toboggan style on to Leyte. I had a wipeout plan at the last second if there was a car coming down Leyte.

I mentioned before that customer service was my forte. No throwing the paper on the lawn or driveway for me. Papers behind the screen door or in mailbox hooks was the practice. If some poor customer didn't have a screen door I placed the paper beneath a rock.

When I was subbing for Glenn, I needed a "cheat sheet" with the delivery addresses written on a sheet of paper. Soon I was delivering papers without the sheet because I had memorized the route. Glenn would alert me as to changes such as customer adds and drops. Today I have recurring dreams that I have been asked to deliver papers on my old route with no cheat sheet. It must be one of those stress type dreams. The strange thing is that I could probably deliver the route today by memory.

The Star would alert me as to changes with add and drop slips in my paper bundle. Complaints were pink slips and if you received too many of them, The Star would "pink slip" you as a Star Boy. Complaint slips came if the paper was wet or dirty or if you missed a delivery. Fortunately for me I received very few complaints with most coming from the nonpaying, deadbeat customers (I wish I could have pink slipped them.)

Our neighborhood was transitional and we had lots of military and government worker families. This was a benefit for me because new people were always moving into houses on my route. The transitional benefit was that paper carriers received bonuses, prizes, and trips if they got new customers. You were never penalized for losing a customer if they moved away. Acquiring new customers was down to a science for me. There were times when customers would alert me that they were moving away and they would give me the moving date. I would watch the house like a hawk for the new tenants sometimes greeting them at the moving truck as they were moving in. For Sale signs were also noted. I made friends with one of my customers who was a realtor, and I received insider information concerning sales and moves.

The Star would give you a check for $5 if you got a certain number of new customers. They ran special nights where if you got one new customer you got a twenty-four bar box of Hershey's Chocolate Bars (Mr. Goodbars were my favorite.)

One time the special item was a Kennedy Half Dollar which was becoming a collector's item. The rules given to us were that when we called in a new customer there would be a bell at certain intervals to indicate we had won a silver dollar. I had two new subscribers and my strategy was to speak slowly and stall until the bell rang. I called The Star and started speaking slowly, "Hi...I'm Gary Dreibelbis...Dreibelbis is spelled D-R-E-I-B-E-L-B-I-S...did you get that?...My first customer is..." DING! (I'm thinking, Wow, I've won a half dollar and I haven't even given them the first customer information.) My plan was going well. I give them the customer information. DING! Another half dollar. By this time I'm really milking things). "OK...The second customer is Frank Osborn...That's Osborn with an "s" not a "z" like the Wizard of Oz..."DING! By the time I finish giving the information for the second customer there are four more DINGS! When I finished I heard a hurried voice on the other end, "OK Gary, we've got it. You've won seven half dollars. Thanks. Bye." CLICK. I could tell that The Star office worker just wanted to get rid of me. The next day my route manager presented me with an envelope containing seven Kennedy Half Dollars. My speed, or lack of it, paid off.

The small prizes were cool because you could win something by getting one customer. The bonanzas were usually given to the top ten paper/salesboys in the DC area. One of the big trips I wanted to win was to Puerto Rico. The Star put out a flyer promoting the trip showing beaches, palm trees, pineapples, and wonders too numerous to mention. Less exotic trips were to places like Philadelphia and Atlantic City.

The contest were always made interesting by The Star because they would put a points sheet in your bundle giving you up to date information on the point leaders. The way the point system worked was that you got 100 points for a daily subscription, 50 points for a Monday-Saturday subscription, and 25 point for Sunday only. Paperboys could watch for point sheet updates the way some fans watch NASCAR points. I was in the top twenty for the Puerto Rico trip but could never crack the top ten so there were no beaches or tasting pineapples for me.

When The Star announced the Atlantic City trip they announced that the top twenty salesboys would go. Relying upon all my faculties and resources I plunged into this contest the way The Diving Horse plunged into the water tank at Atlantic City. The Star's Atlantic City brochure boasted of beaches, The Boardwalk, salt water taffy, and a large horse diving into a tank of water. Wow! I would trade pineapples to see a diving Mr. Ed anytime.

I called The Star with new customers on a regular basis. I took the brochure with the picture of the diving horse door to door to show potential customers. Many people said that they would take the paper for a couple of months so that I could win the trip. I started going over to the route of another boy who was less industrious and asked if I could solicit in his territory. He could care less; he was delivering papers because his father thought it would teach him responsibility.

The Star decided that they would fuel the competition. They announced that the top twenty-five boys in the point totals at that time would get a "preview" of the Atlantic City trip. The Star would fly us out of Dulles International Airport and we would fly over Atlantic City on to a New York City flyover then return back to DC for a sky high day trip. We wouldn't land in either place just fly over it. This sounded great to me because I had never flown before nor had I ever seen Atlantic City or New York City even from the air, so this would be an adventure.

The next day the point standings came out, and I was nowhere to be found. They always listed the top fifty carriers in the point race and I wasn't on the sheet. I looked again carefully and this time more slowly. Then at number twenty in the rankings I spotted route 151, my route, with the name "Grebulis." That had to be me! They were always misspelling my name but at least they usually started it with a "D." Before I started delivering my papers I called The Star to double check. They told me that they were busy with route managers calling in problems and to call back later.

I ran through my route at breakneck speed not bothering to pet any dogs or read portions of the paper as was my custom. When I got home Mom was talking on the phone to a neighbor across the street. "Why can't she walk across the street to talk to the neighbor?" I thought. Several minutes passed and the phone was free. I called The Star's circulation department and asked them if they had made a mistake with the name in the point standings. "What's your route number kid?" questioned the circulation person. "151" I replied. "Yeah that's you kid. What kinda mane is that anyway? Greek?" I said thank you and didn't answer the "Greek" question to tell him that "Dreibelbis" is Pennsylvania Dutch. Things were smoking! I was at number twenty "with a bullet," as

Billboard Magazine would say about their Top Forty records.

Closing for this contest was in five days and I had to keep the momentum going. There was action over at "Mr. Responsibilities" route with two people moving in. I snagged both of them but would it be enough to keep me in the top twenty? Some people on my route who were taking the rival Washington Post heard about the contest from their neighbors taking The Star. They agreed to take The Star for a couple of months then drop it. I debated the ethics of this but decided that as long as I gave them good service I couldn't help it if they dropped The Star. I had five more subscribers in my column and the results would come the following Monday.

My route manager was late on Monday. School was out and I had been home for ten minutes. The grind of The Star truck finally made its way around the corner and my papers were dumped. No time for my route manager to talk; he was late and on a mission. I was on a mission as well. I pulled out the points slip and there at number 20 was "Drubulis 151." No doubt this time and they had even started my name with a "D."

The next day we were given the logistics concerning the trip. Five of us would meet a supervisor at a Virginia shopping center at an appointed time. He would take us to Dulles to meet the rest of the carriers. It was an American Airlines flight to Atlantic City and we would get a snack and lunch on the flight.

Flight day came and Mom was a nervous wreck. She had never flown but she was giving lots of advice. "Make sure you have one of those life vest things. Don't eat too much or you will get air sick. Call when you get to the airport." Dad took me to the shopping center where I met the supervisor and four other boys. The supervisor was reassuring and told Dad that I would be in good hands.

The other boys were nice enough, and one who was near the top of the leader standings started talking about his route. He said that his route was in a high rise apartment building and all he had to do was go to the mailroom and put the paper in the customers air chute and it would be delivered. The other guys had routes in apartment complexes as well. I always said that the boys who had apartment routes could cover ground faster and had more opportunities for new customers than those of us who were delivering in house subdivisions. I didn't say anything and I was just happy to be there.

Dulles International Airport was the largest building I had ever seen with the exception of The Pentagon. It was relatively new and it dwarfed National Airport by comparison. Dulles had large windows and we could see the mobile lounges used to transport passengers to their planes. The lounges were state of the art at the time.

All the kids were excited as we boarded the plane and it was the first flight for many of us. As we entered the plane, we were greeted by smiling, smartly dressed flight attendants. I had seen such scenes in movies but here I was actually experiencing everything as to being a flight passenger. Shortly after we sat down and buckled up the engines revved and the plane rolled slowly down the runway. Soon it was takeoff and we were airborne.

Our flight path took us over the familiar sights of DC: the Washington Monument, the Lincoln and Jefferson Memorials, with the Capitol building in the distance. It wasn't long until we were flying over the ocean and it was the first time I had seen it. The flight attendant came through the cabin with chocolate cupcakes for our snack along with ginger ale. Just as I was beginning to think, "This is living," the kid across the aisle from me began to hurl. A flight attendant was there immediately to pull a barf bag from the seat in front of him to catch the aftermath. The kid looked like his name could have been Poindexter. He appeared to be from one of the more affluent areas of DC such as Georgetown or the Montgomery County suburbs. He probably didn't even deliver his papers and delegated that to his butler. Before I saw the flight attendant with the barf bag I didn't know its intended purpose. I thought it was like a doggie bag for leftover snacks or lunch.

It wasn't long until we could see the beach, Boardwalk, and buildings of Atlantic City. I strained to see the tower of the diving horse but I couldn't make it out. A few minutes later, the pilot announced that we were approaching New York City. We were on the side with the best view so the kids from the other side of the plane got out of their seats and crowded our side. The pilot told everyone to remain in their seats and he would circle the plane so everyone could enjoy the view. We got a great view of the skyscrapers and could make out The Statue of Liberty.

The plane circled and we were on our way home. It wasn't long until we could see the mountains of Western Maryland, the Potomac, and then Dulles. Everyone cheered as we touched down, even the seasoned fliers. If it was that good in the air how good would Atlantic City be in person.

The contest was two weeks away, and I fought to stay in the top twenty; it was touch and go. Finally, one day Mr. Z., my route manager, delivered my bundles and said to me, "Pack your bags Gary. You're going to Atlantic City. Congratulations, you worked hard." I stared at him as he was one of those Publisher's Clearing House people who had come to my door with one of those huge cardboard checks telling me I had won a gazillion dollars. All I could say was, "Thanks." Details of the trip would come to me in a few days.

I went off to deliver my papers without telling Mom. Everything seemed unreal and I delivered my papers in silence not even talking to my favorite dogs. Some of my customers greeted me and I managed a slight smile. When I returned home Mom was making dinner and I told her. Her response was the same as mine—disbelief. Eventually it sunk in that I was going on the biggest adventure of my life and she went into a barrage of questions at Cheetah speed: "What are you going to pack? How many shoes do you need? What day do you leave?"

Every question was answered and in about two weeks I was on my way to National Airport instead of Dulles for the trip to Atlantic City. Mom and Dad dropped me off, and I entered the airport as a seasoned traveler. Inside my stomach felt like the wooden roller coaster at Marshall Hall. Upon entering the American Airlines terminal I saw people I recognized from The Star with signs as well as the four boys I had met on the air trip. Poindexter "The Amazing Barf Boy" was there as well.

We were herded on to a smaller plane than we had taken for the flyover but it was comfortable with friendly flight attendants. We were treated like first class citizens as the chaperones took care of our luggage and other details. Once again the engines revved and we started moving. National's, now Ronald Reagan, runways are very near the Potomac River. As we increased speed I began to panic because I thought that we were going right into the drink. My thoughts ran to the headline in tomorrow's Star: "Plane With Twenty-Five Star Boys Crashes," as well as the announcement on local TV news stations, "Twenty-five Paperboys Crash in the Potomac: Film at eleven."

Just when it looked as if we were going to hit the water we achieved lift off and we were on our way. When you take off from Reagan the monuments and buildings appear much closer and larger than when you take off from Dulles. For those unfamiliar with DC, Reagan is just a bridge away from the city. The view as we left looked like a model railroad layout of DC.

We took the ocean route again. Since it was a direct flight we only had time for a snack. We finished our snacks and we were ready to land. The sights of Atlantic City were in the distance, and soon we were on terra firma. A cheer went up from the entire group and it was the first noise we had made, being the polite Star Boys that we were.

After we secured our luggage, we were loaded into vans and taken to a modest one story motel not far from the Boardwalk. It wasn't the fanciest motel in Atlantic City but it was certainly suitable. When we entered our rooms we found boxes of salt water taffy with "Welcome to Atlantic City" written on them. Poindexter probably consumed half of the box by dinner.

The chaperones organized the group and took us to a nearby Howard Johnson's, where we were told that we could order anything on the menu but we must have a least one serving of a fruit or vegetable. This was bending The Food Pyramid a bit but heck we were on vacation.

After dinner we were given a tour of The Boardwalk and we were back at the motel by our 10PM curfew.

We were told not to leave our rooms at night and that anyone doing so would lose their paper route and be sent home. It was anyone's guess as to how we would be sent home but no one wanted to test the system. My guess was that the poor disobedient soul would receive a one way Greyhound ticket to DC and their parents would have to reimburse The Star COD. I had taken a Greyhound to Baltimore and it was the longest forty miles I had ever experienced. The bus smelled only slightly better than our school bus with the smell of stale alcohol replacing tuna fish as the dominant foul smell. The Star had hired a security guard to enforce the curfew.

The next day we ate breakfast at the Howard Johnson's. The trip itinerary was given to us, including mornings on The Boardwalk, beach time in the afternoon, back to the motel for clean up, dinner at Ho-Jo's, back to our rooms to watch TV, and bed check at 10PM. It seemed like a perfectly reasonable schedule to everyone and besides, The Star was paying for it.

The Boardwalk was wide and wonderful with numerous attractions. The chaperones warned us not to squander our money on games because the game operators were often less than honest. There was no danger of that for me because I wanted to buy some souvenirs for the family.

We finally got to see The Diving Horse on day three. The horse was not as big as the one pictured in the brochure. He, and I'm pretty sure it was a "he," was loaded into some type of contraption and taken to the top of the platform where he was met by a human diver. The announcer blared over the P.A. system along with circus-like background music. Before we knew it there was "One, Two, Three...SPLASH." That was it. The Diving Horse was OK but I guess I expected more. The splash was big but the whole act seemed to be in speed-up. I got the feeling that they had lured enough suckers in to see the act so let's hurry up and get it over with so we can lure in the next group of suckers. Please remember that this whole event before animal rights activists brought people to their senses concerning the possible dangers to the horses.

From the horse it was off to lunch and on to the beach. The beach was becoming more crowded as we got closer to the weekend. It was only Wednesday, but each day seemed to draw more sun worshipers to the warm sands. By Friday I was ready to go home. The experience had been a wonderful adventure and The Star had promised us five days in Atlantic City with us arriving on Monday and leaving on Friday; however; most of us had experienced enough and some kids were homesick.

The trip home seemed faster. For some reason trips home always seemed faster to me than trips to a destination. The descent into National was beautiful. I never tire of returning to DC and the beautiful descent into Reagan, always remembering my first time seeing the famous monuments from the sky. The experience of landing was the reverse thrill of taking off as again it looked as if we were doomed to be in the murky waters of the Potomac. No problem. The pilot had probably landed here dozens of times and with great precision we were on the ground.

Dad was waiting for me at the luggage belt which was conveniently near the exit. I didn't even need the chaperone's assistance and in short order we were on our way back to Oxon Hill through Alexandria and over the "Woody Wilson Bridge." Mom was happy to see me with Doug caring less. I distributed the souvenirs with each person receiving a large box of salt water taffy and Mom and Dad receiving a picture of the Atlantic City Boardwalk mounted on wood. The picture hung with pride on the wall of our back porch/ dining room for a few months until it was banished to the attic for some other "masterpiece."

The trip was memorable not only because of The Boardwalk, beaches, Diving Horse, and taffy, it was memorable because it was the first time I had been away from home without my parents for any length of time. I had been to a safety patrol training camp near Baltimore for a few days when I was entering sixth grade, but that didn't seem to count. Atlantic City was A TRIP! AN ADVENTURE!, far above our "staycations" and without my parents.

"How did it go?" asked Mr. Z. on my first day back from vacation. "Great!" I responded. "We saw The Diving Horse, went to the beach, and ate at Howard Johnson's!" (I could never resist the twenty-eight flavors of ice cream, trying a different flavor every time I went.) "Glad you had a good time. We had some complaints about your sub. Lots of missed papers." frowned Mr. Z. I had entrusted my route to a kid named Ricky who was always bugging me about helping or substituting for me when I was away. Ricky was a little older and seemed like a nice guy but he had the attention span of a gnat. Ricky had two cute sisters who would wash their cars in their bathing suits and would always say, "Hi!" to me. It was a scene straight from the movie Cool Hand Luke with the woman washing her car and George Kennedy lusting after her with repeated moans of "Lucille." Perhaps the sisters were the tipping point in the decision to let Ricky sub.

One night Ricky missed fifteen customers despite the fact that I gave him a clear cheat sheet. To make matters worse his mother thought that he had done a wonderful job, because he had fifteen papers left over. When Mr. Z tried to tell her that this was not a good thing she didn't understand. We can see where Ricky got his genes. So it was back to the job of delivering papers, patching up customer relations, and reuniting with their dogs.

Winning trips and prizes were nice perks for being a Star Boy but one of the other benefits was getting to know the dogs on my route. I love dogs and for the most part the dogs on my route loved me. I fussed over them at each stop and had a supply of Milk Bones for treats. My attention to canines and reading most of the paper from front to back added about 30 minutes to my route. This exasperated my Mom, who also scolded me for "lollygagging around." I never knew what "lollygagging" was. Is this what one did when they were choking on a lollypop?

The dogs were of all breeds with many being what I called "Heinz dogs"—fifty seven varieties. There were some memorable favorites. Angus, a Scotty of course, would run to the front fence without barking. He would follow me to the front door while I dropped off the paper then follow me to the gate tail wagging, and a look of, "See you tomorrow, It's almost happy hour and time for a shot of Old Angus."

During the summertime many people left their front doors open and I would open their screen doors and toss the paper into the living room. One beer drinking customer had a Lazy Boy recliner near the door, and I could literally toss the paper to the side of his recliner without spilling his beer. Now that's customer service. One day I was delivering to a new couple on my route, and as was my custom, I dropped the paper inside the screen door. I turned around and suddenly a beast appeared out of nowhere. It was the largest dog I had ever seen; a gray dog resembling the U.S.S. Enterprise. The conventional wisdom is to show no fear when approached by a potentially threatening dog. Remembering this "wisdom" I tried to fake it as best I could. Suddenly there was a deep voice from the front door, "Betsy, don't eat the paperboy." It was my new customer smiling at Betsy. Betsy started wagging her tail and a waterfall of drool fell from her jowls. She wanted attention so I petted her and fed her my last Milk Bone. On the spot I determined that she was a three bone customer. Betsy could pass as a female version of the comic strip dog Marmaduke and rivaled "The Big M" in gentleness. After consuming the bone in short order, we went our separate ways.

There were exceptions to friendly canine companions. Chihuahuas were my nemeses. Sorry Chihuahua owners when I was delivering papers I never saw one that I liked and believe me I tried The Milk Bone persuasion did not work with these dogs.

The one dog that was a pain in the ass, both figuratively and literally, was a German Shepard named Heidi.

Heidi was a beautiful dog, a female Rin Tin Tin, but must have come from a line of dogs bred by The Gestapo. When I first started delivering "Heidi's Paper" I had to leave it in the front gate. This didn't work, as Heidi became a canine paper shredder. Then I put the paper in a brown paper bag and placed it outside the gate. Neighbors probably thought my customers were subscribing to a porn publication.

I spoke to the customers and they agreed that Heidi was a problem. They were a military couple who had met in Germany and the wife was German. We came to the agreement that Heidi would be locked on the back porch during the late afternoon when I was delivering papers. This seemed to work but at a certain angle as I left the house Heidi could see me from the porch. I could sense that she was even angrier because she was incarcerated. This went on for several weeks and it was a satisfactory arrangement but Heidi was not pleased.

One afternoon I delivered the paper and there was no barking. Was Heidi not at home? Was she at the kennel? Had some Gestapo agent in Argentina wired for her to come home?

It was the calm before the storm. As I was opening the screen door to deliver the paper a black and tan tornado came tearing around the corner of the house. Before I could react, Heidi rushed past me biting my buttocks with every Teutonic tooth ripping my jeans as well as my flesh. I was so scared that I pushed the front door opened. I spilled into the living room where much to my surprise Frau Whatever was sitting in a recliner, watching TV, and wearing nothing but bra and panties to beat the summer heat. She screamed something in German to the effect of "What in the hell are you doing in here, you Yankee scum?!" I think I screamed too and tried to avert my eyes from looking at her. Tried is the operative word here. The spirit was willing but the flesh was weak.

Stuttering and bleeding on her carpet all I could manage was a tearful "Heidi bit me." Frau Whatever went to get her robe and was able to corral Heidi to the back porch. Realizing that she had left the backdoor to the porch open Frau lunged to close it before Heidi could have a second helping of my bacon. She yelled at me, "Get out of here!" Her German accent gave her even more authority.

I had no trouble leaving the premises and once safe, I tried to assess the damage. Besides my butt feeling as if it had been stabbed by two dozen hypodermic needles the seat of my jeans was torn and was ready to flap in the wind like a blue denim flag. There were only about a dozen customers left to deliver so I pressed on hoping that no one would see my torn jeans and bloody buttocks. I was able to carry a pile of papers in such a way that concealed part of the damage. This was especially useful when a girl who was in my school class saw me as I delivered her paper. She took the paper and didn't notice that I looked like a discus thrower as I held papers to my side. I finished my route and took the alley way home so fewer people would see me.

When I arrived at home Mom was on the phone so I went to the bathroom to wash off the blood, patch myself the best I could, and put on a new pair of jeans. All this was accomplished with Mom still on the phone. I emerged from the bedroom to show her my jeans and tell her what had happened but I don't recall her reaction. I think that I was still in a bit of shock.

Suddenly, I noticed a police car in front of our house with two policemen approaching the front door. The worst thoughts came to mind: I was going to be arrested for animal abuse, breaking and entering, and being a Peeping Tom. Mom opened the door and the officers identified themselves before entering the living room. They sat down with one officer asking questions and the other taking notes. The questions were the "Who, What, When, Where, Why" type. After I responded to them the officers ask to see the injury. In one of the embarrassing moments of my life I bore my bloody buttocks to two of Oxon Hill's finest. "That looks pretty serious." said the recording officer. "Go to the doctor and get a tetanus shot." Just what I needed; more pain. To add insult to injury the second officer was trying not to laugh.

The officers said that Heidi would be quarantined for a few days. They left. Dad came home and saw that I was alive so not much was said as dinner was served. Heidi was released a few days later. The customers cancelled their subscription the same day. Perhaps there was too much embarrassment for both parties.

In the circulation rivalry with The Post The Star started adding more incentives for paperboys to sign new customers. One of them was a short evening radio program called "Star Boy." The program was about five minutes in length and included a Star commercial. The program was nothing more than a Star infomercial where listeners got to hear from different paperboys and it was similar to the old TV show Kids Say the

Darndest Things. Mr. Z. nominated me for the show and I was selected. Upon hearing my selection and air date, I told my customers and friends that I was going to be on the show. "Star Boy" aired during the evening drive time on WMAL radio and had a good audience because WMAL had good traffic reports and was always near the top of the ratings. Johnny Wilcox was the drive time D.J. and host of "Star Boy." Wilcox was part of a great WMAL lineup where all the D.J.s tried to be your radio friend.

Show day came and Dad left work early to pick me up and take me to the WMAL studios on Connecticut Ave. We fought traffic to travel across town but we made it in plenty of time. WMAL radio shared facilities with WMAL, now WJLA TV. We walked past the news and several other sets before coming to the radio side. A pleasant receptionist asked us the nature of our business. "I'm here for the "Star Boy" show and this is my father." I said confidently. "You must be Gary...how do you say your last name?" "Dra BELL biz." Dad said trying to sound it our phonetically. "The other answer is with a lot of difficulty." The receptionist laughed and said "Great to meet you. Mr. Wilcox will be with you in a minute." "Star Boy" aired at 5:05 following the local news. Johnny came out to greet us as soon as the news began and led me into the studio, while Dad stayed behind and listened to the news on a waiting room speaker. Mr. Wilcox, as I addressed him, did a quick pre-interview as to my interests, grade in school, what school I attended, and what I like about being a Star boy. "Just talk to me as if you are talking to a friend," said Mr. Wilcox, "Now, let's do a sound check. You can say anything you want but don't say testing one, two, three. That drives me nuts." The engineer pointed at me for the check and I said, "Hello everybody! I'm Gary Dreibelbis, Route 151 from Oxon Hill, Maryland, and it's great to be on Star Boy." Mr. Wilcox smiled as the engineer gave him an "OK" sign through the glass and said, "Wow, that was great you're a natural. Do that during the show and you'll be great. News is ending, then we have a Wilkins Coffee commercial, then we're on."

My heart was racing now. It was not a "fight or flight" feeling, but my juices were flowing as I visualized my family, friends, customers, and thousands of others stuck in rush hour traffic listening to me on "Star Boy." The Wilkins Coffee spot ended signaling the start of the show. The

116

red ON AIR light flashed and it was live radio. A tape of a woman's voice yelling "Star Boy, Star Boy" started the show. Wilcox began, "Meet your neighborhood Star Boy. Today's Star Boy is Gary Dreibelbis from Oxon Hill, Maryland." The receptionist must have tipped him off as to how to pronounce my name. "We'll be right back with Gary in thirty seconds." The Star commercial ran and the ON AIR light flashed again.

Johnny Wilcox began, "We're here with Gary Dreibelbis from Oxon Hill, Maryland, and Gary, we understand that you are a big Washington Senators fan." "Yes, Mr. Wilcox. I love the Senators and can't wait for opening day. My father and I usually go." "Well what do you think about the big trade bringing Frank Howard to the Senators?" quizzed Johnny. The Senators had traded for Frank Howard, a tall slugger who could hit the cover off the ball but was also near the league leaders in striking out. Don Lock was a Senators outfielder with power but also struck out a lot. I was tired of guys trying to hit home runs but striking out all the time.

I responded, "I don't care for the trade. We gave up a good pitcher in Claude Osteen to get Howard and he strikes out too much. Don Lock already does that." I could hear the engineer and the guys in the booth busting out laughing, and Johnny was smiling and trying not to laugh. "Wow, we better get George Selkirk (The Senators General Manager) on the phone with this news." quipped Johnny. The rest of the interview went well and I said "Hi!" to my customers and ended with "Everyone say 'Hi!' to your dogs and tell them that I will be back with bones tomorrow." The interview ended with the Star Boy tape and we were out. Johnny congratulated me on a great job and a staffer took a Polaroid photo of me at the WMAL mic.

Dad and I fought the traffic on the way home. When the traffic had subsided a bit he said, "Nice job," and that was about it. He was never one to lavish praise on me but I knew he was proud.

By the way, I was wrong about Frank Howard. He went on to win two home run titles and was one of the few bright spots for the Senators. Years later when I was living near San Francisco, I went to see a Giants vs. Mets game. Frank Howard was managing the Mets. I took my red Washington Senators pennant purchased in 1962 with my in hopes of getting him to autograph it. Batting practice was in process and I spied Frank near the backstop recording an interview with KNBR's Giants' announcer Duane Kuiper. After he finished the interview I asked him to sign my pennant. Frank took it in his massive hands and said, "Wow! I haven't seen one of these for a long time." He signed and handed the pennant back to me and I said, "Thanks Frank!" I half expected him to say, "That's OK kid." I was in my forties with streaks of gray becoming more evident in my hair but for a few seconds I felt the layers of age peel away, as I reverted back to being a ten-year-old. It was a "Field of Dreams/Kevin Costner" moment. As I went to the snack bar to get a brat and a beer I felt as if I should have been carded.

The Star continued with their incentives.They introduced scholarships in the amounts of $500, $300, and $150 for paperboys who demonstrated excellence in sales and service over an extended period of time. Mr. Z nominated me for a scholarship because, by this time, I was a veteran Star Boy. It turned out that winning a scholarship was easier than winning a trip because service was considered. Within a year I won a scholarship but that wasn't all. The recipients were invited to a banquet at The Shoreham Hotel in downtown DC. The Shoreham was recognized as being one of DC's top hotels and I thought that I had joined the city's elite.

Each recipient was invited to bring a guest so Dad would get to experience the evening. It had been years since he had been at dances at The Shoreham and I think it brought him youthful memories. I chose my Beatles collarless jacket along with a rep tie that Dad had handed down to me.

The Shoreham was on Connecticut Ave. far past the WMAL studios. We knew we were near the hotel when we hit the Calvert Street Bridge with its cement lions standing guard. When we entered the lobby we saw a sign directing us to the banquet and we walked past the Marquee Lounge home of Mark Russell political satirist. Russell has appeared on PBS specials the last few years. We stopped at the entryway for a few moments and heard Russell playing the piano, cracking jokes, and people laughing.

We moved on to the banquet room, and there were assigned seats with our name places on the table. This was by far the classiest event I had ever attended and certainly not the Harvest Dinner held in the church basement. This was the real meal deal.

The banquet was hosted by WMAL's Harden and Weaver, the morning drive-time duo who were DC's answer to New York City's Bob and Ray. Ask any DC baby boomer and they will tell you that Frank Harden and Jackson Weaver ruled DC's morning drive-time for over twenty years. Harden was tall and wore glasses and Weaver was mustachioed, short, and stout. I thought he may have been a walrus in a previous life. My Dad and I considered this affair to be a big deal if Harden and Weaver were hosting.

The entertainment also included a "bubble gum" local rock band which most of us could have done without. Our featured speaker was Baltimore Mayor Theodore Mc Keldin. Mc Keldin gave an inspirational talk on "People pleasing people" which was certainly appropriate for our group. Following the talk the scholarships were awarded and I was in the middle of the pack with my $350 award. Then came to the $500 awards and a few words were said about each recipient. These were the overachievers, The Eagle Scouts, class presidents, saviors of humanity and future Nobel Peace Prize winners. These guys would attend Harvard, Yale, or, if they stayed local, Georgetown. My Uncle Jack had always said that if you can't run with the big dogs stay on the porch. I was staying on the porch for the time being and grateful to have my $350 scholarship. The evening ended with Harden and Weaver shaking everyone's hands as they left the banquet room. Northwest DC and The Shoreham were no more than ten miles from home but it felt like a world away.

My Star Boy service lasted for five years, a long time in paperboy years, equal to a major league baseball player lasting twenty seasons. Mine were good seasons with The Star giving me opportunities I would not have experienced. The paper route taught me responsibility, money management, and social skills. Once, when I looked at a list of people who had been paper carriers it was like a "Who's Who" of prominent Americans.

When I left The Star in the late '60's, the handwriting was on the wall for it and other evening papers across the nation. TV assisted in killing evening newspapers. The Star, once called "The Queen of Washington Newspapers," struggled to stay in the court.

The Washington Star did not go gentle into that good night. Various features were added, such as political cartoonist Patrick Oliphant who came on board to battle The Post's Herb Block better known as "Herblock." For a period of time, DC could boast that it had two of the country's political cartoonists. The Star eventually merged with The Daily

News another DC evening paper which had been on life support for years. The Daily News was a tabloid and was popular with bus riders. Journalism historians can debate as to whether or not Bob Woodward and Carl Bernstein's coverage of Watergate in The Post was one of the nails driven into the coffin of The Star. It couldn't have helped. Time Magazine bought The Star and tried to keep it alive. Time could not save it, and when The Star died, Star employees wore tee shirts stating, "Time Has Run Out on The Star." The Washington Evening Star went to "The Black Ink Beyond" in the summer of 1981.

The fall of '81 I had just taken an assistant professor of communication position at Bradley University in Peoria, Illinois. One of my assignments was to assist in coaching Bradley's national award-winning speech team. An extemporaneous speaker, Andrew Heaton, who is now a successful counsel with Ernst and Young in DC, had a file box with newspaper and magazine clippings for evidence to be used in speeches. During the summer of '81, he had an internship in DC. Taped to the outside of his file box was the top half of the front page of The Star's farewell edition. For a few seconds images of delivering papers in the August heat and January chill, smiling customers, dogs of various nations, The Star truck grinding around the corner at 3:30PM Monday through Saturday and 3:30AM on Sundays, and a trip to Atlantic City came to mind.

Then I looked at the clock, realizing that I could not turn it back and that I had a class to teach in two minutes instead of papers to deliver. I did the responsible thing and went to teach my class.

RELATIVELY SPEAKING

You can pick your friends but you can't pick you relatives. It's a cliché but in my case very true. The sets of relatives were as different as night and day. Another cliché but also true. Dad's relatives hailed from Pennsylvania Dutch Country. Mom's folks came from the hills of Western North Carolina. You can see where there might be some potential differences.

I know more about Dad's side of the family than Mom's. Dad's side of the family took pride in the "Dreibelbis" name, even though it was not a Smith of Jones surname. If I had a dollar for every time I had to pronounce or spell my name either in person or on the phone I could have retired to Palm Springs twenty years ago.

As strange as it may seem Dreibelbis is a common surname in Pennsylvania and there are numerous Drebelbises, or perhaps I should say "Dreibelbi" like hippopotami roaming the towns of Eastern and Central Pennsylvania. In one town there is a beautiful Dreibelbis covered bridge complete with Pennsylvania Dutch hex sign. The bridge must have a perfect safety record because the hex sign is supposed to ward off evil forces. There's even a small town named "Dreibelbis" with its own train station. For my money "Dreibelbis" is a better name for a town than Intercourse, PA (don't get me started here with potential jokes. This is a PG rated book).

The name Dreibelbis is of Swiss-German origin. I mentioned before that many think that it is a Greek surname because of the "is" ending.

The following information comes from an official group, The Dreibelbis Cousins. The Dreibelbis Cousins were around long before ancestry.com, and they really have it down as to tracing ancestry. Now we do a Mr. Peabody and Sherman and return to the early 1700's to Northern Switzerland and Southern Germany, (apparently my ancestors were border runners, indecisive, or both) the original name was "Deubelbiss."

Research indicates that "Deubelbiss" means "bitten by the Devil." This would have been helpful information for me to have had in grade school to explain my behavior to teachers when I misbehaved.

The Deubelbisses, or Deubelbi if you prefer, grew a mysterious plant called "The Devil's Bite." The Devil's Bite could supposedly cure a variety of ailments as well as keeping people in high spirits. I think I can make a claim that my ancestors were growers and suppliers of a special weed or, in short, pushers. Deubelbi would probably be welcomed today in Northern California's Mendocino and Humboldt Counties where Marijuana is a cash crop and slightly behind fishing and micro-breweries as a major industry. If Deubelbi roamed these parts, people might say "Roll me a Deubel." instead of a Doobie.

Several years ago, I traveled to Switzerland in search of information regarding the "Deubelbi." The Dreibelbis Cousins organization provided valuable information as to stalking the wild Duebelbi. In my case they were deceased but they may have been wild in their time.

First I must digress concerning Switzerland. I hope I don't sound like a travel columnist for The Peoria Journal Star (Don't worry, I have friends at The Peoria Journal Star who will like the plug) but Switzerland may be the most beautiful place I have ever visited. The place not only has natural beauty but beautiful people who know that they have something special and appreciate it. You have to love a country where the national pastime is hiking.

There are giant geraniums in front of almost every home. The secret for their care and feeding is cows, of which there are many, and cow manure works wonders on geraniums. Cows seem to be everywhere including within town limits. I was in a small town with a house built over a cow stable and cows roamed in the front yard inside a wooded fence. There was no stench of cows. How do the Swiss do this?

The trains all run on time. I took trains daily throughout the country and they were never late. You know they are on time because there is an identical clock on the platform at each station. Train stations are immaculate and no matter the size of town you can get food and drink. Larger town stations have restaurant service and bars. I was sitting at a bar at one station and a Frenchman, realizing that I was an American, started chatting me up in an unfriendly tone concerning

122

American culture or that we had no culture and stole from every other countries. I raised the issue of jazz and he dismissed my argument. Finally, after my third beer I gave him a brief history lesson as to how the U.S. had saved the French's bacon in two world wars and if it hadn't been for the Yanks, he would probably be speaking German today. I punctuated my remarks by telling him that he could stick his French culture where the sun doesn't shine. He had no comeback for this argument and paid for my third beer.

When you take the train, you see nothing but passing natural beauty. The mountains look like the opening scenes from The Sound of Music and as you pass hills and waterfalls you feel as if you are in an extended natural Disneyland. If you travel to Switzerland be sure to purchase a Swiss Pass, the best transportation value you will ever encounter. A Swiss Pass allows you to ride any form of transportation including trains, ferries, ski lifts, basically anything that moves that is not a cow or horse. I tried using it on a cow that I found in one valley but the farmer politely refused the pass.

I mentioned that hiking is the national pastime and with good reason. The trails are immaculate with wild flowers everywhere and clear signage to direct you. You could have the sense of direction of a mole and never get lost. The signs look as if they send out someone each night to clean them and do a paint touchup.

There is no litter on the trails. The Swiss take pride in their trails and if you threw a Nestlé's ice cream wrapper down you would probably be confronted by a member of the Swiss Army and hauled off to a Swiss jail. This might not be a bad thing because a Swiss jail is probably nicer than many two star motels in this country. The secret of the trails' maintenance is that they are the responsibility of the Swiss Army. This seems reasonable to me because what else does the neutral Swiss Army have to do—sharpen their knives?

OK, back to the story of stalking the wild Deubelbi. Information from The Dreibelbis Cousins indicated that the Deubelbi attended a church in Holderbank, Switzerland. This was comforting to me that when they were not pushing their "Devil's Bite" weed that they would take time out for church. At least they were not complete heathens. There was physical evidence to prove that they attended church, as the Dreibelbis Cousins included a picture of the church on their website along with a "Deubelbiss" stained glass window in the church.

I had been gallavanting across the country when I decided to go to Holderbank. I caught a train to Zurich, then transferred to Holderbank. Upon arrival I was a little disappointed. Holderbank is a factory town, not nearly as attractive as most Swiss towns but certainly cleaner than most factory towns in the U.S.

The church was a short distance from the train station and it looked as pictured on The Dreibelbis Cousins' website. There was a beautiful simplicity about it and it was sooo Swiss. I went inside and felt as if I had traveled back in time with Mr. Peabody and Sherman. I'm not a mystical person but I could feel something come over me as to the spirits of past congregations including some of my ancestors. I looked at the organ and could hear hymns of the Reformation.

Then I saw it. A stained glass window with a knight figure holding a shield. Below the shield was a banner, "Deubelbiss." This was the family crest on the window. On the shield I noticed three tulip-like flowers. I looked at the other windows, and they too had family crests. One window for the Fischer family had fish on the crest. I returned to look at the Deubelbiss crest with great pride. I figured that to have such a window they must have been good tithers and would have made good Baptists.

I stopped outside to view the grounds and found the church cemetery. It was filled with Deubelbi. The headstones went back to the 1700's but were all readable. Each grave was immaculate and would you expect anything less from a Swiss cemetery. My stalking the wild, or not so wild Deubelbi, was successful and soon I would return to the U.S.

Now for Dad's ancestors I have pretty good information. Here in the U.S. his immediate relatives lived in Central Pennsylvania not far from Harrisburg. Dad's sisters were Winnie and Phoebe married to Jack and Bill respectively. His sister Mary died of cancer shortly after I was born and his brother Donald died before Dad was born during the great influenza epidemic following World War I. Dad's mother Ethel, was known to all the grandkids as "Nan." My grandmother Nan was the epitome of unconditional love.

I mentioned Mom's mother Carrie. Sorry to say it, but I never considered her to be my grandmother. Maybe I had too little contact with her but the times I saw her I considered her to be an old woman who just happened to be there.

My grandfathers were nonexistent. Paternal grandfather Mark committed suicide in 1943 by cutting his throat. Dad had to return from duty in England to attended the funeral during the heat of the war. The Army Air Corp refused to keep him stateside and he returned to England shortly after the funeral. Mark Dreibelbis had a successful job working with the Pennsylvania Railroad during The Great Depression and railroad jobs were considered to be jewels. Unfortunately, he lost part of his foot during a rail accident and he was unable to return to work. He tried his hand at barbering and other jobs but fell into deep depression. From information I've been able to assimilate Mark took out most of his frustration out on Dad. Dad was the youngest child and only male so he was expected to do the household chores his Dad couldn't do.

My maternal grandfather, Tom, died of tuberculosis in 1959. My only recollection of him was visiting him in a TB sanitarium in Black Mountain, NC when I was five-years-old. I can remember waiting in a large ward and sitting on the floor. They wheeled him in and he was wearing a robe. "This is your grandfather." Mom said. He was smiling, and later I thought he looked a bit like pictures I had seen of the old entertainer Will Rogers. It's sad, but I probably have more vivid memories of a nearby gas station which had a bear on a chain who drank Coca Cola's.

In my mind Nan was my only grandparent. She demonstrated unconditional love to all her grandkids but she was especially loving to me. She was under five feet tall with black hair she tied into a bun. When she let her hair down for combing it would drop past her waist. Her eyes sparkled and she was active and full of energy into her 90s.

I believe my cousin Billy and I were here favorite grandkids. She loved all her grandkids but had the most contact with Billy because he was Phoebe and Bill's son and Nan spent most of her time living with them. Billy was attentive to her and just an all-around good guy. Billy went on to play with the group The Magnificent Men a group that became a cult favorite in the middle Atlantic states. Their sound was "Blue-Eyed Soul" and they were a white guys' version of a Motown group; in fact, they often opened for Motown groups playing concerts in Philadelphia and New York City. They were "One Hit Wonders" with a song "I could Be So Happy," which went high on the Billboard charts.

Nan loved me in part because she thought that I would grow up to be a preacher and follow in Billy Graham's footsteps. When I decided upon a career in education, she thought that was the next best thing. There was a rotating system as to where Nan lived which was a common practice for families in the 50's and 60's. She spent time with Aunt Phoebe and Uncle Bill, shifted over to Aunt Winnie and Uncle Jack then came to spend time with us for part of the summer. I don't know who figured out the rotation for her to come visit us in the sweltering DC heat.

There are memories of her but two stand out. She was a devoted Christian and she read her Bible daily often without eyeglasses. Nan would sit at the end of the couch and read her Bible for hours. In the room we designated as her bedroom she had a small sign on her nightstand, "Prayer Changes Things" and back in the day she would be considered what was called a "Prayer Warrior."

My other favorite memory of her was that she loved baseball. I think she acquired this from Mark and other family members who were avid fans. Mark taught her how to keep score in a scorebook and she would break from her household chores to listen to ball games and score the game while he was at work. Nan was able to look at her scorebook and give him a re-creation of the game before dinner.

There were hot humid nights at our house with Nan and I sitting on the front lawn, watching fire flies, listening to cat fights, and listening to the Senators game on a large transistor radio. If the Senators were lucky enough to get a rally against the opposition, which was rare, Nan would say, "Oh, I bet those guys are mad," meaning the competition. She died in her late 90's from complications following a broken hip. A piece of me went with her as she was laid to rest in a cemetery in central Pennsylvania filled with old Drebelbi'. The thoughts of the old hymn, "I'll Fly Away," lifted my spirits.

As mentioned, cousins were Gwen and Jackie, belonging to Winnie and Jack, and Pam and Billy belonged to Phoebe and Bill. Doug and I were by far the youngest, with the span ranging from sixteen to two years difference.

For some reason I always felt that our family was were the black sheep of the extended family. We weren't mistreated but the Pennsylvania relatives had nicer homes, certainly not mansions, but with more than one bathroom, nicer appliances, and nicer yards. Aunts

Winnie and Phoebe were always well dressed, belonged to clubs, and fitted the June Cleaver mold. Uncles Jack and Bill worked some types of government jobs at a military depot. Uncle Bill was a true gentleman and was always well spoken. I can remember him doing such "gentlemanly" things as tucking his tie in his dress shirt when eating spaghetti and expertly twirling the noodles with his fork and spoon.

Uncle Jack was much more colorful and my favorite uncle. He was balding with slick black hair, a mustache and glasses. He had been a bit of a rogue before settling down and marrying Aunt Winnie. During the Depression he was a glorified hobo, riding the rails, thumbing rides, and being an early-day Jack Kerouac. He eventually landed in Southern California and scored several plumb jobs such as being a chauffeur for movie stars such as Lionel Barrymore. He eventually returned to central Pennsylvania, met, courted, and married Winnie. The running joke in the family was that Nan and Mark thought that Jack was a rogue and if they were sitting on the porch when he came calling they would leave the porch and retreat inside. Everything worked out with Winnie and Jack being married for over sixty years.

A major part of the fun of traveling to Pennsylvania was the journey itself. Before the Interstate Highway System it took about four or five hours to make the trip. We would drive all the way through DC to Northwest DC and hit Montgomery County Maryland. Miles up the road was Frederick, MD with its historic red brick road houses. There were signs everywhere for Barbara Fritchie's Candystick Restaurant. I asked my parents about Barbara Fritchie as to whether she made good candysticks, and if we could eat at her restaurant. They didn't respond and we never ate there.

Later I discovered that she was a woman in her nineties who stood up to Confederate troops during the Civil War and waved a Union flag in the middle of the street to antagonize Stonewall Jackson's troops during the Maryland Campaign. This may be legend, but she was the subject of a John Greenleaf Whittier poem Barbara Fritchie:

> "Shoot if you must this old gray head,
> But spare your country's flag," she said.
> sadness, a blush of shame,
> Over the face of the leader came;

The nobler nature within him stirred
To life at that woman's deed and word;
'Who touches a hair of yon gray head
Dies like a dog! March on!" he said...

Historians can argue all they want as to whether or not this actually happened but it's still a great story and a poem that I had to memorize in grade school. If I had been armed with this valuable piece of historic and poetic information my parents may have stopped at the Barbara Fritchie Candystick Restaurant.

Up the road we saw Burma Shave signs along the road at what seemed to be ten-mile intervals. Boomers can recall these on trips because they were a major part of Burma Shave's advertising campaign up until 1963 when Interstate Highways became the preferred mode of travel. The signs were placed along the road side at interviews with a rhyming message:

Big Mistake
Many Make
Rely on Horn
Instead of Brake
Burma Shave

We eventually hit Gettysburg, PA, and the town was before you got to the battlefield. There was an old Rexall Drug Store on the town square with a huge sign on the second story, "This is Where Lincoln Wrote The Gettysburg Address." There is some debate as to where Lincoln wrote the address. He may have written it in the building long before it became a Rexall Drug Store selling tacky Lincoln and Gettysburg souvenirs, including miniature cannons and fake beards. Some say that he wrote it on the back of an envelope while riding a train from Washington, DC, to Gettysburg. Others say that he wrote it while exchanging shots of whisky with General Ulysses S. Grant (There are few historians who subscribe to this, but it does make one hellava story.) Lincoln's two-minute masterpiece of oratory followed windbag Edward Everett's two-hour oration.

A few miles from the town square was the Gettysburg Battlefield with the cannons pointing at us along the roadside. Next to the cannons were cannonballs stacked pyramid style. Most historians agree that Gettysburg was the turning point of The Civil War for the Union. The more I learned in school and in later research the more I became amazed at the tactics used and the loss of life. Today the battlefield had a large visitors' center and helicopter rides with views of the battlefield.

Next was one of the highlights of the trip at least for us kids, the Pensupreme Restaurant. The restaurant had chrome soda fountain stools and vinyl booths and served great hamburgers. The piece de resistance was the hot fudge sundaes. The fudge was always hot and it melted the ice cream so you had to eat fast with your long fountain spoon. You always got ice cream headaches but we could have cared less.

Leaving Pensupreme and heading up Route 15 you hit Distelfink's on the left with its bright neon sign. The sign is still there, but the snack bar is long gone. I've tried to convince a lawyer friend of mine who lives in Gettysburg to place it in his front yard. He has declined. Distelfink's was only a few miles from Pensupreme but we had no problem getting Dad to stop. He was an ice cream fiend. The ice cream was soft similar to a frozen custard. The sidekick was a large soft pretzel with lots of salt. The combination of the salty, doughy pretzel and soft ice cream can't be beat. Add mustard on the pretzel, and you have a triple play combination. If you are wondering as to what is a Distelfink it is a mythical Pennsylvania Dutch bird of good luck.

Since we are talking snacks and food let's discuss Pennsylvania Dutch food. There are three categories: The Good, The Bad, and The Ugly. First The Good. As mentioned, Pensupreme ice cream of any kind is good. The hot fudge sundaes were to die for and if you ate too many of them you probably would. The old restaurant on Route 15 is gone but you can still buy Pensupreme in stores. It is a regional brand and it is to ice cream as regional beer brands are to microbrewing.

Distelfink's ice cream has also been discussed, and it is of a bygone era; however, soft pretzels are still with us and they can now be found throughout the country. As far as I know they are not banned in Boston and if so Red Sox, Patriot, Bruin, and Celtics' fans are missing out. While soft pretzels may be found throughout the country I maintain

129

that they are of Pennsylvania Dutch origin. The first one I ever had was at Distelfink's and the first time I ever had mustard on one was when I saw Dad doing it. Like father like son. I firmly believe that putting mustard on a soft pretzel was the creation of a creative Pennsylvania Dutch woman. Yes, I said woman because only a woman could come up with something this good. I put mustard on my pretzel during Giants' games at San Francisco's AT&T Park and people looked at me as if I had said, "Willie Mays doesn't belong in the Baseball Hall of Fame." Teaberry ice cream has also been discussed, and I've never seen it in any other part of the country.

I don't know if Rakestraw's ice cream in Mechanicsburg still exists but if was right up there with Pensupreme and Distelfink's. The great thing about Rakestraw's was that Aunt Winnie and Uncle Jack lived five doors down from their factory. You walked two hundred feet and you could get almost any flavor imaginable. They had egg nog ice cream year round.

We move on from ice cream to another healthy food; potato chips. My two regional favorites are Charles Chips and Utz. There is something about the thickness and right amount of salt that make Charles some of the best chips I ever tasted. Charles made their way out of the Pennsylvania Dutch region to other mid-Atlantic states. I'm not sure you could buy them in stores. In Oxon Hill we had a guy in a delivery truck come to our house. The deliveryman had a gruff voice and smoked a cigar. He'd ask Mom, "Do ya need any chips today?" It was the same kind of voice you associate with a stranger driving up to a kid and asking,"Do you want some candy little girl?" The chips came in a mustard yellow and brown can to preserve freshness. The chips man would pick up your empty can and supply you with a full can of chips. We always got two cans because on a good day I could finish half a can. Charles Chips can be ordered on-line so you can make the decision yourself as to their quality. If you don't like them don't bug me about a refund until this book makes The New York Times Bestseller List. Even then, don't hold your breath for a refund.

My other chip favorite is Utz and I stock up on them whenever I'm back in the DC area. Utz is a little lighter than Charles but still has the right salt content. Utz also makes killer hard pretzels and cheeseballs. I've been able to find the cheeseballs here on the West Coast but not the pretzels.

There is a dessert delicacy called Shoe Fly Pie. This is pure heaven for anyone with a sweet tooth. The best way to describe it is to compare it to pecan pie without the pecans. Powdered sugar is spread on top. You can see why four out of five dentists love this pie. Nan was a specialist at making Shoe Fly Pie and one pie was enough to satisfy anyone.

Birch Beer is another Pennsylvania Dutch specialty and it is their answer to root beer. It has a slightly lighter taste than root beer with true sassafras flavor. When you pour it you see a slightly reddish color. I know that birch beer is sold in the mid-Atlantic states, but I haven't found it on the West Coast.

Lebanon baloney, so named because it comes from Lebanon, PA, and not from the country, is great with any meat combo sandwich. Uncle Jack used to bring us CARE packages when he came to visit, and Lebanon baloney was always included.

As for The Bad, we can skip it because there is no Bad, and we can go straight to The Ugly. Two major candidates for this category are red beet eggs and scrapple. Red beet eggs are hard boiled eggs in pickled beet juice. This may sound great to some, but I can't stand hard boiled eggs, and the thought of having them in pickled beet juice is repulsive. This was another Nan specialty, and for some reason she thought that I loved them. Sorry Nan, you had the wrong grandchild.

The other candidate is scrapple not to be confused with Snapple. Scrapple is appropriately named because it is the scraps of the pig that are left over after everything else has been processed. It is considered by many a delicacy preferable to sausage. I believe that I have added at least five years to my life avoiding scrapple.

I was very fortunate that most of these ugly items were never brought to family reunions, with the exception of Nan's red beet eggs. She always brought four quarts and they seemed to go fast; either that or someone left the picnic area and dumped them into the Susquehanna River.

I can only remember two family reunions that my family attended. My relatives had more, but my folks decided not to go because of the distance or Mom's health. I know that The Dreibelbis Cousins organization has family reunions, and attending one is on my bucket list.

Like Fox News, I wish that I could be "fair and balanced (don't turn me off CNN fans) but I had less contact and information about my relatives from the Tar Heel State. Mom came from a family of eight but I can only recall meeting four of her siblings. There are many strange stories about Mom's family, and one of the strangest concerned her sister Mary. Mary was about twenty years older than Mom and lived in a town not far from Mom's home. Mom can remember receiving a letter from Mary saying that she would see the family on Sunday. Sunday came and there was no Mary and no one ever saw or heard from her again.

I'm no Alex Haley but I have been able to ascertain that many of my ancestors were Cherokees from Western North Carolina. The trips to North Carolina were less frequent and could take up to eight hours; again, this was before Interstate Highways. The trip was about 400 miles, and up until I went away to college near Chicago, it was the greatest distance I had been from home. The route to Western North Carolina went through towns large and small. By the time you hit Richmond, VA, and were on the way to Winston Salem, NC, you knew you were on Tobacco Road as you passed large plants such as R.J. Reynolds. We also went through Charlottesville, VA, home of Thomas Jefferson and The University of Virginia; sadly, we never stopped.

Once we got to Winston Salem we knew that we were in the home stretch of the trip. When my grandmother was alive we would visit her at her farmhouse near Statesville. This was roughing it because there was only a roof over our heads. I was only five and Doug was one. When I say roughing it I'm not exaggerating. Even by 1950's standards the house was primitive.

First there was no indoor toilet. There was an outhouse about 100 feet from the house. Thank goodness it was supplied with honest to goodness toilet paper instead of pages from a Sears' catalog or corncobs. Next, no bathtub or shower. There was a pump on the enclosed back porch which was your only source of indoor water. You heated buckets of water then poured the buckets in a large tub for your bath. Heat came from a wood stove and needless to say there was no air conditioning for comfort during the hot North Carolina summer nights.

Worst of all there was no TV. At a time when the U.S. Census Bureau reported that there were more TV sets than bathtubs or refrigerators we could say that my grandmother's farm had none of the above. "The entertainment center" consisted of a radio, which probably reported Truman's victory over Dewey, and a phonograph with a fine collection of 78 RPM records.

The farm had once hosted livestock such as pigs and cows but nothing exciting such as horses. The grounds had potential but had been neglected. About the only redeeming quality about the farm was going to Josh Davison's store where he treated me to Lance peanut butter crackers and Dr. Pepper. At Josh's store I could drink Dr. Pepper ten, two, and four.

When Granny passed away we spent time at Aunt Blanche and Uncle John's farm in the mountains near North Wilkesboro. Uncle John was known as "Frail" and I have no idea why. My cousins were Carol, Joyce, and Jerry. Carol and Joyce were college students and Jerry was the closest to me in age. The trio of cousins was highly intelligent with Jerry eventually graduating from med school.

Uncle Frail had built a serviceable, comfortable house in the Brushy Mountains near Moravian Falls. The house was on a curvy dirt road where vehicles had to honk their horns to alert oncoming traffic. Compared to Granny's house it was The Ritz Carlton complete with indoor plumbing, a refrigerator, freezer, AND a TV. In the years long before satellite and cable TV you received two stations out of Charlotte, one clear, the other snowy.

Uncle Frail was a farmer by hobby. His day job was working as a laborer for the Carolina Mirror. Aunt Blanche tended the home fires and tended them well. Hers was my first experience with farm cuisine and eating schedule. Farm life, even for hobby farmers, was hard work. The morning consisted of a FULL breakfast of bacon and eggs, biscuits and gravy, and of course, grits. Grits are a southern staple for breakfast. Years later when I was a guest lecturer at The University of Georgia I stopped at a store outside of Athens, which featured an entire row devoted to different brands of grits. Mid morning there was some kind of snack usually small sandwiches. The noon meal was referred to a supper, not lunch, and it featured dinnertime-type food. Another snack came mid afternoon.The evening meal was complete with roast beef or fried chicken, all the side dishes, and a homemade dessert.

You would have thought that Doug and I would have gained ten pounds—not true. There was a sizeable vegetable patch across the road from the house which needed basic tending and we were up to the task. There were two horses as well. Lucky was a gentle riding horse and even we city slickers could manage him. There was also an old fashioned swimming hole just down the road for hot afternoons.

Some evenings we would journey down the mountain to watch Jerry pitch for his boys' club team. The snack bar had one of my favorite southern treats, slaw dogs, hot dogs with cole slaw. The other evening excitement was going to a movie theatre in North Wilkesboro which showed what I guess they called second-run films. I'm not sure you could call what this theatre ran as "second run." I got the impression that they would show any film that wasn't a silent Charlie Chaplin or Buster Keaton film. Today such a movie theatre would be called an "art house." I can remember seeing the Robert Mitchum film Thunder Road in the early 1960s. It had to be at least ten years old. It was good enough with lots of action about traveling moonshiners. Perhaps the theatre owner had analyzed his demographic.

Speaking of which, one afternoon following swimming and before dinner I went hiking in the woods behind the house. As I walked along, I stumbled upon a strange looking metal contraption. When I returned to the house I said to Aunt Blanche, "I found some strange metal thing out back in the woods." Aunt Blanche responded, "Oh, that's Uncle Frail's st...." She caught herself and said, "I mean that's Uncle Frail's special bar-b-quer." Visions of some really fine ribs started dancing through my head. "Wow, when is Uncle Frail going to bar-b-que?" "Oh Gary, he just uses that for 'special' occasions," she responded. I thought that it was pretty special that we had driven 400 miles to see them but I decided that it was impolite to press the issue.

"Besides, I think it is broken." she added. A few years later I put two and two together and knew the real use of Uncle Frail's "Special Bar-B-Quer." He could have made some fantastic Jack Daniel's-like bar-b-que sauce in that thing.

My love of dogs was satisfied when we visited our Moravian Falls relatives because Aunt Blanche and Uncle Frail had several. My favorite was Foxie—a red Border Collie mix. She was friendly, super intelligent, and always wanting kids' attention. One day Uncle Frail had a brilliant thought probably after a snort or two from his "special grill," to breed Foxie with a neighbor's large Chihuahua. The result was supposed to be a "speed ball" coon hunting dog. Yes, they actually do hunt coons in Western North Carolina.

The next time we visited, we saw the result. The red fur of Foxie and the light tan of the Chihuahua made for a short-haired dog that was a close to pink as a dog could get. The dog had pointed ears, a pink

134

nose, and curly tail. Neighbors called the dog "Frail's Folly," while the family named it Piglet. The dog was a dead ringer for the A.A. Milne's character with the exception of walking on four legs. If you put a stuffed Winnie the Pooh next to the dog and photographed them you would have the spitting image of A.A. Milne's dynamic duo. Several days after we laughed at Piglet he was killed on the dirt road as a driver came barreling around a blind curve. Everyone felt remorse for laughing at poor Piglet. Piglet, RIP.

I was always thankful when our Pennsylvania relatives came to see us. It was good to see them but it also meant that we would actually "do something." By this I mean that Dad was not one for sightseeing and the only time we were able to take advantage of the Nation's Capital's attractions was when our relatives would come. The first time I visited Ford's Theatre, The White House, Arlington Cemetery and the Wax Museum was when the relatives came. There may have been other firsts but these were the most memorable.

Ford's was nothing like it is today. The theatre part of Ford's did not exist. Today it is a working theatre with excellent seasons of productions. There is also a fine two-actor production dealing with the aftermath of Lincoln's assassination. In the late 50s and 60s, there were exhibits of artifacts and pictures but no theatre.

Across the street from Ford's is the William A. Petersen house where President Lincoln was carried for treatment and where he eventually died. The blood stained pillow on the bed where Lincoln died is still there. It was disturbing to me when I first saw it because we had just finished a unit on Lincoln at our school.

I found the Wax Museum to be disturbing as well. I think that wax museums have the potential of being eerie to little kids. I've been to a few wax museums over the years but the one in DC is one of the best. The White House was a treat because I knew that was where the Kennedy Family lived. The other fun aspect of The White House trip was that cousin Billy had the courage to sit in every chair in each of the rooms we visited despite being reprimanded by The White House Guards. It's amazing to me how little security there was in those days.

On one relatives' visit, we went to Arlington Cemetery to see the changing of the guard at the Tomb of the Unknown Soldier. Even as a child I appreciated the discipline and control of the guards in ninety-plus degree heat. For those who have never been to Arlington Cemetery you can become overwhelmed with the visual reminder of human sacrifice for our country. When I visit Arlington today, I always try to process that sacrifice, then my mind proceeds to another consideration. It is amazing to me that the great Confederate general Robert E. Lee lived on the grounds in the Custis-Lee Mansion overlooking the Potomac River and Washington, DC less than a mile away. This may have been a question of location over loyalty in his decision to fight for the South. I will leave that up to the historians.

We visited Arlington before JFK and RFK were buried there. As I mentioned, as one who appreciates excellent political rhetoric from members of both parties, I am taken by the RFK quotations inscribed on a wall near his gravesite. When I see the excerpts, I recall Frank Capra's great film, Mr. Smith Goes to Washington. There is a classic scene where a young boy is reading Lincoln's Gettysburg Address from the wall of The Lincoln Memorial to his grandfather. The grandfather with failing eyesight having memorized the speech years ago prompts him when his grandson stumbles.

The other advantage of the Pennsylvania relatives coming to visit was that they were dropping off Nan for an extended stay and that Mom would make her special spaghetti for them. I've heard many say that their mothers were the best cooks they ever knew and that they could make a special dish. I could not claim the first part for Mom. She was not a great cook and lacked imagination as to food preparation but we never starved. Her spaghetti was different. I never knew her recipe but I've had spaghetti from New York City to North Beach in San Francisco and hers is the best. The relatives always wanted jars of it to take home and it was a fair trade for the Lebanon baloney and teaberries for teaberry ice cream.

Unfortunately, my relatives from both sides have passed on or scattered to parts unknown and I have no contact with them. In this age of technology and social media I suppose that there is no excuse for this. If I can stalk the wild Deubelbi in Switzerland I should be more proactive in tracking down my few remaining relatives here in the States.

Maybe I inherited my parents' genes in that we didn't socialize with our relatives the way other families did. When all else fails we can blame our parents. A couple of holidays and reunions just don't cut it. Holidays were solitary affairs with just the four of us. This may be part of the reason I experience some anxiety today when I'm involved with Eileen's family gatherings. There is no logical reason for this because they have accepted me and love me, warts and all.

Perhaps recalling memories, as few as they may be, will be motivation for me to reach out to the remaining relatives. If I do succeed that will be another story for another time. As for relatives in general I am reminded of the old Woody Allen joke about the guy who goes to the psychiatrist and says, "I'm worried about my brother. He thinks he is a chicken." "Why don't you have him hospitalized?" asks the psychiatrist. "Because we need the eggs." responds the patient.

Perhaps that's the deal with relatives. Despite their foibles, in the final analysis, we still need the eggs.

DUCK PIN BOWLING

No self-respecting book about baby boomers growing up in and around DC is complete without mentioning duck pin bowling. You may be asking if this is a self-respecting book. Come on, give the book the benefit of the doubt. This will be a shorter chapter. If you are a Bible reader consider this to be similar to the short books near the end of the New Testament such as Jude. I've always said that you can read the book of Jude in less time than it takes to listen to The Beatles "Hey Jude." The scary thing is that some theologians agree with me.

I reside in the town of Vacaville, CA, population of approximately 100,000. Vacaville is located about 30 miles from Sacramento, 55 miles from San Francisco, and within driving distance to Lake Tahoe. Nearby industries include a Budweiser brewery and the Jelly Belly Jellybean (President Reagan's favorite snack) factory. What more could you ask for—beer and jellybeans. The King of Beers and The Queen of Beans.

So you may be asking, "Why are you talking about your current hometown when this is a book about growing up in DC?" Take it easy Sherlock and you will see. One day I was walking to the strip mall near my house and I saw a sign on the front window of the Rite Aid drug store reading "Closing Soon. Everything Must Go!" I could have seen the handwriting on the wall clearer than Daniel (Wow! Another Bible reference). The store was using only half of its huge building space, had a poor line of merchandise, and they charged through the nose. All this plus there was a CVS drug store opening in the strip mall across the street.

When Rite Aid closed the building sat vacant for months. One day I said to a friend that if I had a few dollars I would open a duck pin bowling alley. "Oh, what's a duck pin bowling alley?" my friend politely asked. The question was polite in tone but his nonverbal contradicted his verbal. He looked at me as if I had come from the planet Uranus (have you ever noticed that there is no way to pronounce the name of this planet without sounding obscene?) I gave him an abbreviated description of the rules that I will now give to you. Following this, you can impress your friends with your vast sports knowledge at your next Super Bowl party.

Duck pin bowling began in the late 1800's in Charm City, better known as Baltimore, MD. I have no idea why they call it Charm City. Perhaps it was because Baltimore was the place where DC government officials went to have affairs. Now they stay closer to home and have affairs in places such as The Oval Office. In the words of Mel Brooks in the film Blazing Saddles, "Gentlemen, the affairs of state must take precedence over affairs of state." Some historians say that John J. McGraw, the New York Giants' great baseball manager, was one of the inventors of the game. Duck pin bowling eventually made its way to DC and the rest of the Mid-Atlantic region.

Duck pin bowling has almost the same rules as ten pin bowling. The major difference is the size of the balls and pins. Duck-pin pins are shorter and reach the red bow tie of ten pins. The balls are smaller weighing between three and four pounds with no holes. You simply palm the ball and hurl it down the lane as fast as you can similar to fast-pitch softball. The other difference is that you get three balls a frame instead of two. Scoring is exactly the same: one ball, all pins down a strike, two balls, a spare, and the third ball is whatever is left. Scores are significantly lower in duck than ten pin. If you have an average of 120 or over you are pretty good. Lane length, ball return, and pins sweep are all the same.

Duck pin bowling ruled DC, Baltimore, and parts of southern Pennsylvania during the post war era. Fairlanes was a chain of duck pin alleys and there was a time when there were more duck pin alleys and leagues than ten pin. One of the reasons for duck pins popularity could have been woman and children. The ball was easier for kids to handle and of course with kids come women. Women's leagues were the rage in the post war DC Metro area. Perhaps moms loved to escape the noise of the homes for the relative serenity of forty lanes of crashing duck pins.

My first experience with duck pin bowling was with my church's Sunday school class bowling at the Fairlanes in Marlow Heights, MD. I fell in love with it. Next, there was a neighborhood summer day camp that took us to Fairlanes once a week. The manager opened the lanes early and for $1 you could bowl three games and get shoe rental. My first trophy of any kind came when there was a contest to out-score our camp counselors. I bowled out of my mind and beat my counselor earning a patch and trophy and I thought that I was a little Don Carter.

I continued bowling until I went to college just outside of Chicago. To my dismay there were no duck pin lanes. I was met with the same reaction I was met with years later in Vacaville, a reaction indicating that I hailed from that planet with the obscene name (this coming from people who play with an oversized mush softball without gloves known as "Chicago Softball.")

I'm pretty sure there are lots of boomers from the metro DC area with memories of the petite pins. Perhaps someday when my ship comes in I'll find another empty Rite Aid and open some duck pin lanes. The vision of families, company teams, and kids after school is fun to ponder. In the meantime, I'll always have the satisfaction of having beaten my counselor five decades ago when duck pin bowling WAS bowling.

CHURCHIN' UP

I've attended church ever since I can remember. Now, you don't have to be afraid and turn to the next chapter. There will be no preaching, fire and brimstone, or altar call here. I am well aware that many have a major distaste of organized religion and that some of the worst wars have been religious ones. I won't get into other reasons why some are turned off by organized religion.

Now you may be wondering how I can talk about religion and church after some of the comments I've made in this book. My faith is important to me. I think the key is that I take my faith seriously without taking myself too seriously. A friend of mine who attends Alcoholics Anonymous meetings tells me that part of the success of the organization is the concept of attraction and not promotion. AA also has such slogans as "Keep it Simple." Maybe organized religion could learn a thing or two from AA.

My denomination du jour is Presbyterian. Why? Maybe because there have been more Presbyterian Presidents of the U.S. than any other denomination; well, maybe that's not such a good reason. Presbyterians are a thinking denomination, and perhaps sometimes we think too much. There's an old joke "How many Presbyterians does it take to change a lightbulb?" The answer—37. You need have five committees of seven to discuss the idea, one person to tell the custodian to change it, then the custodian to change it. Presbyterians are ruled by members of the congregation who are elected as elders. These elders are called the session and session meetings can rival congressional proceedings as to their durations.

It has been said that Presbyterians are Baptist who now drink—but only in moderation of course. A rip roarin' time for a Presbyterian women's group is when someone decides to substitute caffeinated coffee for decaf at their book study.

Presbyterians eventually get things done, but if it has to be done quickly give me a Baptist or Quaker any day. Here's why. About fifteen years ago there were a number of black churches in the South that were burned down by arsonists. A number of Presbyterians in Northern

California mobilized and traveled South in order to assist in rebuilding the churches. Quakers also joined the numbers. They seemed to have the most information as to where there was the greatest need. Their organizational skills were amazing and their efficiency put everyone to shame. I felt like a slacker in comparison. I came to the conclusion that Quakers could travel half way around the world before Presbyterians could get their luggage packed. Perhaps I've been too hard on Presbyterians but I figure if Garrison Keillor can make millions making fun of Lutherans I can at least make pizza money poking a little fun at the Presbies.

So how did I get to this denominational point? I started out a Baptist over fifty years ago. Fountain Memorial Baptist Church was within walking distance of our Minnesota Ave. row house—you simply walked down an alley and you were at church. If you walked down the same alley today you may find yourself in the middle of one of the aforementioned crack cocaine deals.

The pastor was Rev. Charles Holland who peppered his sermons with humorous stories of his Kentucky childhood. There was no fire and brimstone and the basic message was that Jesus loved you. I've already mentioned his keen sense of audience analysis in moving the Sunday evening service to an earlier time slot to avoid competing against Disney and Ed Sullivan.

We had some minor celebrities who attended Fountain Memorial. One was "Pop" Curtis, who owned Curtis Brothers Furniture which boasted "The World's Largest Chair" in the store's parking lot. "Pop" was a jovial man who was a generous giver to the church and visited shut-ins.

The other was "Fishbait" Miller who was the Doorman of the U.S. Congress. For the State of the Union Address Fishbait would bellow, "Mr. Speaker, The President of the United States." Almost every church had their TVs tuned to the address not to hear the President but to see Mr. Miller.

Fountain Memorial was a beautiful stone church. There was a beautiful stained glass window of Jesus in the Garden of Gethsemane in the front of the church. Each side of the church had stained glass windows of significant events in Jesus' life. The baptismal in front of the church had a mural of the river Jordan.

Wednesday night prayer meetings are an important tradition in the Baptist church. Pastor Holland recognized that there was a problem as to workers getting home late and choking down dinner in order to make it to the prayer meeting. The problem was solved by faithful women who prepared dinner for all attendees before the prayer meeting. Dinner was at 6PM and the service at 7. This allowed people time enough to get home and enjoy the popular TV show Wagon Train. Dinners were full meal deals with fried chicken, ham, or roast beef with all the fixings. Women congregated at the church mid-afternoon and tried to outdo one another as to side dishes and desserts. The men enjoyed coming to church to eat because in a number of cases the food was better than what they were getting at home.

As with most churches Sunday School was before the church service. Thinking back it now seems strange that men used to smoke right outside the church in between Sunday School and the church service. The big treat for kids was Vacation Bible School. VBS took up half of the day and was a relief for moms who didn't have to work it. VBS included Bible stories, music, games, and crafts. The crafts usually included ample popsicle sticks and toilet paper rolls.

Refreshments were cookies and Kool Aid. When we moved to Oxon Hill and attended Forest Heights Baptist the big attraction was Kool Aid served out of a garbage can. Mr. Kofink, yes that was his real name, would buy a new garbage can each year, clean it thoroughly, and make gallons of Kool Aid. The kids loved it but the moms thought it was repulsive. The last night was parents' night, with music and skits. We also got to present our crafts to our parents.

Today VBS is a multi-million dollar industry with publishing houses competing for churches' business. Publishers not only provide curriculum, but decorations for sets, posters, CDs, tokens, you name it. A medium-size church could easily spend thousands of dollars if they bought the entire package. Years ago parents themselves developed all the above and everything went well. I don't have anything against publishers but VBS becomes a "paint by numbers" proposition if parents don't use some of their own creativity.

The Rev. Charles Warford was our pastor at Forest Heights. He was young, studious looking, and a teacher instead of a brimstone preacher. I guess our family was lucky in that regard. One major advantage for Forest Heights was that it had so much land. It is near the Capital Beltway and the land must be worth hundreds of thousands of dollars today. The church was conveniently located across the street from John Hanson Junior High School.

One day the pastor called our house and asked to talk to me. "Gary, I've been thinking about you for a long time and I'm wondering if I can talk to you Thursday after school." My mind raced immediately to a recent church softball game where I had argued with an umpire for being called out while trying to steal second base." All I could do was mumble, "Yes" to the pastor.

That Thursday I could not focus in class. I had visions of being scolded by Pastor Warford, or worst yet, being kicked off the church softball team. The dismissal bell rang and I slowly crossed the street to the church. I felt like dead man walking. Once inside the church Pastor Warford greeted me and we went to his study. Many pastors call their offices "studies." It seems more pastor-like. He asked me if I had accepted the Lord. I thought, "Wow! This is a piece of cake. I'm not kicked off the softball team." I told him yes. He asked me if I would be willing to "come forward" during the altar call. Coming forward indicated that one was accepting Jesus Christ as Savior and Lord. I'm not sure if I've ever had anyone had ever looked at me the way he did. It was not threatening. It was perhaps the most honest, caring, earnest look I had ever seen. I was used to seeing that from dogs on my paper route but not from a human being.

I agreed to come forward. That Sunday I didn't hear the sermon. My only concern was coming forward. The moment came as the piano played the old hymn "Just as I Am." "Just as I am without one plea..." I started getting cold feet...Wow! All these people will stare at me...My algebra test wasn't half as difficult as this. Finally, my feet took on a life of their own as I walked to the front of the sanctuary. My parents didn't know that I was going to do this; in fact, we had tickets for a Senators' baseball game. I guess it was appropriate that they were playing the Angels. Rev. Warford was smiling as the hymn ended.

My parents didn't say much on the way to the game. They were surprised but pleased and they figured that I knew what I was doing. We got to the game in the second inning, and there was plenty of baseball to come because it was a doubleheader. The Senators won the first game and perhaps it was appropriate that the Angels won the second game.

A few weeks later I was baptized. Baptist believe in total immersion where you go all the way under water. Presbyterians think that sprinkling will suffice. Rev. Warford was referred to as "Dr. Dunk," because when he dunked you, you knew you were dunked. Wearing a white baptismal robe I was dunked and tried not to sputter as I climbed the stairs out of the baptismal.

Aside from the serious stuff at Forest Heights there was lots of wholesome fun. The Baptists had an organization named The Royal Ambassadors which was the Baptist answer to The Boy Scouts. We went hiking and camping but we also learned Bible verses as well as information about missionaries.

The Royal Ambassadors, or RAs, were heavily into conservation and preserving the creation. I remember reading Rachel Carson's book Silent Spring one of the first publications to warn about the hazards of DDT.

We also learned that deforestation of the rainforest could cause climate change. This was long before Al Gore and others warned of global warming.

Besides the education information there was plenty of outdoor fun. The Shenandoah mountains were within easy driving distance of DC and they became our playground. Our RA leaders, Mr. Frank Knight and Mr. Jackie Wyatt, took us hiking in portions of the Appalachian Trail and we climbed Old Rag Mountain, so named because of its rocky bald peak.

Boy Scouts were often in the same area of the mountains and there was a bit of competition between The Scouts and RAs. One time we came across a Scout who was bragging to us about the number of merit badges he possessed. One of our group challenged him to a knot tying contest. Somehow the whole contest evolved into the Scout being tied to a tree and all of us fleeing with glee. The Scoutmaster came to our leader and complained. We were chastised by our leader in front of the Scoutmaster and told we had exhibited poor sportsmanship, camping etiquette, and that "we were poor Christian witnesses." When the Scoutmaster left our leader giggled and said, "OK guys, time to make s'mores."

Another competitive issue was when we came across a troop that seemed to use enough charcoal lighter to make cement burn. In comparison, we built fires the natural way and some of our group could start a fire with flint. We started calling charcoal lighter "Boy Scout Water."

Besides RAs, we had church league softball. It was pretty easy to get enough churches to form a league because it seemed as if there was a Southern Baptist church on every street corner in the DC area. We didn't have far to go for our home field because it was in front of our church.

Little Leagues get a bad rap as to bad sportsmanship but they had nothing on church league softball. It seemed as if the parents and fans left all their piety at home, and all the frustrations of the week came spilling out at church league games. Players were also colorful with their razzing of opponents. Some teams had "ringer" kids who didn't even go to church. Coaches always rationalized that they were trying to bring the boy "into the fold." I played church softball into young adulthood when I came home from college. The unsportsmanlike behavior continued on the adult teams only it grew more intense. It's amazing because later I played in city leagues in some dicey parts of towns against all kinds of teams. Some teams had factory workers from places such as Caterpillar and John Deere. These guys looked like they could hit a home run every time at bat and that they could hunt bears with a stick. In some cases we would drive through parts of town where there were abandoned cars and refrigerators on the front lawns to get to the softball fields. The city league games were always civil, no fights, no arguing with umpires, just good sportsmanship all around. No matter who won or lost there were handshakes and the captains would ask, "Hey, do you guys want to go out and get a beer?"

Softball aside, Forest Heights and Fountain Memorial churches were major parts of my young life. They taught me the basics of how one should live and the importance of The Golden Rule. I remained a member of Forest Heights throughout my college years. I returned home and was the summer youth pastor at Forest Heights for four summers. At that time, drugs and alcohol were becoming major problems for youth in Oxon Hill. Drugs were creeping over from the nearby DC city limits and the drinking age in DC was eighteen. It was easy to get a fake ID or pay a buck to a wino sitting outside a liquor store to buy beer. My job was basic—teach young people how to make good choices and have some fun while doing so. I grew closer to the kids each year and I think that the Summer of '77 was the best summer of my life. It was my last with the kids before heading off to graduate school at Northern Illinois University.

Years later when Dad died, I felt lost. I had returned home from California just in time to see him on his death bed. The day after he died was Sunday and for some reason I instinctively drove to Forest Heights Church. I had not set foot in the church for years but I was greeted by numerous people who recognized me despite the touches of gray in my hair. A half dozen of the older men greeted me with, "So how have you been all these years?" When they heard the news about Dad they asked where the post funeral dinner was going to be. It had been less than twenty four hours since Dad's death and I said I didn't know.

Doug Norwood, one of the members of the group, immediately volunteered use of the church's social hall and said that church members would prepare a meal. It was an amazing offer. Following the funeral service all in attendance went to the church for the meal. The members had prepared a feast in the typical Southern Baptist style; in other words, if you went away hungry it was your own fault. There is a passage from the New Testament book of James which reads, "Faith without works is dead." The dinner and the kindness of the church members were living examples of this. I think that is a big part of my faith, that, and keeping it simple.

Forest Heights also introduced me to two of the most significant people in my life—Pat and Jack Hansen. They were the volunteer youth directors at Forest Heights and they were living models of how life should be led. The Hansens came from Boston. Pat was a nurse who had graduated from the University of Maryland, and Jack was a graduate of MIT and worked as a physicist at the Naval Research lab.

For Bible studies and Sunday School they were always dealing with current issues, such as situational ethics and trying to get us to think about how to make right choices. Some critics have said that many in Christian education are long on piety and short on brains. That was not the case with Pat and Jack. The couple stressed service work and helping others. To them the concept of "Love your neighbor as you would love yourself" meant that anyone could be your neighbor.

149

One Saturday they took us into Anacostia with boxes of roller skates. I don't know how they discovered this community center but we had been invited to teach the kids how to skate and have an afternoon skating party. Most of the kids were black and had never been on a pair of skates. We demonstrated how to put on the skates with a skate key and soon they were on their way.

It became a Christmas tradition for us to pile into cars and go Christmas caroling to shut ins. Sure, lots of churches do this but Pat and Jack had a knack for finding people who were desperate for human companionship. One Christmas I was depressed and I didn't know why. Maybe it was because of the ways things were going at home or that I wasn't dating anyone. I really didn't know the cause but I thought that going caroling might improve my mood. Kids piled into cars and there were kids stuffed in the luggage areas of station wagons. Once again Pat and Jack had found the people who needed human contact the most. We visited the elderly, the wheelchair bound, and even the Scrooges who probably didn't want us around. Even their hearts were softened.

I would probably never have attended college had it not been for Pat and Jack. One Saturday they took us to a Christian college fair at a church in northern Virginia. We arrived at the church and there was a large room with dozens of displays and representatives from Christian colleges. The representatives were from colleges across the nation and there was even one representative from a college in Hawaii (Gee, college in Hawaii. This sounded great, but I'm not sure I would have studied very much.)

One school caught my eye—Wheaton College. Wheaton is a non-denominational college located twenty-five miles west of Chicago. I looked at the display and the campus brochure and there was information about the campus radio station and the Communication program. The representative was a kind, soft-sell type of guy. Some of the other representatives gave me the impression that my soul was going to hell if I didn't attend their school. Wheaton's rep gave me the information and told me that he would be in touch with me within a week. He gave me a brochure from Wheaton with the caption, "Are You Wheaton's Kind of Student?" The photos in the brochure included smiling, well-scrubbed, well-dressed students walking around campus and others doing important stuff, such as looking through microscopes

150

and playing violins (have you ever noticed that almost all college promotional commercials aired at halftime of college sporting events, include students in white coats looking through microscopes and looking as if they have just discovered air?)

True to his promise, Wheaton's rep called me within a week and asked if it would be OK for him to come and visit me at our house. I thought, gee maybe I'm Wheaton's kind of student. I asked Mom and she was in shock. She managed to pull herself together and give me a possible date. I arranged the date with the rep and he said he would be there to see me.

Wheaton's rep, and I believe his name was Mr. Mitchell, came one evening and had dinner with us. Mom made her famous spaghetti and Mr. Mitchell talked about Wheaton. After dinner, we got down to business. Mr. Mitchell had checked my grades. This was in an era before all the confidentiality stuff that we have today. They were OK but not Harvard material. He started asking about my school activities and was impressed.

Then he broke the news to me. I did appear to be Wheaton's kind of student; however, there was one problem. Wheaton was at full enrollment for the fall quarter. If I was willing to postpone school until the March quarter then I would be admitted to Wheaton. He mentioned the tuition figure and it seemed staggering. My parents didn't even respond. The expression on their faces were, "Good night and thank you for playing. Your parting gift is a quart of homemade spaghetti sauce." The tuition was reasonable compared to other schools, but we had no frame of reference; it just seemed like a big chunk of change.

Then came the good news. If I decided to come in March, I would get massive amounts of financial aid.

Wheaton was also trying to build its Communication department and I wanted to be a Communication major. This all sounded too good to be true. I wouldn't be going to college in the fall but I could earn and save more money for over six months. I ended up going to Wheaton in March of '72 and graduating in August of '75. My college education is due to Wheaton College, financial aid, professors who cared, Pat and Jack Hansen, and people who practiced the concept of "Faith without works is dead." As for the present, I feel that if I can work my faith and have faith in my works, everything will be OK.

PHOTOS FROM WAY BACK WHEN...

Program from the infamous
Pearl Harbor Game,
Redskins vs. Eagles
December 7th 1941
-- Author's collection.

The Old Post Office Building now a Trump Hotel in D.C. My father
and I watched both JFK's inauguration parade and funeral procession
from the steps of the Old Post office.
-- David Blackwell

JFK's grave site
looking towards D.C.
-- David Blackwell

One has to appreciate the
simplicity of RFK's grave site.
-- David Blackwell

On April 17, 1953 The New York Yankees Mickey Mantle
hit a 565 ft. home run off the Washington Senators' Chuck Stobbs out of Griffith
Stadium. I was born the same day at D.C.'s Providence Hospital.
-- Author's collection

The intersection of Pennsylvania and Minnesota Avenues. I spent a number
of my early years in a row house a block from this intersection.
-- District Department of Transportation (DDOT) Library, Pennsylvania and
Minnesota Avenues SE. Dated 1947

Barney Circle where you could transfer from a bus in Southeast D.C. and travel by streetcar to Downtown.
-- District Department of Transportation (DDOT) Library, Aerial photo of Barney Circle. Date unknown.

Congressional Cemetery final resting place for numerous members of Congress. March King John Phillip Sousa is also buried there. As kids we played hide and seek here.
-- David Blackwell

J. Edgar Hoover's grave site. Groundkeepers report that many pairs of pink high heels are left on the gravesite. Draw your own conclusion.
-- Davis Blackwell.

Snow has always been the bane of D.C. area residences who simply do not know how to drive in it.
-- District Department of Transportation (DDOT) Library, Snow and snow removal in DC. Date unknown.

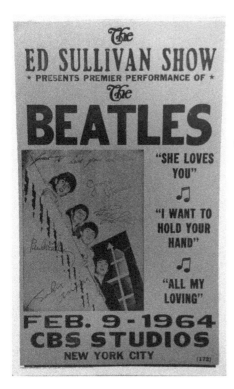

Poster for The Beatles first U.S. appearance on The Ed Sullivan Show. The first Public appearance was at The Washington Coliseum in February of 1964.
-- Author's collection

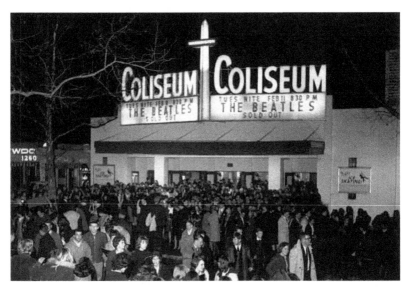

Outside the Washington Coliseum the February night of the Beatles' first public concert after The Ed Sullivan Show. 8,000 attended and paid $2 to $4 for tickets
--- District Department of Transportation (DDOT) Library

The former Washington Coliseum site of the first Beatles performance now the cornerstone store for REI Campiing and Outdoors Equipment stores.
-- David Blackwell

The carousel at Glen Echo Amusement Part.
Black were not allowed to swim in the parks huge pool.
-- David Blackwell

Great Falls a favorite of my family staycation destinations.
George Washington attempted to build a canal to circumvent the falls.
-- David Blackwell

The castle entrance to The Enchanted Fores which was in Ellicott City, MD.
Many of the attractions from the Enchanted Forest have been removed to
Clark's Elioak Farm and preserved there.
-- Elioak Farm

Little Toot, a working tug boat, was an attraction
at The Enchanted Forest
--Elioak Farm

Harper's Ferry WVA another staycation favorite. John Brown stormed
the arsenal there in 1859 in what many historian consider to be
the true beginning of The Civil War.
-- Photo by Don Burgess, Harper's Ferry Historical Society

Scene from the April, 1968 D.C. riots following the assassination of
The Rev. Dr. Martin Luther King. Dozens of D.C blocks were destroyed
and black owners escaped damage to their businesses by tagging
"Soul Brother" in front of their stores.
-- District Department of Transportation (DDOT) Library

Another riot image. It took The District nearly
30 years to recover from the damage.
-- District Department of Transportation (DDOT) Library

The riot fires, which had started on 14th Street, spread to Seventh Street and to H Street in Northeast
- Emil A. Press Slide Collection, Historical Society Of Washington, D.C.

14th and U Streets, the epicenter of the rioting is now a thriving business district.
-- David Blackwell

Small business owner Larry of Larry's
Clothing near 14th Street.
-- David Blackwell

Recent shot from the swimming hole of the
new National Habor. Some things do change.
-- David Blackwell

Shot of sunset on our old Potomac
swimming hole.
-- David Blackwell

Some down and out souls we passed on our way from school to home.
David Blackwell titles this, "Bad Financial Advice."
-- David Blackwell, Copyright Library of Congress

Distlefink's Ice Cream
store neon sign.
The store has closed
but the sign remains.
-- David Blackwell

Yours truly at the mic doing the
Star Boy show on WMAL radio.
-- Author's collection

The final edition of The Washington Star,
August, 1981. I was a Star Boy for five years.
-- Author's collection

The Dreibelbis Covered Bridge in Eastern, PA.
It is on the National Historic Register.
- Eric Dreibelbis, The Dreibelbis Cousins

J. Willard Marriott in front of a D.C.
familyfavorite, Hot Shoppes.
- The Marriott Corporation

WMAL Radio's Frank Harden and
Jackson Weaver who ruled morning
drive time in D.C.
- Tom Buckley--WUSA

The Joy Boys

WRC Radio's The Joy Boy featuring Ed Walker
and Willard Scott were D.C. evening favorites.
The two met at D.C.'s American University.
- Tom Buckley--WUSA

Walker and Scott at the WRC
- Tom Buckley--WUSA

Felix E. Grant Jazz Archives, University of the District of Columbia

WMAL's Felix Grant was D.C.'s Evening Jazz Man.
Here he is with the great Chuck Mangione.
- Tom Buckley--WUSA

Pick Temple was a
D.C. kids' show icon.
Here's Pick
Strumming
a Western song.
- Tom Buckley--WUSA

Other D.C. kid show hosts drop by Pick's ranch: Ranger Hal Shaw, Romper Room's Miss Francis, Pete Jamison, and Captain Tugg played by Lee Shepard.
- Tom Buckley--WUSA

My HEALTH Rules

Washed my hands
before meals

Brushed my teeth
morning and evening

Cleaned my
fingernails

Drank all my
fruit juice

Drank all
my milk

Ate all
my bread

Finished all
my meals

Played outdoors
in fresh air

Read or colored
in good light

To bed
on time

My RANGE Rules

Came first time
I was called

Remembered to say
please and thank you

Looked both ways
before crossing street

Dressed myself

Hung up
my clothes

Remembered not to
interrupt others

Watched my
table manners

Was polite
to everybody

Put away
my toys

Followed orders
with a smile

My CITIZEN Rules

Be proud of my Country
and its glorious Flag

Be ever respectful of
my Mother and Father

Be obedient to the law
and its representatives

Be honest and trustworthy
in my every action

Be helpful to my
friends and neighbors

Be alert to the protection
of the property of others

Be mindful of cleanliness in
thoughts, words and deeds

Be careful of my health
habits for a strong body

Be willing to do my share
for Country, Community
and Family

Be animated always by the
spirit of fair play in my
association with others

DON'T PUT OFF UNTIL TOMORROW WHAT YOU CAN DO TODAY

Pick's Range Rules were sent to every child who wrote to Pick.
- Tom Buckley, WUSA

Pick on his steed with dog Lady making
the turn off Pennsylvania Ave.
-- Tom Buckley, WUSA

Ranger Hal Shaw was
an early morning kids' favorite.
Here's the Ranger calling
the fire tower.
-- Tom Buckley, WUSA

172

Ranger Hal with the stars of Lassie,
Robert Bray and Lassie.
-- Tom Buckley, Milt Grant

The Jim Henson Memorial Statue of Jim and Kermit in front
of The Stamp Center at the University of Maryland.
-- John Consoli, University of Maryland

Milt Grant was a D.C.
teen favorite and a forerunner to
Dick Clark's American Bandstand.
Tuesdays were referred
to by some as "Black Tuesday"
when blacks were allowed
to appearon the show
-- Tom Buckley, WUSA

Max Robinson and Gordon Petersen were news
ratings winners at WTOP-TV. Max was one of the
first black news anchors in the nation.
-- Tom Buckley, WUSA

Warner Wolf was a sports fixture in D.C. at WTOP-TV. In high school people compared me to Warner.
-- Tom Buckley, WUSA

Warner and Washington Redskins' great Sonny Jurgensen with their crutches following Warner's knee injury and Sonny's Achilles injury.
-- Tom Buckley, WUSA

Blues Alley was and is part of the Goergetown music scene.
-- David Blackwell

A converted Little Tavern Shoppe in Georgetown. Jackie Kennedy supposedly stopped at this location for coffee when she was a photographer for The Washington Times Herald.
-- David Blackwell

The Balloon Man was a
fixture in Georgetown.
Where else can you get
an inflatable 747?
-- David Blackwell,
Copyright Library of Congress

The old Georgetown Theater marque.
-- David Blackwell

The Jefferson Memorial where I spent many
lonely nights before heading to college.
-- District Department of Transportation (DDOT) Library

Dart Drug beer. On a
good Sunday, or bad
one depending on your
perspective, you could
get a six pack for 98 cents.
-- Tom Buckley, WUSA

The garage in Northern Virginia where The Washington Post's
Bob Woodward met Deep Throat.
-- David Blackwell

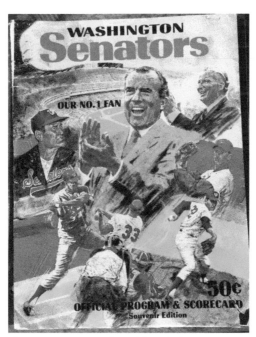

Washington Senators program from 1970 their next to last year in D.C.
President Nixon, owner Bob Short, Frank :"Hondo" Howard, Ted Williams,
and pitcher Dick Bosman are on the cover.
-- Tom Buckley, WUSA

1515 L STREET, N. W. 223-6000
WASHINGTON, D.C. 20005

May 8, 1995.

Dear Gary Dreibelbis,

     I was most interested to learn
from your Mother that you have been
a Washington sports fan, and a Povich reader,
for so many years.

     It is always warming to know that
one's stuff isread, and liked, and it was
a very warm note I received from your
Mother in Oxon Hill.

     I am sure you suffered with me
in so many of those rough years with the
Senators, and the Redskins, but we remember
the highlights, too; don't we.

     With my best wishes, always,

Shirley Povich

Letter from the great Washington Post Sport Writer Shirley Povich.
He responded to a letter that my Mom wrote him saying
thatI appreciated his work.
-- AUTHORS COLLECTION

180

Hot Fudge Ice Cream Cake
- The Marriott Corporation

Mighty Moe's
- The Marriott Corporation

HOT SHOPPES RECIPES

Turn back time for you tummy with these Hot Shoppes recipes
- Courtesy of The Marriott Corporation

MIGHTY MO
Yield one serving

Sesame Seed Hamburger Roll uncut—one each

Oleo margarine—1 tablespoon

Hamburger patties, ½ pound—2 each

Salt—To taste

White pepper—To taste

Lettuce shredded—1 tablespoon

American cheese—I slice

Mighty Mo Sauce—4 teaspoons

Dill pickle chips—2 each

PREPARATION

Prepare Might Mo Sauce according to the instructions given on recipe.

Cut sesame seed hamburger roll crosswise into three equal sections.

Spread bottom, top and one side of center cut of bun with softened oleo margarine.

Grill bun until browned and heated throughout.

Shape hamburger into thin 4 inch diameter patties.

Grill hamburger very lightly in both sides—DO NOT OVER-COOK.

Grill second hamburger very lightly on one side, turn and top with one slice of American cheese and grill lightly.

Spread 2 teaspoons of Mighty Mo sauce on bottom of roll.

Top dressing with shredded lettuce, then hamburger.

Top hamburger with middle layer of bun, grilled side up and spread remaining 2 teaspoons of Mighty Mo Sauce.

Top with cheeseburger.

Place 2 dill pickle chips on cheese.

MIGHTY MO SAUCE

Catsup—1/2 cup

Chili Sauce—1/4 cup

A-1 Sauce—1 ½ teaspoons

Worcestershire Sauce—1/2 teaspoon

Tabasco Sauce—2 drops

Sweet Pickle, finely chopped—1/2 cup

Mayonnaise—1 ¼ cup

Yield is 2 ½ cups

PREPARATION

Combine catsup, chili sauce, A-1 Sauce, Worcestershire sauce, and Tabasco Sauce.

Finely chop sweet pickles and add to sauce.

Combine the sauce pickle mixture with mayonnaise, stirring until well blended.

Store in a tightly sealed container until served and refrigerate.

TWEEN TWIST

Ham, thinly sliced—4 oz.

American Cheese-cut in half lengthwise—1 slice

Tomato Slice—2 each

Lettuce,shredded—As needed

Tartar Sauce—1 tablespoon

Oleo Margarine, soften—As needed

Twist Roll, sliced lengthwise—1 each

Yield one serving

PREPARATION

Spread both sided of sliced roll with softened oleo margarine.

Place the two halves of American cheese on bottom half of roll, covering as much of the roll as possible.

Separate thinly sliced ham and place on top of the cheese, covering as much of the cheese as possible and covering to build full volume.

Place sandwich on grill with ham touching the surface of the grill or frying pan. Place top half of roll on grill.

Heat until ham is hot.

Remove from heat and top ham with 2 slices of tomato. Cover with shredded lettuce.

Spread 1 tablespoon of tartar sauce on the top half of the grilled roll and place on top of the sandwich.

Cut in half diagonally and serve as desired.

HOT FUDGE ICE CREAM CAKE

PREPARATION

Plain yellow cake, day old—3 inches by 3 inches by ½ inch—2 slices

Ice Cream Square, 3 inches by 3 inches—1 each

Hot Fudge, heated—4 tablespoons

Whipped Cream—2 ½ tablespoons

Maraschino Cherry, half—drained—1 each

Yield 1 serving

PREPARATION

Place 1 square of plain yellow cake on serving plate.

Top with the ice cream square and place the second square of plain yellow cake on top of the ice cream.

Drizzle 1 tablespoon of hot fudge over each of the four cake corners, taking care to leave the center of the cake free from fudge.

Place approximately 2 ½ tablespoons of whipped cream in the top center of the cake square. If desired, use a pastry bag to pipe whipped cream onto the top of cake in a rosette shape.

Top center of whipped cream with a well drained maraschino cherry half to garnish.

ORANGE FREEZE

Orange juice—fresh or reconstituted from frozen—3/4 cup

Orange Sherbet—1 cup

Orange slice, twised—1/4 inch thick or Maraschino Cherry, quarter—1 each

Fresh Mint—1 sprig

Yield one serving

PREPARATION

Freeze 14-16 ounce soda glasses by placing clean, dry, room temperature glasses in the freezer.

Remove glasses from the freezer as needed.

Place orange juice and orange sherbet in a blender and mix until well-blended to the consistency of a milk shake.

Pour orange freeze mixture into a frosted soda glass to within ½ inch from the top of the glass.

Garnish top with a whole orange slice twisted or ¼ maraschino cherry and a sprig of fresh mint.

Serve with a straw and a spoon.

Little Tavern was famous for their mugs of "Good Coffee."
-- AUTHORS COLLECTION

LET'S EAT

Most cities can lay claim to having an official food. For New York City I don't know if it is official but my vote would be for the Big Apple's "slice" of New York style pizza. Another choice for me, and certainly not official, is the food served out of carts in Midtown Manhattan. For some reason the food always tastes good to me, and it is amazing that you can get a full breakfast from one of these carts. Coffee is memorable to me in New York no matter where I go. My first time in New York I ordered coffee and the server asked, "regular?" Thinking that 'regular" meant black I said yes. My coffee came with cream and sugar and I soon learned the meaning of "regular" in regards to coffee.

Buffalo has its wings and I think they are best with bleu cheese. Philadelphia has it cheesesteak and maybe that's why the epithet on W.C. Field's tombstone reads, "On the whole I'd rather be in Philadelphia." Cincinnati has its chili, and you can have all the chili cook-offs you want, but give me that sweet taste of Cincinnati Chili with noodles anytime.

Moving westward, St Louis and Kansas City battle it out for ribs, Denver has Rocky Mountain Oysters, (I'll pass, thank you) and then there is Chicago. No, I didn't flunk geography but I saved it for last because I consider Chicago to be my second hometown. My votes for favorite Chicago foods are Chicago style hot dogs and deep dish pizza.

The Chicago style hot dog is a meal in itself with tomatoes, pickles, the best relish you've ever tasted, celery salt, and some stuff I've forgotten. Deep dish pizza is, well, deep dish, and you have to experience a Chicago deep dish pizza and not one of those knock offs served at chains around the country. For my money Lou Malnati's is the best, plus you can have it shipped to you anywhere in the country.

You may be wondering why I'm mentioning food from all these cities when this is a book about DC. Am I trying to curry favor with potential readers in these cities? If you are flying to one of these cities and reading this am I trying to make your mouth water? Wrong on both counts, Sherlock.

The point I wish to make is that, in my mind, DC has no official food which it can call its own. To that I say to the powers that be, "Come on!" even Peoria has its official food—the Butterfly Pork Chop Sandwich, and it's a darned good official food, too!"

With this in mind, and since this is a "memories" book, I will explore the food and eating places of my youth. Keep in mind that most medical experts claim that we lose approximately forty percent of our taste buds by the age of forty so many of my choices are "pre-forty."

DC can't lay sole claim to crabs and crabcakes. This must be shared with Charm City, Baltimore. I believe that the crabcakes in these cities are far superior to those on the west coast. The Dungeness crab cakes of San Francisco are great but nothing brings back taste bud memories like Maryland crab cakes made with Blue Crab. The only problem with regional crabcakes is that some have too much filler. A real treat is mini crab cakes sandwiched between two saltines. I used to get these at old Memorial Stadium during Baltimore Colts' football games.

Then there is the old fashioned DC/Maryland/Virginia crab feast. The first time I encountered one was on a Saturday afternoon on my paper route. I stopped at one house and heard people laughing while a Senators' game blared from the radio. Peaking around the corner of the house I saw what appeared to be some barbaric ritual. There were people smashing crabs with wooden hammers on a picnic table covered with newspapers. Corn on the cob plus beer were being served in copious amounts.

The customer spied me spying and invited me to join them. I was near the end of my route, so I accepted their invitation. For the next fifteen minutes I gorged on crab, corn on the cob, potato salad and other goodies.

The host produced two Rock Creek Ginger Ales to wash everything down. I have been a lover of crab feast ever since and the more barbaric the better. The heck with crab bibs. Guys take off your shirts and women may resort to halter or swim tops and let the crab fall where it may. One of the great things about a crab feast was that there were panel trucks up and down nearby highways selling crab fresh from the Chesapeake Bay. In most cases it was from bay to mouth in less than a few hours.

Turning to burgers, everyone has an opinion as to gourmet burgers but that not what this is about—it's about kids' memories. Little

188

Tavern has already been mentioned. Perhaps it is the memories more than the quality of the burgers. Contrary to the name, Little Taverns sold no beer, and the stiffest drink you could get was their strong coffee or creamy hot chocolate.

Little Taverns may have developed "The Slider Concept" before White Castles in the Midwest. The slogan was "Buy them by the bag," and at one point you could buy a bag of mini burgers for a buck. It was a treat for hard working moms when dads decided to bring home a bag for dinner. The Little Tavern buildings were small but distinctive white tile building with green roofs and The Little Tavern sign. Most of the interior was a long snack bar. The coffee mugs were a distinctive white and green with the Little Tavern logo. I have about twenty of them that I ordered on e-bay for old times' sake. In its heyday, Little Tavern had forty stores in the DC/Baltimore area. The larger chains contributed to the demise of LT.

When considering memories I must mention Mc Donald's. "What!?" you may ask. The mega chain that you can find in places like Moscow and Beijing? Are you a stock owner or something? I understand your burger bombast but I can make my case. Before there was a Mc Donald's on every other city street block (Can you say Starbucks? I once saw a Starbuck's across the street from another Starbuck's in Northern California) Mc Donald's were one of the first chains which appealed to families.

The Mc Donald's closest to us was in Forest Heights, MD, and it was one of the first in the country at store number 12. It was not enclosed and you walked up to the window in the DC heat or cold blowing off the Potomac River to place your order. There were a few outside seats but for the most part you ate in your car or took your food home.

Mc Donald's takes a bad rap today, and in a recent national poll they ranked last in the quality of their burgers with Burger King and Wendy's right there with them, but for the time it was decent food at a low price. I can remember TV commercials with the jingle, "Forty-seven cents for a three course meal at Mc Donald's, the drive in with the golden arches." The menu was a burger, fifteen cents, fries, twelve cents, and the milk shake was the highest priced item at a whopping twenty cents.

Mc Donald's signs were memorable and eye catching. The red sign with the iconic golden arches had a neon Mr. Speedy at the top and a scoreboard displaying how many burgers had been sold. It was always a big deal when the sign switched to another million sold.

Another chain, which was smaller and served the DC/Baltimore area, was Hot Shoppes. Today when we hear Marriott we think of the international, high quality hotel chain. J Willard Marriott's empire started with humble beginnings; it was a root beer stand in Northwest DC. His next step was Hot Shoppes restaurants resembling Howard Johnson's with restaurants sporting orange roofs. They didn't have as many flavors of ice cream as Howard Johnson's but the quality was good and the ice cream desserts were better than Ho Jo's.

Later, Marriott opened Hot Shoppes Cafeterias which were a hit with government workers wanting a quality, fast lunch and with churchgoers who didn't want to cook but just go home and nap or watch the Redskins. J. Willard went on to other food opportunities such as catering food, this at a time when you could get a decent meal on a plane. Marriott also opened several American Graffiti-type restaurants called Might Mo's where you could receive car service from car hops and eat your meal in your car. No skating servers were involved. The featured item was Mighty Mo which was a forerunner of The Big Mac and, in the opinion of this burger critic, at least five times better. A submarine type sandwich, the Teen Twist, was also a favorite.

Hot Shoppes eventually went the way of other local chains with many older customers lamenting the closing of the cafeterias. The Marriott Corporation decided to put its energy and resources into the more lucrative hotel business.

Another long gone chain was Topp's, "Home of the Sirloiner." Topp's was one of the first chains in the U.S. to offer Kentucky Fried Chicken long before KFC started its own chain. Colonel Sanders appeared on local kids TV shows promoting Kentucky Fried Chicken at Topp's. Today, fifty years later, we have an imposter Colonel Sanders hawking chicken on KFC commercials.

Currently, the DC area has many fine eateries featuring various types of cuisine but I'm not going to do a Washingtonian magazine top fifty review of them. My review is based upon my memories and the fact that if we ate at a Downtown restaurant, it was a special event. Hogate's was a seafood tradition in DC. One could argue that there were better seafood restaurants in the DC, area but Hogate's and its rum buns were loved by both locals and tourists. Hogate's was located on the Potomac and may have served more fried oysters than any place on the east coast. I tried my first fried oyster there in an act of bravery for my young palate and I loved them.

The Florida Ave Grill was one of my Dad's favorites many years ago. The Grill was located near old Griffith's Stadium, home of the Redskins and Senators, and was a favorite of soul food connoisseurs. I've been to some quality soul food restaurants in my time and I believe that the Florida Ave. Grill is tops. This is authentic soul food with pig's feet on the menu (not that I would order them but I just wanted to verify that this is a REAL soul food restaurant.) I've never been a big fan of sweet potato pie but I will take two pieces of The Grill's pie any time and there are at least two U.S. Presidents who would agree.

The Hawk and The Dove restaurant and bar is located on Capitol Hill and it was a place we would go in high school if we wanted to impress our dates. In an era when congressional members could step across the aisle and cut deals with one another the Hawk and The Dove was a place where deals were often made.

Before Colonel Sanders came along, Kentucky style fried chicken was on the menu of many DC area restaurants. As we traveled south it seemed, as if Maryland style fried chicken was the more popular item on menus. I could never tell the difference; they both tasted like chicken to me. Chinese food has always been a favorite of mine and I maintain that DC has some of the finest in the U.S. DC's Chinatown is smaller than those in other U.S. cities but in this case size isn't everything. One of my favorite dinner memories was when Dad would bring home the little white containers of Chinese food. At first I think I was more intrigued with the containers than eating the food. It wasn't long until I was savoring the food inside. Chinatown in DC, with its classic gate, is located just north of the Verizon Center, for those who want a bite to eat before a Capitals' or Wizards' game. I will always remember the Chinatown of old long before surrounding development.

Now, back to oysters. Those who have been to the east and west coasts will debate on which coast has the best oysters. It's pleasing that I'm within driving distance of Pt. Reyes near San Francisco where I can get fresh bay oysters. Californians have mastered the art of bar-b-quing oysters. West coast oysters seem fresher to me so my head would go with them; however, my heart goes with east coast oysters because they seem a little meatier. I guess I didn't leave my heart in San Francisco as far as oysters are concerned.

I mentioned Cincinnati Chili earlier in this chapter, but Clyde's in Georgetown is a close second. It doesn't have the pasta and isn't as sweet but it does have some sweetness and is meaty. Clyde's was a high school hangout for us when visiting Georgetown and wanting a treat. Today tourists take home cans of the stuff setting off metal detectors at Reagan, BWI, and Dulles Airports.

Today's diners may refer to The Washington Post's Style section when considering DC's fine dining choices but my favorite as a youth was The Old Ebbitts Grill. Old Ebbitts always featured hearty food and was a favorite of some U.S. Presidents. I always try to visit there when I return to DC to relive history and my personal memories.

Many boomers will take me to task for omitting some of their favorite eateries or foods. I know some will remember Eddie Leonard's Sandwich Shops, and while I never ate there, I can always remember the radio jingle:

"Eddie Leonard's Sandwich Shops you should try 'em.
For the very best in sandwiches just buy 'em
No matter where you are, you'll find that you're not far
From an Eddie Leonard Sandwich Shop

Every sandwich it will please, fifteen varieties
Open late every night, you'll enjoy a taste delight
Pick some up take some home,
once you do you'll never roam
From an Eddie Leonard Sandwich Shop.

So take a short drive, for a long, large measure
Of sandwich and pizza pleasure
At an Eddie Leonard Sandwich Shop
You're never far from an Eddie Leonard Sandwich Shop"

Some will take me to task for not mentioning Gino's but I consider that to be a Baltimore institution; still, the two Baltimore Colt greats, Gino Marchetti and Alan "The Horse" Ameche offered good burgers and there were some stores that made it to DC.

While DC may not have had an official food, I know that I never went hungry. I think by recalling the foods mentioned in this chapter my taste buds reverted back to those of forty years ago.

MY GREEN CATHEDRAL

Phillip J. Lowry has written a wonderful book, Green Cathedrals chronicling ballparks of a bygone era. I can identify with the choice of "Green Cathedrals" as a title because a ball park is my other church. The great New York Yankee's catcher Yogi Berra once said, "Baseball is like church. Many attend but few understand." I believe he was spot on with this quotation.

I attended a convention of the Society For Baseball Research back in the 1980's in Arlington, VA. One of the best presentations was given by an architect concerning ball parks. One of his claims was that in theory the entire earth is a baseball park. Unlike other sports with boundaries, the foul lines have no limits and, in theory, extended into infinity. This argument may have been a stretch, but the baseball romantic in me buys it.

I can't remember if this guy was associated with one of the large architectural firms that later built retro ballparks such as Camden Yards in Baltimore or those which followed but he was retro all the way. He spoke of past ballparks which were "Green Cathedrals" and that baseball needed to return to playing the game in "parks" instead of the so-called multi-purpose concrete doughnuts. He was prophetic, and any park built after 1990 was a retro-style ballpark.

My first green cathedral was a concrete doughnut, DC Stadium, later renamed RFK Stadium. Before continuing I must discuss some "pre-me" history. My team, the Washington Senators, was certainly not the New York Yankees. During their seventy year history they won the American League Pennant three times and the World Series once. The Senators or Nats were romanticized in the Douglas Wallop book The Year The Yankees Lost the Pennant which later became the hit Broadway musical Damn Yankees. The plot revolved around a Senators' fan who loved the team so much that he was willing to sell his soul to the Devil if he would make him the greatest baseball player alive. I loved the Senators but not enough to deal with the Devil on those terms.

The Senators were actually respectable when Dad came to pre-war DC, and they challenged for the pennant in 1944 and '45.

One of Dad's early jobs was that of a soda "jerk" at the Peoples' Drug Store on F Street N.W. This may not seem like a big deal but Peoples' was in the heart of the theatre district in DC with people coming to the snack bar before and after show for refreshment.

It wasn't long until Dad noticed people going to the basement of the store. Curious as to what was going on, he followed the crowd to the basement and found that there were small bleachers, radio equipment, and a large gong. With the equipment was Arch McDonald, "Voice of The Senators." Mc Donald recreated Senators' away games by looking at a cryptic piece of AP wirecopy and giving the impression he was at the game. He would strike the gong when a runner reached base and hit it four times for a home run.

Baseball re-creation was common because of the expense of the technology of the day in order to transmit away games to home fans. Many stations did re-creations and President Ronald Reagan got his start as "The Great Communicator" by re-creating Chicago Cubs' games for radio station WHO in Des Moines, IA, using the moniker Dutch Reagan.

During Dad's first years in DC The Senators could have been a team rivaling The Yankees for years to come. OK you ask, "How?" Please let me make my case and show that I'm not a "homer." Griffith Stadium was home to The Senators and also home to The Washington Grays perhaps the finest team in The Negro League. The Grays fielded such greats as Josh Gibson and Buck Leonard who were the Ruth and Gehrig of The Negro League.

Dad recalled that The Senators would play a day game on Saturday afternoons and draw 3,000. He and his buddies would adjourn to The Florida Ave. Grill for food and drink, and then return to Griffith to watch The Grays. The attendance would be 30,000 for the Grays' night game. The Grays were tops and the competition was fierce. The great pitcher Satchel Paige lead another top- tier team, The Kansas City Monarchs, and the Grays/Monarchs' rivalry was legendary.

Now here's where the "new New York Yankees" concept comes into play. The Senators were owned by Clark Griffith who was a fixture in DC baseball. "Griff" had been a quality pitcher, winning over 200 games before managing the Senators and eventually becoming their owner. Griffith was dubbed "The Old Fox" and with good reason. Not only had he been a shrewd pitcher but he was also a shrewd businessman. He owned Griffith Stadium and rented it to the Redskins, circuses, boxing promoters, and other events. The Grays were one of the tenants.

Griffith considered integrating the Senators long before Branch Rickey integrated The Brooklyn Dodgers with Jackie Robinson. If he had done so the Senators, who at the time were a good team, would have become a great team. Not only would they have acquired Gibson and Leonard, Griffith could have hired Paige who would pitch anywhere, including Cuba, if the price was right.

Griffith's shortsightedness won out. He was making so much money from renting the stadium to The Grays that he never integrated Senators. It was probably one of the worst decisions ever made by a baseball owner.

I only saw Griffith Stadium from the outside. By the time I was becoming a baseball fan the Senators were moving to the Twin Cities to become The Minnesota Twins. Griffith's nephew, Calvin, took over the team after Griff's death and race was an issue in the move. Calvin made the statement that blacks didn't care for baseball and liked "wrasslin" better. He rejoiced in moving the team to the Twin Cities to "play in front of hard working white people." Others speculated that he did not want to move into the new DC stadium and pay rent.

The move took the city by shock. There had been some rumblings about a possible move but most people could not envision The Nation's Capital without baseball. I have vivid recall of watching Bozo the Clown on WRC Channel 4 when a newscaster interrupted the show and broke the news that the Senators were moving to Minnesota; however, baseball had decided to put an expansion team in DC which would become "The New Senators." Los Angeles would get a new team, the Angels, expanding the American League to ten teams.

The 1961 Senators opened at Griffith Stadium vs. The Chicago White Sox, and President Kennedy threw out the first ball. The Senators managed to escape the cellar with a group of players who were has-beens and never-weres as they finished ninth over Kansas City.

Most fans can recall with great clarity their first baseball game. Mine was in May of 1962, The Senators vs. Cleveland. Fans often recall the green of the grass as they entered the archways of the ballpark. The brightness of the green was especially striking to me during the pre-color TV era. The giant scoreboard in right field caught my eye with the People's Drug, Washington Post, and First Federal Savings' ads on top. The Senators wore their home whites with "SENATORS" in red letters across their chest. They wore blue hats with a red "W." Cleveland wore their road grays and "CLEVELAND" across their jerseys with blue and red hats. A nondescript Senators' player, Ken Hamlin, hit the first home run I saw in person. The Senators won 4-2. The hot dogs were cold, the coke watered down, but I was in heaven.

Without doubt, my favorite player was Senators' centerfielder Jimmy Piersall. Piersall was the subject of a book and movie Fear Strikes Out. Both dealt with Piersall's struggles with mental illness. The movie, starring Anthony Perkins as Piersall and Karl "The Streets of San Francisco" Mauldin, took major liberties with Piersall's story and went way over the top. Piersall was one of the most colorful players I've ever seen as well as being an outstanding defensive centerfielder. He was never an offensive threat like Mickey Mantle or Willie Mays but he made up for this with his defensive skills.

As for the colorful side, Piersall was as colorful and stormy as they come. He was ejected from games four times in one season by the same umpire. The umpire, Al Salerno, once ejected Piersall before the game even started. He would dance the Twist between innings to organ twist music. He once disputed a strike call by pulling out a squirt gun from his uniform and washing off home plate. When he hit his 100th home run as a New York Met he ran the bases backwards.

Jimmy Piersall was my hero beyond the field. I knew of his struggles with mental illness and I figured if he could conquer it Mom could too. He became a hero for Mom, and she improved for a short period of time; unfortunately, my hero was not enough for her battle.

One of the nicest things Mom ever did for me was to write a letter to Jimmy Piersall requesting that he write a letter to me. He wrote back to me from L.A. on hotel stationary: a letter of thanks for being a fan. One of the things he wrote was, "Some fans are fair weather ones. You are for me all the way, good days and bad."

Years later, Jimmy Piersall went on to team with the legendary Harry Caray to announce Chicago White Sox games. Piersall and Budweiser Ambassador Caray were a team of announcing bad boys—

you never knew what you were going to get. I lived near Chicago during their reign and it was as if the Lord thought that I needed a good dose of Jimmy Piersall to get through grad school.

As for my baseball summer of '62, there was a long drought between my in-person baseball experiences.

I mentioned the August 1st twi-night double header against The Yankees in front of 48,000, the largest baseball crowd in DC history. The thing that hit me, besides the enormity of the crowd, was that players such as Mickey Mantle, Roger Maris, and Yogi Berra were human beings. You might ask, "Well, what did you expect?" For me to see them in-person, and not on a TV screen, was an unforgettable experience.

The Senators faired poorly that season but I continued to be a fan. Trips to the ballpark were few but I followed The Senators on WTOP-TV and radio. Dan Daniels and John MacLean called the games and I maintain that MacLean was one of the most underrated announcers of all time.

The great Washington Post sportswriter, Tom Boswell, wrote a wonderful book, Life Begins on Opening Day. I like the way Mr. Boswell thinks. Throughout the 60's and early 70's, I knew not only how many days there were to opening day but how many minutes. I see that major league baseball teams share my feelings by having a clock on their websites ticking down the days and hours to opening day.

Opening Day in Washington was always special with military bands and the President or worthy substitute would throw out the first pitch. Presidents continued William H. Taft's tradition of throwing out the first ball from the Presidential Box into a sea of players from both teams trying to catch it. By the way, we have President Taft to thank for the tradition of the seventh inning stretch. President Taft, our only 300 pound President who had a bathtub custom built to hold his ample girth, was getting a bit antsy being stuffed into a stadium chair. During the middle of the seventh inning Taft stood and stretched and the rest of the fans stood out of respect to the President; hence, the beginning of the seventh inning stretch. This later became a tradition for desperate beer drinkers to run to the refreshment stands to order their last beer because beer sales now end at the end of the seventh inning stretch.

I had the pleasure of seeing Presidents Kennedy, Johnson, and Nixon throw out first pitches. If The Senators won it was always great to open up the next day's sports' page and see the Senators at the top of the standings at 1-0. It was great to be in first place if only for a day.

As opening days progressed I had a new hero to replace the departed Jimmy Piersall. Frank Howard could slug the ball for tape measure distances and was about the only thing Senators' fans had to cheer about from 1965-'71. Howard was famous for his mammoth home runs, and management painted seats white in the upper deck to indicate where his blasts landed. Hondo, as he was nicknamed, halted the 1969 All Star game in DC when he blasted a home run and fans gave him a five minute standing ovation.

The second division Senators had a glimmer of hope when Hall of Famer Ted Williams became Senators' manager. Williams worked with Howard and others to improve their hitting and he was successful. The Senators made it to the first division and over .500 baseball for the first time in years. A plus for me was getting Williams to sign a copy of his autobiography, My Turn At Bat.

Robert Short was the owner of the team during the late '60's and early '70's, and for long-time Senators' fans he remains a villain. Short may go down in history as one of the worst owners of any sports franchise. The bright side is that Los Angeles basketball fans can be thankful because he moved the Lakers from Minnesota to LA. If you ever wondered why the name "Lakers" for an LA team that's the reason. Short was also one of the worst promoters of all time. One of his most infamous promotions was Saturday Night Panty Hose Nights where packages of panty hose were distributed to female attendees. Evidently Mr. Short never heard of Bat or Bobblehead Days.

In 1970 he made one of the worst trades in baseball history trading slick fielding shortstop Eddie Brinkman and star third baseman Aurelio Rodriguez to Detroit for pitcher Denny McLain. McLain had won 30 games in 1968 for the Tigers but it was common knowledge among major league scouts that his arm had seen better days.

The Senators blasted the A's on Opening Day 8-0, before a sellout crowd of 45,061. Master Sgt. Daniel Pitzer, a former prisoner of war of the Viet Cong, threw out the first pitch. The mood was festive for the most part but there were some rumblings in the air. My friends and I were standing near The Senators dugout and saw a long-haired Maury Povich, yes the same Maury Povich of daytime TV fame, filming a sports report for WTTG-TV. We couldn't hear what he was saying.

We went home that night to watch WTTG news and there was Maury's report. Basically, he said that if fan support for The Senators did not improve this could be the last opening day in Washington. My friends and I as well as most fans, did not take the warning seriously.

McLain stunk, The Senators stunk, and Williams was losing interest in managing the team. Short wanted a million fans for the season's attendance, and everyone knew that this was impossible given the team the Senators fielded. No number of Panty Hose Nights could save the team.

In September the rumblings became real and it appeared as if the team was on its way to Texas. A lack of fans and TV revenue were the excuses. Joseph Danzansky, CEO of Giant Food, put together a bid to keep the Senators in DC but Major League baseball owners voted to allow Short to move the team to Texas, where they would become The Texas Rangers. Washington, DC would become the only city to lose a Major League team twice. I would assert that in both cases it was due to poor ownership.

The Senators' final game, September 30th, 1971, was part tearful farewell and part ghoulish delight. My friends and I were part of the crowd of 14,460 who came to RFK Stadium to pay our final respects to the team. Every Senators' player was given a standing ovation worthy of World Series heroes. Even those not hitting their weights were cheered.

The biggest ovation was for Frank Howard, and the crowd of 14,000-plus sounded like the 45,000 who had cheered his home run in the 1969 All Star Game. The humble Hondo was overwhelmed and finally tipped his cap.

Mike Kekich was on the mound for The Yanks and Dick Bosman for The Nats. These were not The Bronx Bombers of old and they had fallen on hard times in the post-Mantle, Maris, Berra, Ford era. On paper it was a meaningless game for both teams but for the Senators it was their last hurrah.

In the seventh inning, Frank Howard came to the plate with The Nats down 5-1. Mike Kekick threw a high fast ball and Hondo drilled it over the left field fence and it hit the back wall with such force that it could have left a cannonball hole. As Hondo circled the bases the fans roared at a decibel level rivaling that of 50,000 at a Redskins' game. He finally made it to the dugout but the fans wanted a curtain call. Those sitting in the high priced box seat behind the dugout (Oh, did I mention that The Senators had the highest priced tickets in the league? Higher than New York—this for a tenth place team) were screaming and some were standing on the dugout.

Hondo eventually came out and tried to quiet the fans but to no avail. He finally came out of the dugout and threw his helmet into the stands. Kekick just stood on the mound and smiled. Some say that in this meaningless game Kekick grooved the ball to Hondo. So what if he did? As much as I love baseball, it really is show business, a diversion, the candystore of life. Kekick provided a show if he grooved it; besides, Hondo had to hit it, and hit it he did.

There were signs all over the place. Two women had a sign with a picture of a broken heart with the words, "We'll Miss You!" There were numerous farewell signs but others were not so kind. A vertical banner unfurled from the leftfield grandstands with "Short Stinks" in block letters. Another sign dropped an "F Bomb" on Short. That sign lasted about a New York minute before ushers, who should have been given battle pay, ripped it down. Obviously a photo of that sign could not appear in the local press. Earlier I described the air as "ghoulish delight." Years later I was able to obtain a CD of Ron Menchine's play-by-play on WWDC radio and the background noise is almost disturbing. There is a low steady roar instead of cheering and not unlike the sound one would hear in a Halloween fun house.

The Senators eventually took the lead, and the score was 7-5 going into the ninth inning. At that point, things became truly ghoulish as the crowd began yelling "We Want Short!" It was close to lynch mob mentality. Joe Grzenda got out the first two Yanks and The Nats appeared headed for a victory but then the floodgates opened. Fans poured on to the field. They ran the bases, cut pieces of turf, took letters off the scoreboard, and ran to meet the Senators' relief pitchers who were running from the bullpen and hoping to arrive in The Nats' dugout. The game could not continue as anarchy reigned. The ushers ran for cover and the DC police were undermanned. The umpires called the game and ruled it a forfeit. The Senators lost the game officially by a score of 9-0, the score for a forfeited game. My friends and I wandered onto the field and looked up at the lights to say that we were there. My Green Cathedral was broken but still there.

For some reason, I wandered up to the press box. Most reporters had scattered, not only to meet deadlines but also to avoid bodily harm. Game notes and press releases were left behind. I picked them up for souvenirs which I still have. I looked over to my right, and there was the legendary Washington Post's sportswriter, Shirley Povich, Maury's Dad, typing away and finishing his column on what could have been an old Underwood typewriter. I stood in silence and watched while chaos continued on the field.

Of all the oddities of my life, and there have been a few, I have the distinction of being one of the few people who can say that they have attended two forfeited games. My second one was at a Chicago White Sox game in the mid-1970's. The Sox were playing a doubleheader and the Promotion was Disco Night. This was during the Bill Veeck era of ownership where you could expect just about anything at "The Old Ballpark."

The promotion asked for fans to bring a disco record to burn and there would be an explosion of the records between games. Fans brought records by the thousands and they were heaped into a huge pile in centerfield. Chicago D.J. Steve Dahl emceed the proceedings and record explosion. Fans stormed the field after the explosion and the field became unplayable. Chicago forfeited the game.

Frank Howard, Ted Williams, and the rest went on to Arlington, TX, to become the Texas Rangers. Some baseball purists believe that a city loses a piece of itself when it loses a baseball team. Perhaps so, but Major League Baseball has always come to the rescue by providing a new team to fill the void or the city was a two- team town where one team remained. Philadelphia lost the A's but still have the Phillies. Boston lost the Braves but still has the Red Sox. The same was true in K.C. when the A's left and were replaced by the Royals, and in Seattle when the Pilots left (And who remembers them?) the Mariners came. Finally, in St Louis, the Browns (Perhaps the worst franchise in Major League history) left, but the Cardinals remained.

Such was not the case for DC, as I monitored events from far away as I became an adult and was always disappointed. Other teams teased DC with thoughts of moving to The Nation's Capital but there was no follow through. I had recurring dreams of a team coming to DC, and of sitting in the first base mezzanine watching The Washington What Cha Ma Call Its, and cheering them to victory.

During the summer of 2004, I was a visiting lecturer at the University of Georgia, and I started hearing rumors that The Montreal Expos were headed to DC. Pinch me! It can't be true. Friends begin e-mailing me that it's a done deal. Fall comes and it does look like a done deal but there are political hurdles. I started thinking, "Only the DC government could mess this up." Finally, The Washington Nationals are christened.

Opening Day 2005 featured President Bush throwing a strike for the first pitch. It's was all good. The Nationals beat The Arizona Diamondbacks. As Nats' radio broadcaster Charlie Slowes would say, "Put a curly W in the record book!" because of the curly W on the Nats' hats. All was right with the world.

A decade later, it's spring and I'm hungry for baseball. There's an exhibition game on the tube and The Toronto Blue Jays are playing in Montreal. I get the feeling that Montreal was treated like DC. As I watch the game and see the enthusiasm of the Montreal fans, many wearing Expos' gear, I say to myself, "I hope it isn't a thirty-three year wait for you guys.

ON THE RADIO AND TV

Radio and TV of The Boomer Era was personalized and localized. The personalities on both mediums were your friends who just happened to be visiting you through a box. Today's fare is syndicated on TV and managed by large radio groups on the audio side.

Ask a Boomer about TV and radio in their day and they can, with a little prompting, provide you with a rundown of the personalities and shows they loved. The long term memory lasts longer; it's the short term memory that kills you. The great Bob Hope once said that there are four stages to memory loss: "First you forget names. Then you forget faces. Then you forget to zip up. Then you forget to zip down." I'm at stage 3.5.

During the '50's and '60's, long before kids' programming went to cable and syndication, almost every city and town had local kids shows. The following is a case in point.

I was teaching at Bradley University and living in Peoria, IL, during the '80's and early '90's. My house was a block away from the campus in an old neighborhood known as The West Bluff. I would jog around a two block area where one lap equaled a mile.

It was a hot summer day and I passed a man in his front yard. He had a Van Dyke beard and was sitting on a reclining lawn chair. Each time I jogged past him I would wave and he would nod or wave in return. One afternoon after a jog in ninety degree heat I started walking to cool down. When I reached the house with the reclining man I waved and he came over to me. "Young man, would you run down to Super Liquors and get me a six pack? He gave me some cash and told me to get something for myself. Super Liquors was a couple of blocks away so it was no big deal. I returned with the six pack and gave him the change having not bought anything for myself.

This went on for awhile when one day a neighbor informed me that the man in the recliner was "Captain Jinks." At first I thought he must be a war hero. "Yeah, that's Captain Jinks. He used to be on every Monday through Friday with Salty Sam on Channel 25. Every kid in town watched them." Sure enough, the maritime duo were favorites with Boomer Kids. They definitely "Played in Peoria."

So what about DC? I've already mentioned that our 17 inch RCA Victor TV was my window to the world with a cast of characters flickering into my living room. My fascination with TV increased when I saw a TV show being produced. My cousin, Lynn was involved with a local program Chapel of the Air, a religious program tailored to military personnel. Lynn invited Dad and me to visit a taping of the program and I was intrigued with the lights. cameras, and production equipment. One thing I never forgot was a stained glass window projected on the set. The creation of the window was simple; coat hangers arranged in a pattern over a spot light. I knew when I was six-years-old that I wanted to be involved with making TV shows.

On the homefront, it seemed as if as if there were numerous characters to keep me company. The basic premise was that a host, who was usually some type of character and the "glue" of the show, sold products and was the transition to film segments such as cartoons, The Three Stooges, or silent films. Some of the content was racist such as cartoon crows speaking in black dialect. Turning the dial quickly to adult fare, Amos and Andy, which aired on CBS and was cancelled due to racial controversy, continued on DC airwaves during the March on Washington in 1964.

Switching the dial back to kids' fare (Sorry, we didn't have remotes back then) all four commercial stations had kids' programs, mornings and afternoons. Maybe I was ahead of my time but I loved Jim Henson's Muppets on Sam and Friends and WRC Channel 4. Jim Henson was a homegrown product from Hyattsville, MD, and started at WRC when he was a teenager. He continued at WRC when he attended the University of Maryland. Henson and a friend answered an ad to do a puppet show at WTOP Channel 9. The show only lasted a few weeks but Henson landed on his feet with Sam and Friends at WRC. The star Muppet, Sam, looked like a Muppet prize fighter who had purchased his clothes at Chez Goodwill. He was joined by an assortment of other Muppets, including Kermit the Frog.

In many ways, Sam and Friends was more adult oriented in humor than kid oriented but I still loved it. During the '50's and early '60's, local news aired for only twenty-five minutes. Sam and Friends filled in the final five minutes. They were the lead-in to Chet Huntley and David Brinkley with the NBC national news, which was the top-rated network news program at the time. I wasn't awake to see the show airing after the late local news and lead-in to The Tonight Show. Sam and Friends reaped the benefits of program placement. The early evening placement was appropriate for kids and adults and the late show was more adult oriented. The content was satire with The Muppets lip syncing to popular songs of the day. The musical bits were the forerunner to MTV.

We still lived on D. Street and I was a five-year-old with the measles. As I mentioned, the conventional wisdom of the time was that children with measles should not watch TV because it could cause blindness. My parents allowed me to watch the five minutes of Sam and Friends each evening and that was the extent of my TV viewing.

Jim Henson would go on to network TV, Sesame Street, movies, and other projects. He was fifty-three-years-old, still working on Sesame Street and working on a formal agreement with Disney, Inc. when he died of complications from pneumonia. Doctors say that if he had arrived at the hospital two hours earlier they might have saved his life with antibiotics.

Former Today show weatherman, Willard Scott, worked with Henson at WRC-TV recalls, "I just loved Jimmy. We worked together on the afternoon show, Home. He was very creative and was always working with the technicians as to special effects. NBC came and wanted him to sign a network deal. I told him that he could sign anything he wanted but not to sign away The Muppets, because they were too valuable."

Henson's memorial service in New York City was attended by hundreds and later a statue of Henson and Kermit the Frog was dedicated at The Stamp Memorial Union at The University of Maryland. Today, students and visitors stop by the statue, leave flowers and stuffed Muppets dolls, while others take photos. Some bow their heads and pray.

Other stations had different kids fare. WTTG-5 had an afternoon host, Bill Johnson, who featured the usual cartoon fare along with puppets and some unique in-studio creations.

Johnson had a futuristic contraption called "The Gyrodenameter." "The Gyro" had flashing lights and twirling objects and it signaled that something good was going to happen on the show. Dad made me a semblance of a "Gyrodenameter" complete with a twirling, battery-operated star, knobs, and cranks.

Another WTTG favorite was Captain Tugg. Captain Tugg had a creative set where he stood at the boat's wheel and could turn away from the wheel and walk through the boat's interior. The set was so well done that the viewer had the feeling of actually being on a boat. Sound effects of the boat's engine and water waves enhanced the realism.

Captain Tugg's specialty was Popeye cartoons and he had a tugboat full of them. The questions that I have concerning Popeye cartoons are why is the bully in the cartoons called "Bluto" in the early episodes and "Brutus" in the later episodes. The other burning question is if Popeye and Olive Oyl weren't married, who is the father of Sweet Pea? This falls into the category of does Donald Duck promote pornography because he doesn't wear pants?

Mornings on WMAL-7 began with Pete's Place, starring Pete Jamieson. Pete's Place was similar to Bill Johnson's and Captain Tugg's shows in that it featured a lot of in-studio activity to go along with the cartoons. Pete's show was famous for contests. One memorable contest was when a new polar bear cub arrived at The Washington National Zoo. Kids were asked to send in post cards with a name for the cub. Prizes were offered and the contest attracted hundreds of post cards from DC area kids. My suggestion was "Miss 49'er" which had nothing to do with the San Francisco football team but because Alaska had just been admitted to the union as the forty-ninth state. My entry went into the circular file with hundreds of others and the winning entry was "Snowstar," or something to do with snow in the name. Highly original— NOT!

Ranger Hall ruled the airwaves on WTOP-9. The Ranger was portrayed by Hal Shaw who knew so much about the outdoors that he could have been a real forest ranger. He was joined by a large rabbit puppet named Oswald which was appropriate because most of the cartoons in the WTOP vault were Oswald cartoons.

Now for a cartoon side trip or down the rabbit hole. "Oswald The Lucky Rabbit" was the creation of Walt Disney. Disney had a good run with Oswald, whose cartoon adventures were distributed by United Artists. After good commercial success, Disney wanted more money per episode for Oswald. United Artists refused and pulled Oswald out of Disney's hutch and brought in animator Walter Lantz to create new Oswald episodes. Lantz eventually became known as the creator of Woody Woodpecker, Andy Panda, and other characters.

After his dismissal from United Artists in New York Disney went home to Los Angeles to lick his wounds. The legend goes that while he was on the train, he came up with the idea of a mouse character named Mortimer. Disney's wife Lillian thought that Mortimer was too pretentious and suggested the name Mickey. As we know, Mickey became the cornerstone of Disney's billion dollar empire. Years after theatrical runs, Oswald wound up in the vaults of WTOP and other local stations.

Ranger Hal usually had had a good moral lessons, as well as education concerning the environment long before Earth Day and decades before the book An Inconvenient Truth (Al Gore are you reading this? You should be because you are a native Washingtonian.) Ranger Hal was a popular guest at the opening of various DC stores. Hal Shaw was the kiddies' pal and had a long run on WTOP. Sam Donaldson and the news preceded Ranger Hal each morning shortly after WTOP signed on-air.

Bozo the Clown was a WRC-4 afternoon hit featuring Willard Scott as Bozo with a live studio audience of kids. Scott would clown around with the kids and was very acrobatic in those days lying on the floor and clapping his big shoes high in the air. Scott was able to take his clowning glories forward to develop the original Ronald Mc Donald.

Bozo the Clown was the first TV show I saw in color. It was at a neighbor's cottage during our annual summer Potomac River beach trip. The color could be rather garish if you didn't adjust the tint control, but heck, it was still color. Color was a novelty during The Boomer Wonder Years with most color programs being games shows, soap operas, kids' shows, and any show that had established set lighting. Filmed programs shot in color, such as Bonanza, also aired in color. The majority of TV homes did not have color TVs until the late 1960's.

Bozo aired in other cities with different performers as Bozo. One of the most notable examples was Chicago where the show aired at noon as kids were coming home from school to eat lunch. Chicago's Bozo aired on kid friendly WGN-TV with a live audience of kids. The show had a waiting list of kids to be in the audience that was years long and the running joke was that when women became pregnant they would send post cards to WGN to reserve a place for their child in the audience.

Perhaps my favorite DC kids' show was Pick Temple. Pick Harrison Parker Temple was a guitar playing cowboy in the Gene Autry mode with animal sidekicks Lady the Collie and Piccolo Pony. Lady was a friendly collie willing to shake paws with anyone, anytime, and Piccolo was willing to shake his hindquarters and leave equine deposits on the set. Skillful off-camera stagehands removed the evidence. I always wondered what it was like for a stagehand to go home for dinner and a spouse ask, "How was your day, Dear?" The response might have been, "It was a good day. Piccolo only dumped once."

Pick's film fare included cowboy films, assorted film shorts, and cartoons, but Pick and his animal friends were the stars of the show, delighting both the in-studio and TV audiences. He was also a walking, talking infomercial for Giant Food stores and their Heidi Bakery. His signature greeting was "Heidi Partner" instead of "Howdy Partner." Heidi birthday cakes with a riding cowboy and horse jumping a fence sold as fast as they were made.

Pick's show was not only entertaining but contained information on how to be a better kid-citizen. You could sign up to be one of Pick's Rangers and you received some trinkets and a membership card with Pick's Pledge. One memorable point was, "Don't put off until tomorrow what you can do today." As an adult it is amazing how many times I have disobeyed Pick on this principle. Tomorrow is always the busiest day of the year. The strange thing is that when I procrastinate I often hear Pick's voice.

If Pick's show was a Giant Food infomercial every other DC kids' show was a video sales show as well. Kid-Vid hosts were not only your best adult buddies they were your best adult buddies selling you something. The products were usually seasonal. During the weeks before July 4th, fireworks kits were the rage. You could get the small assortment of six to twelve fireworks but hosts always hawked the mammoth kits of sixty-four. Hosts always emphasized that these were "Safe and Sane" fireworks.

When it came to fireworks, my Dad was about as "safe and sane" as one could get; however, one firework almost "got" him. One of the final pieces in our kit was a Roman Candle, and Dad lit it holding it away from his body as instructed. The candle backfired and sent a row of flame up his arm. He wasn't harmed but the flame sent a bald racing stripe up his hairy arm. During the next few weeks his co-workers probably thought that he was sporting a new fashion statement.

Throughout the year there were numerous live in-studio demonstrations of products. Silly Putty was a sure bet and it would bounce and stretch every time as well as lifting the ink off comic books. I remember seeing a host trumpeting the fact that Coke was now in twelve once bottles. In the Big Gulp era, where anything less than an oil drum full of soda won't do twelve ounces probably sounds like barely a mouthful. The host had three glasses filled to the brim with ice. There was so much ice one could barely see any spaces in the glass. The host proceeded to carefully pour Coke into the glasses. He boasted that you could get two and a half glasses of Coke over ice. He should have said that you could get two and a half glasses of ice with some Coke.

Snack foods were also big commercial items. Seven-Eleven was all over the airwaves when Slurpees were introduced. I maintain that there was no sensation quite like a Slurpee headache on a hot day. Ranger Hal's show hawked Tastykake products with puppets lip-syncing the theme, "Clap, clap, clap, and yum, yummy, yummy, Tastykake cakes and pies, so much fun to put in your tummy, Tastykake cakes and pies."

There were film commercials as well and these could be deceiving as to what their products could actually do. Lionel Trains were accurate most of the time. The action cars on TV did pretty much the thing in real life with the exception of the helicopter, which was unpredictable and could fly across the room and your smack grandmother between the eyes.

There was a company that was very deceptive concerning their toys—Remco. Remco, and even the brand name sounds phony, would show toys doing such amazing tasks that any kid would want one. One toy, The Whirlybird helicopter, had a commercial showing the copter actually flying through the air. Come Christmas morning and eight flashlight batteries later the only thing The Whirlybird could do was putter lazily across the floor and the movement wasn't enough to keep a cat interested. Another toy was the Drive-In Movie Set (teenagers making out not included). The commercials showed that you could show movies with the set; in actuality, you got a plastic screen with a light and film strip. Remco's slogan was suspect as well—"Every boy wants a Remco toy!" Eventually as an afterthought they added, "...and so do girls." Maybe girls were the smart ones who didn't want Remco toys.

Romper Room was on TV stations throughout the nation and aired on several DC stations throughout its history. Romper Room featured a TV classroom with a live host, "Miss 'Fill in the Blank." and kids trying to look interested. The big attraction was saved for the end of the show with the teacher looking through "The Magic Mirror" and naming kids at home that she could supposedly see. "I see Billy...I see Debbie...I see Andy..." and this went on for about a minute. Kids would press their noses to the TV screen hoping to that their names would be called. I always felt sorry for kids with unusual names such as "Felix."

By the time I reached fourth grade I pretty much had my fill of kids' shows and turned my attention to real world fare. For some reason, I became a news and political geek at a young age. Dad watched Walter Cronkite report the news and he became what pundits called, "The Most Trusted Man in America." Long before he received this title, Mr. Cronkite cut his teeth at WTOP-TV, DC's CBS affiliate, before eventually heading to CBS in New York. He was a seasoned print journalist having been one of the Associated Press' top war correspondents. He flew with missions shortly before D-Day and later experience combat first hand.

While at WTOP, Cronkite attempted to make news more visual with maps and charts. Most TV newscasts lacked visual support and were radio newscasts with "talking heads." Cronkite's use of visual support was a forerunner of what newscasts would use. After going to CBS, Cronkite hosted their morning news show which was supposed to be the answer to NBC's Today. His co-host was a lion puppet named Charlemagne.

For some reason few DC newscasters stand out for me the way the kid-vid hosts did. I do remember one weather forecaster, Louis Allen. Weathercasters didn't have today's technology and drew fronts, temperatures, storms, you name it on maps. Louis Allen was a master of this, and after the forecast he would draw a cartoon, Woodle, for the sponsor PEPCO—The Potomac Electric Power Company.

As I got older, there were two newscasters that I came to appreciate—Gordon Peterson and Max Robinson on WTOP-TV. They were one of the first black-white news tandems in the country. Peterson was smooth, serious, but always had a dry sense of humor, which was evident during the "hand offs" to weather and sports. His career spanned four decades of TV news and he ended his career at WJLA, formerly WMAL.

I always admired Gordon and thought that he was the epitome of what a local newscaster should be but it was Max Robinson who caught my attention. It wasn't because he was black, although there were few blacks on TV in those days. Robinson had eyes that burned through the camera lens and into your living space. His voice was deep but not too deep. He would have been great as Othello. I remember his doing a news special, "A Place Called Shaw." The special was about the Shaw neighborhood of DC, which was a neighborhood of substandard housing, unemployment, and liquor stores, all within blocks of the White House. It was an award winning piece of work.

Robinson went on to ABC News and was the anchor reporting network news from Chicago. He was the first black network anchor. In the late 1980's, he was diagnosed with AIDS and died in 1988. One wonders how much he could have contributed to network news had he lived.

I must give a "shout out" here to Jim Vance of WRC-TV. Jim came later in my childhood/teen years and was much more an influence in DC TV news after I left home for college and moved to other parts of the country. He was a fixture in DC news for four decades, and I always appreciated the fact that whenever I came home, there he was reporting the news in his cool, authoritarian style. Jim Vance battled and beat drug addiction and became the face of DC news. Again, I mean no disrespect to Mr. Vance, it's just that most of his work came after I left DC.

As for sports, Warner Wolf was my favorite sportscaster, hands down. Warner hit DC by storm and became one of the top sportscasters in the nation. He started his DC career and became more popular during my high school years. Part of Warner's success was that he was a sports fan who realized that sports is the candy store of life and that it is show business. He didn't take sports seriously and it wasn't as if he were trying to cure cancer. Warner had lots of gimmicks, and he played them well.

Videotape was taking the place of film as to visual support. There was a three second lead-in to videotape, so technicians had to be precise in rolling the tape so it would be seen at the proper time. Most sportscasters had typed scripts but Warner would ad lib from notes written on pieces of paper. In order to give the proper cue for technicians to roll the videotape Warner would say, "Let's go to the videotape." It was simple, but it became his trademark in DC and in New York. A typical story might be, "Senators in New York tonight to play the Yanks, Phil Ortega for the Senators, Mel Stottlemyer for the Yanks. The action heats up in the third inning. Let's go to the videotape..."

He had other gimmicks. His "Boo of the Week" was for something he disliked in sports during the past week. Warner would come up with ideas such as, "In baseball it's called a foul pole. Why don't they call it a fair pole? If you hit it it's a home run, it's fair." Warner had a point.

Warner went to ABC Sports and was one of the voices for Monday Night Baseball and was a contributor to the Winter Olympics coverage, for some reason, he never quite made it at the network level. He did make it in The Big Apple on WCBS-TV. He maintained his trademark, "Let's go to the videotape." Warner returned to DC but it was never quite the same and he boomeranged it back to New York.

He went on to pair with Don Imus on Imus' "Imus in the Morning Show." I visited him a few years ago at WABC studios at 2 Madison Square Garden and watched him in action. Some things don't change. The only difference was that now it was, "Let's go to the audiotape."

Perhaps the thing which demonstrated that sports really is the candy store of life was when Warner gave eyewitness coverage from his apartment of the events at The World Trade Center during the 9-11 attack. There was no going to the videotape—it was alive and real.

A non-kid vid, or news program that was memorable to me was The Milt Grant Show. It was a teen dance show and it preceded Dick Clark's American Bandstand by a couple of years. If you've ever seen the Broadway show or movie Hairspray you have some idea as to the concept behind The Milt Grant Show. Milt featured teenagers dancing to popular records of the day, live talent lip-syncing their hits, and live commercials for sponsors such as Topp's Drive-Ins with the world famous Sirloiner.

One of the regular show features was an unofficial "Black Tuesday," which was the day that black teens would appear on the show. Milt also promoted live acts at DC's Howard Theatre, a predominantly black theatre in Northwest DC.

As I recall the video images of my early years, I assert that one of the reasons they were special was not only because we boomers were young and impressionable, but because TV was still relatively new and we didn't take it for granted. TV competes with so many other technologies today, and TV receivers don't wear out—they seem to last forever until you want to buy something bigger and newer. The most likely fate for an old TV receiver is to give it to children or elderly parents.

The other reason why we didn't take TV for granted was that at a moment's notice, your TV set may go on the blink and you would have to call the dreaded TV repairman. The TV repairman made house calls and would poke around with a tube tester to see if the set could be repaired. If not, your TV set went to "The TV Hospital" for a week, so unless you were one of the families fortunate enough to have a second set you were left staring at a glass screen sans picture tube in a piece of polished furniture.

In many ways, TV and radio were in the same boat of transition during my wonder years. Local TV stations started producing fewer local shows. Kid vid, news, and sports were still locally broadcast, as well as some public affairs programs; however, station management discovered that it was less expensive to buy syndicated shows than to pay talent and tech crews for live shows. All they had to do was to roll tape and sell commercial time.

On the other hand, network radio was dying in favor of local programming. Network radio news was still strong, but stations began relying upon local talent for programming. One of the last attempts to save network radio was NBC's Monitor in the mid'50's. Monitor was the invention of NBC's programming guru Sylvester "Pat" Weaver (Sigourney Weaver's dad). Monitor began on Friday nights and covered the entire weekend. You could expect anything from any place on earth as program content. Program announcers were dubbed "Communicators" and included the likes of Henry Morgan, Bill Cullen, and Gene Rayburn. The Monitor ID was a sound dubbed "The Monitor Beacon," which sounded like alien communication from outer space. Monitor lasted until the early '70s, but the rest of network radio with the exception of news, sports, and special events was on life support.

On the DC front, Harden and Weaver were the kings of morning radio on WMAL Radio 63. Frank Harden was the tall straight man and Jackson Weaver was the short, rotund, mustachioed funny man of numerous voices. They steered Metro drivers through morning rush hours with skits, traffic reports, and humorous treatment of commercials. They once got into trouble with the Federal Communication Commission for going overtime with their commercial ad libs. Two features which were unique to their show were The Hymn of the Day at 6:55 AM and The March of the Day at 7:20AM. One can only speculate what would happen to a commercial radio station today if they played a morning hymn.

Harden and Weaver were heavily into public service and personal appearances, and it seemed as if they were ubiquitous. They were always a presence at DC's Cherry Blossom parade, which was one of the year's major events. Weaver was the voice for Smoky the Bear Public Service Announcements with his signature, "Only you can prevent forest fires."

Jackson Weaver was always the host of our band concerts at Oxon Hill Senior High School. Somehow our band director, Mr. William Johnson, befriended Weaver and he never missed hosting a concert. His baritone voice was perfect for the introduction of each selection. Harden and Weaver seemed to be indefatigable, doing numerous appearances at night then turning around and being fresh for their morning show.

DC stations had identifiable D.J.s holding down time blocks and playing the station's musical format. Most of the big stations were Middle-of-the-Road format while the youth listened to WPGC and WEAM. As much as I listened to the two rockers I have difficulty recalling the names of D.J.s. It seemed as if many of the D.J.s at these stations stayed in DC for a short period of time then moved on to larger markets. WPGC did have its distinctive jingle of "W-P-G-C—-Good Guys Radio."

Young listeners of the era, and anyone of the former DC D.J.s who are reading this, are free to disagree, but I thought that the DC rocker D.J.s paled in comparison to those in other cities. At night my friends, known as The Merry Pranksters (with apologies to Ken Kesey) and I would tune in out-of-town stations for a sampling of jocks. New York had Cousin Brucie and Murray the K who was one of the early promoters of The Beatles. We could receive two 50,000 watt blow torches, WLS and WCFC Chicago featuring the likes of Larry Lujack and John "Records" Landecker. For some reason we thought that it was radio magic to listen to stations from New York and Chicago.

The big DC stations fought to maintain their evening audiences during the late 50s and throughout the '60s, despite the fact that TV was the king medium. The audience may have been people who didn't care for TV programming, people driving, or folks who just wanted an audio companion. Two major shows satisfying any or all the above were WRC's The Joy Boys and WMAL's Felix Grant.

The Joy Boys, Willard Scott and Ed Walker, were the evening version of Harden and Weaver, except they aired after the evening rush hour. Each night they hit the airwaves with their theme, set to an old vaudeville tune, "We are The Joy Boys of radio, we chase electrons to and fro..."

Walker and Scott met when they were students at DC's American University. In some ways they were more versatile than Harden and Weaver in that they could both do character voices for sketch comedy. Like Harden and Weaver, they often took liberties with commercial copy often to the delight of sponsors who reaped increased sales. One of their most memorable spots was for The Old Stein Grill a popular German restaurant in N.W. DC. The background music gave you the feeling that they were in a Munich beer hall and part of their copy read "We have knockwurst, bratwurst, and the best of the wurst." If your product aired on The Joy Boys, you could expect more business.

Few listeners knew that the late Ed Walker was blind. He would read from Braille scripts and benefited from what seemed like a near photographic memory. Ed Walker and Willard Scott continued their friendship until Ed's death in 2015.

WMAL had something completely different in Felix Grant and "The Album Sound." Grant was a jazz aficionado and his program was a seminar in jazz. His encyclopedic knowledge of jazz was put to good use Monday through Friday nights, as he played jazz records and gave you the back story behind the selection and artists. Grant had thousands of albums in his S.W. DC apartment, and he had listened to them all. I can say a major "Thank You" to Mr. Grant for introducing me to the likes of DC's own Duke Ellington, Dave Brubeck, and Miles Davis.

The first DC baseball announcer I can recall was Hall of Famer Bob Wolfe. Wolfe held forth as The Washington Senators' announcer on TV and radio throughout the 50s. Wolfe's philosophy of announcing was mirrored in his book, "It's Not if You Won or Lost, It's How You Sold the Beer." "You always knew who was winning," he once remarked, "and you knew it wasn't The Senators." Wolfe's play-by-play heard from The White House to Wheaton was putting perfume on a pig. Not only did he sell beer, but he sold the struggling Senators. Perhaps one of his most famous gimmicks occurred during a game when it appeared that The Senators were headed for another defeat. Wolfe told the TV audience that one of the cameras was equipped with a magic ray and that if the fans concentrated on the TV screen the ray would cause the opposing team to make errors.

It worked! Ground balls which should have been easy outs became a comedy of errors for the opposition. The Senators had a chance to tie the game but it was too good to be true. A Senators' hitter grounded a ball to the shortstop and ended the game. Wolfe's response, "Someone must have left the screen or wasn't concentrating hard enough." It was an adult version of Romper Room's Magic Mirror.

Local TV and radio personalities have gone the way of the dinosaur. The death of the species took years, but economics and stations' pursuit of profits won out. Today's social media pretty much ensures that local personality media is a thing of the past; still, the sights and sounds of DC's best on-air talents remain in Boomers' memories. They just need to turn the mental dial and with a little prompting the sights and sounds return. No technology can top that.

THE BEST MOVIES I EVER
AND NEVER SAW

Prior to duplexes, multiplexes, and Netflix on your home theatre, DC, as with other cities, had its share of movie theatres. They fell into three classes: the big downtown theatres, Lowe's Palace and RKO Keith's; dozens of neighborhood theatres, most of them owned by Fred Wineland, and Drive-Ins. I was fortunate through my childhood to live within walking distance of theatres. The exceptions were the Drive-Ins, but they were within easy driving distance. Both neighborhood and Drive-In theatres are pretty much relics with many Drive-Ins now serving as ideal locations for flea markets.

My first movie theatre attendance was when I was three years old at the Highland Theatre on Pennsylvania Ave. near the aforementioned pizza place where I had my first slice. The film was Walt Disney's Lady and the Tramp. Unlike a first baseball game I'm not sure how many people remember their first movie. It might be a generational thing where Boomers were bombarded with fewer media so events such as movies were truly special. Kids today are media/tablet savvy and if you are an older media luddite all you have to do is find a four-year-old for assistance. I advise against pulling up in your car stopping a kid street-side, and asking, "Hey kid, want some candy? How about helping me with my I-Pad?"

Back to the Highland and Lady and the Tramp. I remember walking into the theatre lobby and it being very dark. Of course the snack bar and popcorn maker were well illuminated and the boxes of candy were huge theatre-sized ones. My parents discouraged buying candy even though our dentist was only three hundred yards away across Pennsylvania Ave. Later when I went to movies solo or with Dad, who had a sweet tooth, I favored Welch's Pom Poms or Bit 'O Honey. For me these two candy treats were a great value because they were long-lasting. There was a great jingle for Bit 'O Honey commercials featuring a six-headed monster enjoying the gooey treat: "Bit 'O Honey goes a long, long way, if you have one head it will last all day." Some advertising genius at Leo Burnett probably got a corner office for that one.

My folks would usually settle for popcorn with no butter and soda out of those vending machines famous for dispensing soda but forgetting to drop the cup. When this occurred you had to deal with the theatre manager who always asked, "Why don't you just buy soda at the snack bar?" to which you wanted to respond with, "Why don't you just get rid of your stupid soda machine?"

I was surprised by the darkness of the theatre and I had to stay close to my parents. One of the first things I remember was a blue neon clock near one of the front exits with "Highland Theatre" around the rim. To my surprise there was a tremendous amount of "stuff" going on before the feature. It seemed as if there were an endless amount of previews. Dad told me that they were not the movie we were about to see but what was coming to the theatre. Following the previews and out of the blue was a Mickey Mouse cartoon. The old Mickey cartoons always started with a huge Mickey face coming out of a sunburst. The image popped up on the screen and there was a huge Mickey face staring at me. At first I was startled because this was not a Mickey on a seventeen inch black and white TV; this was mammoth Mickey.

Lady and the Tramp followed. I don't remember everything about the film but I do remember the classic dinner scene in the alley behind the restaurant with Lady and Tramp sharing spaghetti. Tramp rolls a meat ball to Lady and the couple shares a spaghetti strand. I include this in my top ten romantic scenes in celluloid history.

Disney films were pretty much my movie menu until I was six-years-old. Mom and I hopped the streetcar at Barney Circle several times to go to RKO Keith's just a block away from The White House and across from The Treasury Building.

One of the surprising things to me was that blacks seemed to congregate in the theatre's balcony. Years later I discovered that this was out of habit but also to avoid confrontation. There was no formal segregation during this time at DC theatres but there had been. The balcony was often referred to as "The Crows Nest."

Dad took me to movies downtown on his days off. He worked numerous weekends so he often had Tuesdays and Wednesdays off. This was great because there were fewer movie attendees on Tuesdays and Wednesdays and the matinee prices were cheaper.

One memorable downtown movie trip was to see Disney's Bambi. Of all the Disney animated features I put it in my top three favorites. When I was five-years-old Dad took me to Lowe's Palace, one of DC's largest movie theatres, to see Bambi. I enjoyed the film so much that I asked Dad if we could watch it again. Dad with the patience of Job, said "Yes." They didn't clear theatres then like they do today and you could watch the film all day if you wished. We noticed some peculiar smelling people in the back row as we first came in. My guess is that they were homeless and that "The Palace" was their daytime home. We watched Bambi for a second time, at least I did. My guess is that Dad took a nap for most of the film.

We returned home and Dad discovered that he had lost his wallet. Retracing his steps he knew that the only place it could be was in the theatre because he had last used it to buy popcorn. He bought movie tickets, popcorn, and Pom Poms and came straight home. Worst yet, we had stopped by his work to pick up his pay check and it was in his wallet.

We hopped back into the car and drove to Lowe's. I waited in the car and held my breathe thinking that I was in trouble. If we hadn't stayed for the second show and Dad's nap he may not have lost his wallet. He returned to the car and he was smiling. The manager said that an usher had found his wallet and took it to the office. Dad gave the manager a $10 reward to give to the usher. The chances of retrieving your wallet from a Downtown business today are about as good as hitting the DC Lottery.

My first non-Disney flick was Cecille B. DeMille's The Greatest Show on Earth, a drama about Ringling Brothers and Barnum and Bailey Circus. Greatest Show was the Oscar winner for Best Picture in 1953 and was in its umpteenth run at the Anacostia, our other neighborhood theatre. The old Anacostia is now a neighborhood museum and a branch of The Smithsonian.

Mom thought that Greatest Show would be good kids' fare because it was about the circus. The film is typical DeMille, filmed on a grand scale with a great storyline. Jimmy Stewart portrays a clown who is always in makeup because he is on the lam. Stewart is a doctor who euthanized his wife because she was suffering from a terminal disease and because he loved her. Other intense elements of the film include Tony Curtis as The Great Sebastian falling from a trapeze after refusing to perform without a net and a train wreck with escaping tigers. I didn't sleep for a week after Greatest Show.

Our film attendance fell off during Mom's illness but this didn't stop me from acquiring an appreciation of film thanks to TV. The Early Show, The Late Show, and The Late, Late Show all featured older films including classics. Some of the films I first saw on TV were Sgt. York, Pride of the Yankees, Bridge Over the River Kwai, Around the World in Eighty Days, and The Marx Brothers' Duck Soup, just to name a few. There was a period of time when network television, long before cable, seemed to have movies every night of the week.

By the time I hit junior high school a new strip mall was constructed across from the school. Oxon Hill Theatre was one of the finest suburban theatres and featured the same first run films as the Downtown houses. The theatre had a spacious lobby, huge snack bar, and a mural with caricatures of movie stars.

I went from zero to sixty as to my film diet. This was the era of the anti-hero with films such as Butch Cassidy and the Sundance Kid, Cool Hand Luke, Bonnie and Clyde, The Graduate, and others. My friends and other teenagers loved this diet because it was entirely different from anything we had seen. We always thought that Butch, Sundance, Bonnie and Clyde and other anti-heroes would pull it out in the end. They didn't. The Graduate had an unresolved ending as Dustin Hoffman foils the wedding of the one he loves but the tandem escapes to who knows where.

Eventually I graduated to Drive-In movie fare. Cramming kids into the trunk of an older kid's Buick was great cheap fun, and we had two Drive-Ins within five miles of each other on Indian Head Highway: ABC and The Super Chief. The ABC was your standard Drive-In; however, its big plus was that the screen faced the highway. There were kids who swore that they could read lips and refused to pay admission parking outside and watching the screen while eating and drinking stuff brought from home. The drinks were often "adult beverages."

The Super Chief was by far my favorite of the two. It had a large roadside marquee with a neon Native-American chief. You drove down a road lined with pine trees until you got to the parking area and screen. It was traveling to another world when you went to The Super Chief.

Both Drive-Ins had great snack bars with burgers, dogs, fries, pizza, egg rolls, you name it. It wasn't unusual for people to bring their own crab feast with crab they had purchased from panel trucks just up the highway.

As for the films I never saw you may have guessed that these were at the Drive-In but I will not cover this in detail. I never kissed and told. I did know when to show restraint if a young woman was engrossed in the movie. It was a losing battle to make serious advances when your date was really involved with a flick. Love Story was a definite "no-no" as to fooling around. You knew not to try anything more than hold hands, and hold hands tighter during scenes that elicited "faucet works." For films like Love Story, I always read the reviews first and sometimes broke down and read the book so I could give thoughtful insights. Young women always seemed to appreciate this.

Doctor Zhivago was a big investment. One knew that getting to first base would be difficult, and you dare not attempt anything else unless you wanted a Whitey Ford pick off move to first base. You took young women to see films such as Doctor Zhivago and Romeo and Juliet because they were special dates and really wanted to see the film. In a way it was a good gesture as to your credibility and in a sense you were paying it forward. If you really wanted to pay it forward you took your date to Pistone's with their great pizza or Italian beef steaks then stop at Hovermale's Frozen Custard just up the road from the Drive-In. The Super Chief snack bar was used only for drinks, and if you had room, for popcorn.

I did actually "see" most of the films when I took a date to the Drive-In. To paraphrase the words of the singer Meatloaf it wasn't exactly "paradise by the dashboard light," but it was exactly purgatory either. Let's just say that I was pretty much a PG rated date and when I went to pick up my date parents mostly got what they saw as to my gentlemanly demeanor.

Some of the content I saw at the movies came in handy as to real life. In the film The Graduate, Dustin Hoffman's Benjamin character is given advice by one of his father's business associates. The advice comes in one word—"Plastics." The associate believes that plastics is the business of the future. I found this advice valuable when dealing with my high school guidance counselor Mrs. L. I discussed my distaste for high school guidance counselors earlier in this book. Whenever I went into her office she always asked me if I had thought more about my future. I told her numerous times that I wanted to get into broadcasting and journalism. She wanted me to opt for something interesting such as pharmacy (at least she wasn't suggesting the results of the Cooter Preference Test which showed that I would be a good cowboy or forest ranger.)

One day the question came concerning my future. "Plastics," I said. She looked at me and quietly repeated, "Plastics" in a pensive tone. "Well, at least you seem to have your future in hand." I was off her futuristic hook. The other big plus was that she didn't ask me to take her daughter to the Valentine's Day dance.

The movies in both theatres and Drive-Ins provided me not only with memories of dates and fun it increased my interest in film. I eventually enrolled in undergraduate and graduate level college film classes. This led me to teaching history of film at the college level.

The great Brooklyn Dodgers' catcher Roy Campanella, one of baseball's first black players, was once asked by a socialite at a party what he did for a living. Campanella responded, "I play baseball." Then as an afterthought he added, "And I get paid for it too." That's the way I thought about teaching film—I loved it and I got paid."

While teaching at Bradley University the Peoria, IL, ABC affiliate WHOI asked me to be the evening news film critic. I guess they thought I knew something about film. For four years I was the one who told what played in Peoria. I also played in Peoria. The great Groucho Marx once said, "If you play in Peoria you can play anywhere." Thanks Groucho. I always said that Groucho was a wise man as well as being a wise guy.

HAIL TO THE REDSKINS

The Dallas Cowboys have been dubbed "America's Team." There was a time when The Washington Redskins could have made that claim. Now, Cowboy fans before you start sending me hate e-mails and start questioning my ancestry, which by the way was well documented in a previous chapter, please hear me out. The operative words are, COULD HAVE MADE THAT CLAIM." I'll explain my analysis of this a few pages from now in a manner of which Tom Landry would be proud.

Before we cover my history with The Redskins, I'll provide you with a brief history of "The 'Skins." The Redskins began as The Boston Redskins in the early 1930s and played at Braves Field, home of The Boston Braves baseball team. George Preston Marshall, the owner of the team, dubbed his team The Redskins because of the Braves connection.

Here comes a point of contention. Approximately every five to ten years there is an outcry concerning what people consider to be the racist nature of the name. These critics call for a change of the name. First, the likelihood of name change is remote. Whether or not you think there should be a name change the NFL follows The Golden Rule: The one with the most gold rules. I have been told by a number of people in the business world, who know much more than I, that a name change would be a merchandising nightmare for DC. Second, right or wrong, The Redskins have one of the richest traditions in the NFL. They had the first, and in my opinion best, fight song of any NFL team, "Hail to Redskins."

They were the first pro team to have a halftime show and many rivaled the spectacles at the Roman Colosseum. Fortunately, no one has been killed during a Redskins' halftime show and there have been no lions involved even when Detroit is in town.

Finally, I did my part on behalf of a name change. I thought a logical solution to the problem was to name the team "The Redhawks." The team could keep the colors and logo, or at least modify it and keep the team fight song with some lyrics changes. I think I developed this idea after a few adult beverages during the fourth quarter of a game where The 'Skins were getting pounded by Dallas.

Anyway, I was sober enough the next day to draft a letter to then Redskins' owner Jack Kent Cooke—a gazillionare who owned The Chrysler Building in New York and half of L.A. It was one of my "Give peace a chance/Let's hold hands and sing Kumbaya moments." The letter included my idea for the name change along with advantages.

Within a week I received a letter with Redskins' letterhead from Mr. Cooke. He thanked me for my interest in the Redskins and my loyalty to the team. It was signed "Jack Kent Cooke." There was no mention of the name change. I suspect some lackey stamped the letter with Cooke's signature.

Another consideration against the name change is that Congress would probably call for a government shutdown—OK, I guess that weakens my argument.

The Redskins are Washington's team, something that binds the DC Metro area like nothing else. The fans range from government officials, members of Congress, and common working folks who really make the city run. Democrats and Republicans can sit next to each other as well as high and low level government workers. Dogs and cats have been known to lie together during Redskins' games. During The Redskins' RFK Stadium days you were lucky to get a ticket. It's a little easier now that The 'Skins play at 90,000 capacity Fed Ex field. The buzz on the streets is that The 'Skins plan to build a new stadium, designed by a Danish firm which features a moat surrounding the D.C. stadium.

The city shuts down when The 'Skins play, crime decreases, and the water pressure drops from toilet flushing during commercials. There are other great football cities, Dallas being one of them, but The Redskins have longevity on their side.

In the 1930s, The Boston Redskins played well but did not draw. They played well enough to win the NFL Eastern Division Championship and Marshall moved the game to New York for better attendance. Marshall had roots in DC, and he moved the team the next season. The Redskins were an immediate hit playing to huge crowds at Griffith Stadium. The team's popularity was due to the on-field success and because Marshall was a master promoter a la P.T. Barnum. Marshall's entertainment elements have been discussed. He was also a promoter as to his dry cleaning business. He once took out a full-page blank newspaper ad. In the corner of the page in small type was, "This page cleaned by Palace Cleaners."

Marshall's flare for promotion was also reflected in the team's personnel. He hired a Native-American coach, Lone Star Dietz. Dietz did a good job with the team but Marshall ruled with an iron hand. Once he ordered Dietz to kick off rather than receive if the team won the coin toss. Washington won the toss and Marshall headed up to the press box. When he arrived, The Redskins were in receiving formation. An angry Marshall picked up the phone to the bench and yelled "Dietz! I thought I told you to kick off!" Dietz responded, "We did. They ran it back for a touchdown."

Another bit of promotion that paid dividends on the field was drafting quarterback Sammy Baugh from Texas Christian University. Baugh arrived in DC wearing a ten gallon hat and cowboy boots. He had never worn western garb before; it was another Marshall stunt.

Slingin' Sammy Baugh may have been one of the NFL's best players of all time. Today's fans often scoff at me when I say this the same way Dallas fans scoffed at me a few paragraphs ago. I make this statement not because Dad saw him lead the Redskins' to championships but because Baugh excelled on both sides of the ball. He was not only a pin point passer but also an excellent defensive back who often led the league in interceptions. Add to this the fact that Baugh was one of the best punters in NFL history. The lean Texan was in the first class of inductees for Canton's Pro Football Hall of Fame. Not every Baugh moment was successful. He was the quarterback during The Chicago Bears 73-0 rout of The 'Skins in the 1942 NFL Championship game. The Bears revealed the T Formation, and Washington was defenseless as the Monsters of the Midway rolled.

Now, as promised, let's get to my point about The Redskins' being America's Team long before The Dallas Cowboys were a glimmer in the NFL's eyes. Once the Redskins' established their on-the-field success the promotion-minded Marshall began building a radio network throughout the South. Remember that this was long before Southern teams such as The Atlanta Falcons and Tennessee Titans were in existence. Marshall persuaded cities and towns throughout the South to

227

carry Redskins games. Southern cities, such as Richmond, Charlotte, Atlanta, and dozens of others, came on board to form The Redskins Radio Network. The slogan for station WSB in Atlanta was, "We blanket the South like dew." The Redskins did too. They were truly a national team.

George Preston Marshall brought attention to the NFL when college football was still king. He marketed to both men and women providing a collegiate atmosphere to 'Skins games with halftime shows, cheerleaders, and other features. One of his plans, which never came to fruition, was to limit games to 10,000 premium seats and charge premium prices.

Looking at Marshall through today's lenses one may question his position on race. Marshall, like Clark Griffith, was short-sighted as to the benefits of integrating their teams; instead, they settled for short-term financial gain. Civil rights aside, money ruled. Despite his shortcomings, he was one of the first inductees into The Pro Football Hall of Fame.

Let's fast forward to get to my history with Washington's team. My first big year as a fan was 1962. The Redskins had just moved into DC/RFK Stadium, which would become their legendary home. I'm not sure there has ever been a stadium that provided such a home field advantage. Today's fans talk about the decibel levels in stadiums such as Seattle, Kansas City, and others but the noise at RFK was beyond compare. For many years, RFK was the NFL's smallest venue, with a capacity in the high 50,000 range, but that number could sound like twice as many. The concrete doughnut nature of the stadium held sound. I can remember attending games and attempting to hear player introductions for The Redskins. The P.A. announcer might as well have turned off the mic and drank a beer. The players' names were inaudible. The only way you knew who was introduced was by their number or physical features.

The other scary thing about RFK was that the lower grandstand would undulate as if hit by an earthquake. A large section of the stands was on rails enabling change from a baseball configuration to football. Fans could jump up and down and make the stands bounce. I was at one game next to a father and his young son when the bouncing started and the boy yelled, "Make 'em stop Daddy, Make 'em stop!" Good luck kid.

228

There was an on-field advantage as well. A gate near the east end zone could be opened and breezes would flow off the Anacostia River. The breezes raised havoc with opposing team kickers. If an opposing team was attempting a field goal a stadium hand would open the gate and the breeze would flow. This contributed to a number of "wide left" field goal attempts. This was long before Tom Brady and The New England Patriots' "Deflategate."

Along with the new stadium in 1962 came an exciting new player from The Cleveland Browns, Bobby Mitchell. The excitement concerning Mitchell transcended the playing field. Bobby Mitchell was the first black to play for The Redskins, this at a time when blacks had become the majority racial group in DC. The Federal Government got into the act as to the Redskins integrating the team. DC Stadium was built with Government money and if the Redskins wanted to play there, they would have to integrate. Not only was the stadium state-of-the-art at that time, it held over 10,000 more fans than Griffith Stadium. One of the reasons given by historians for the Redskins' non-integration was their huge southern radio network, and that the team did not want to alienate southern fans. It was another case of D.C sports team not integrating a team where money was an issue. In the history of DC sports, money was as strong as race as to non-integration.

Bobby Mitchell came to The Redskins in a round-about manner. The Redskins drafted the great Syracuse running back Ernie Davis who was black. They traded Davis to the Cleveland Browns in return for Mitchell. Davis died of leukemia shortly thereafter and is the subject of the film, The Express: The Ernie Davis Story.

Bobby Mitchell was my first Redskins hero. There was an unforgettable game during the 1962 season, where the Browns were determined to shut down Mitchell. They were successful until one play where Mitchell carried the ball to the sideline and made an amazing cut freeing him for a touchdown run. Years later Mitchell would say, "God did that."

Some of the kids in Oxon Hill did not share my admiration for Bobby Mitchell. Mom knew that I was a Bobby Mitchell fan so she dyed a sweatshirt Redskins' burgundy and sewed a white "49" on the shirt. This was long before NFL properties. I went to one of our street football games wearing my new "jersey." Two kids who came from another block were playing with us and one asked, "Why are you wearing that N****'s number? "Because I like him." I responded. I wasn't trying to be some social justice hero; it was an honest answer. I was colorblind and I flat out loved Bobby Mitchell. Mitchell was converted to a wide receiver, where he became a perennial Pro Bowler and was inducted into the Pro Football Hall of Fame. He later became a vice-president for the Redskins.

My next hero would come a couple of years later—Adolph Christian "Sonny" Jurgensen. Sonny came to the 'Skins via a trade with Philadelphia. The Duke alum may have been the best pure passer I've ever seen. Fans will argue that quarterbacks of more recent times had better arms but I always tell them, "You never saw Sonny." As a stunt in practice he could pass the ball from behind his back.

The rotund redhead had good receivers in Mitchell, Charley Taylor, and Jerry Smith, but The 'Skins had no running game during his tenure. It was pretty much Sonny and his posse scoring points with the defense giving up just as many. The 'Skins didn't have winning records during my early years as a fan, but they were never boring.

My first Redskins' game came in August of 1963, an exhibition game against The Chicago Bears. The game was sponsored by The Shriners as a benefit for their hospitals. The 'Skins played the championship caliber Bears to a 15-15 tie, but unlike my first baseball game, I remember fewer details about my first football game.

The thing I remember most was the spectacle. The Redskins' band performed before the game and at halftime. The band was always high quality, because it had a number of its members from area military bands. I think that band members got $10 a game and a free game ticket.

Long before The Dallas Cowboy Cheerleaders The Redskins had cheerleaders dressed as Native-American princesses wearing faux buckskin and a single feather. The costumes were not as revealing as today's cheerleaders. The halftime show was a typical Redskins' spectacular with the band, cheerleaders and dozens of Shriners riding in small cars and doing parade maneuvers. The climax of the show was when they turned out the stadium lights and the P.A. announcer asked for everyone to flick their cigarette lighters or light a match as a collective flame of hope for Shriners' hospitals. The stadium went dark. In those days almost everyone smoked or knew someone who did, so you had

50,000 flickering flames looking like a huge rock concert. The Redskins' cheerleaders, known as The Redskinettes, marched in circles and carried large torches. A Redskins' halftime show never disappointed.

The regular season shows were also spectacular. The final show of the season was the Christmas show and The Redskins' pulled out all stops. The major draw was an appearance of Santa Claus and he would arrive on a different mode of transportation each year. One year George Preston Marshall was especially creative and had Santa parachute from a helicopter flying over Griffith Stadium. Everything went as planned until the prevailing winds blew Santa past Griffith Stadium. The resourceful Marshall produced a back-up Santa, demonstrating that Santa is truly omnipresent.

I attended a classic Redskins' game on November 28, 1965, when they played The Cowboys. The Cowboys owned The Redskins for the first half. The 'Skins couldn't even make a PAT after their lone touchdown.

Things were different the second half. Jurgensen, using mostly down and out routes to Mitchell, Taylor and Smith, led Washington to four second-half touchdowns and held Dallas to one. The game ended in the finals seconds, with Dallas threatening to tie the score with a field goal. The kick was blocked and the final score was Washington 34, Dallas 31.

Dad and I never saw as many Redskins' games as Senators' because the tickets were scarce and expensive. The only way that we could attend games was if a co-worker gave tickets to Dad or sold them at a bargain rate. For some reason it always seemed as if we saw memorable games.

Another classic game was The 'Skins vs. The New York Giants. The game was the highest scoring one in NFL history: Washington 72, New York 41 on November 27, 1966. Redskins' Hall of Fame linebacker Sam Huff told Sonny Jurgensen, "Don't let up. Don't let up," because the Giants offense was potent as well.

The Redskins shocked the sports world in 1968 with the hiring of the great Vince Lombardi as Head Coach and Team Vice-President. Lombardi won the first two Super Bowls with The Green Bay Packers and had taken a top level front office job with "The Pack." Apparently, the front office was boring for "The Great Lombardi," and he listened to overtures from Redskins' President, Edward Bennett Williams, one of the nation's most successful trial lawyers. Williams persuaded Lombardi to coach The Redskins along with front office considerations and other perks. Some joked that Lombardi had been offered a piece of The Washington Monument. Within months, Washington sports teams had acquired the services of two major sports icons: Lombardi with The Redskins and Ted Williams with The Senators.

I remember seeing Lombardi at The Redskins' summer training camp in Carlisle, PA. The 'Skins practiced at Carlisle College, formerly Carlisle Institute, the alma matter of the great Jim Thorpe. Uncle Jack and Aunt Winnie had moved to Carlisle so Uncle Jack invited me to Carlisle for a visit and to watch The Redskins practice. Training camp was nothing like today where hundreds of people fill the stands to watch players run around in their underwear. Some teams charge fans to watch practice.

Uncle Jack and I drove over to camp and there were a few dozen people watching. A chain link fence surrounded the field, and you could walk up to it for a close-up view of the action. Uncle Jack and I were watching a play when suddenly we heard yelling a few feet from us. It was Vince Lombardi in all his glory verbally undressing some unfortunate rookie lineman. Lombardi was dressed in a polo shirt, shorts, and visor. The harangue lasted for several minutes and by the time it was over, the poor rookie probably wished that he had been drafted by The Colts.

I had seen NFL films of Lombardi yelling and coaching in the heat of battle but film did not capture the dynamism of the man. This was an early practice session in Carlisle that was meaningless but here was Lombardi coaching as if he were in The Super Bowl. To Lombardi you practiced the way you were going to perform.

His method worked. Future Hall-of-Fame linebacker Sam Huff came out of retirement to play for Lombardi. Known for being a prince of DC nightlife, Sonny Jurgensen modified his ways. Lombardi didn't have to yell at Sonny to do it. The two had utmost respect for each other.

The Redskins went on to have their first winning season, 7-5-2, in well over a decade, and hopes were high for greater things. Then, the news that shocked not only DC but the entire sports world—Vince Lombardi had cancer. The cancer grew swiftly. The Great Lombardi of Green Bay Packers' fame and the future of Redskins hope died on September 3, 1970 at Georgetown Hospital. His widow Marie donated funds for a cancer research center. Today the Georgetown Lombardi Comprehensive Cancer Center is one of the finest cancer facilities in the nation and a living memorial to the man many call the best coach in NFL history.

The Redskins, obviously rocked by Lombardi's death, returned to mediocrity the next two seasons; exciting, but mediocre. Edward Bennett Williams had tasted victory and wanted more. Out of the west from The Los Angeles Rams came George Allen. Allen had success with The Rams and had been a successful assistant coach with The Chicago Bears but had never been to a Super Bowl. Both Allen and Williams were hungry and on the same page. Williams even joked in a press conference, "I gave George Allen an unlimited budget and he managed to exceed it."

Allen's philosophy was, "The Future is Now." He had little patience with draft picks, rookies, and the tomorrow philosophy be damned. Why waste time developing rookies when you could get established players who knew the ropes. He traded the 'Skins' top draft picks, and sometimes picks he didn't have for veteran players.

The first wave brought veteran Rams' players such as Jack Pardee, Richie Pettibon, to The 'Skins, and DC scribes dubbed them "The Ramskins," but the label that stuck and is remembered by Redskins' fans is "The Over the Hill Gang." Many of the players could have become AARP members in a little over a decade if the organization had existed.

Allen and his 'Skins helped to keep me sane during my post high school graduation days (more about this later.) Excitement hit DC in the fall of '71. I remember seeing a news interview with Redskins' tight end Jerry Smith, who was attending the last Senators' game in September of '71. He expressed sorrow at losing the Senators but told DC that The Redskins would make D.C. proud the coming season.

The 'Skins did and the Allen formula worked. It was not without problems. Allen favored Billy Kilmer at quarterback instead of the free throwing Jurgensen. Kilmer was ball control and Jurgensen was the vertical game. The choice produced controversy with the fans and "I Like Billy" and "I Like Sonny" bumper stickers appeared all over the Metro area. Dad and I were Sonny guys but we did admire the gutsy, wobbly-duck ball passing Kilmer.

The Redskins made it to the playoffs for the first time in my eighteen years on earth. This was new territory for most Boomers but San Francisco popped the bubble as the 'Skins lost to the 49ers in the playoffs.

The 1972-'73 team brought DC its first Super Bowl. I was away at college, and I watched the success from afar. The Billy vs. Sonny controversy continued and the two QBs went crying all the way to the bank. Allen attempted to drive a wedge between the two but to no avail. The party hardy duo continued to be friends no matter who played.

Washington's first Super Bowl came against the undefeated Miami Dolphins. The 'Skins were unable to muster any offense against the tough Dolphin's defense, and their only seven points came on the infamous muffed pass play by place kicker Garo Yepremian intercepted by Mike Bass and returned for a touchdown. Washington did not return to The Super Bowl until 1983 in a rematch with Miami. John Riggins busted a tackle on a run late in the game for a touchdown to give Washington its first Super Bowl victory. It happened a few weeks before my thirtieth birthday.

Joe Gibbs would lead Washington to two more Super Bowls. By then I was a tax paying adult living and teaching in Illinois and later California. The Super Bowl victories were sweet, and after over five decades, I remain a Redskins' fan. The Redskins of my childhood weren't great but they were bigger than life to me. They remain as one of my connections to DC. I hope that The Redskins return to The Big Game before I start drooling on myself and require live-in care. That would be pure burgundy and gold tonic to my soul.

AUGUST

      Judith Rossner, author of the disco-age best seller Looking for Mr. Goodbar, wrote a novel entitled August. It never took off the way Goodbar did but I loved the premise. August was a time of reflection and in some ways a "throw away" month—not quite summer, not quite autumn.

      I shared some of that sentiment but not all. For many in the DC area, August was truly a throw away month. The city became a ghost town. Congress shut down for a month as legislators scattered to their respective states or to choice vacation spots. This left over 25,000 congressional staffers with vacation time as well. People with other jobs traversed to beaches such as Ocean City and Bethany. Others had cottages on the Chesapeake. Some preferred the mountains and journeyed to The Blue Ridge.

      The major reason for the DC exodus and the city looking like the exodus scene from the film The Ten Commandments was the horrible heat. The average temperature ran between 95-100 degrees, and the humidity was about the same. There is only one city in my experience that rivals DC with heat and humidity and that is St. Louis. I have been in The City of Cardinals a couple of times in August and I swear that I could cut the air with a knife. It was as if someone held a hot Mississippi mud pack over my face.

      Kids in The Boomer Era could care less about the heat. We looked at the calendar and knew that summer vacation was half over and the countdown was on for Labor Day. We knew what that meant—SCHOOL. August was a weird time for us as to sports. Interest in the Senators waned because we saw the handwriting on the wall of another trip to the American League basement. Football was beginning to capture our imaginations as The Redskins started training camp. This reflected in our play as we slowly turned from playing baseball to sweating out football games on the high school field.

      Schools in California now begin school the middle of August when kids should be playing and reducing the epidemic of childhood obesity. Yes I've been on this soapbox before but I see no logical reason for school to begin before Labor Day. How many in-service days do teachers need? If you don't know how to teach perhaps you should consider other career options (Would you prefer paper or plastic?) I don't understand the half day calendar and I really don't understand showing popular videos which have nothing to do with lesson plans to kill time. Which of you Boomers agree with me? Not that I'm going to do anything about it but it's nice to have vicarious support. Back in the day if schools started in mid-August in the DC area the peasants would have been carrying torches in mass uprisings.

As it was, we had a few sweltering weeks of freedom. There was a major issue of how to stay cool. Not all parents could afford the Atlantic beach accommodations. We weren't like New York City kids who had functioning fire hydrants to release geysers of cooling water. Desperate heat called for desperate measures.

The late George Carlin mentioned in one of his monologs that his friends mentioned that he had good health and they wanted to know the reason. Carlin's response: "I swam in shit!" George spent many summers swimming in New York's heavily polluted East River. He maintained that this greatly enhanced his immune system. "I have an immune system with AK-47 rifles armed and ready to eliminate any germ that comes into my body." he remarked.

People often ask me the same question about my good health. I never get sick. My hospitalization record is birth and tonsillectomy, the later I believe was unnecessary. At the first sign of a cold I do three things: alert my immune system with their AK 47s (There is no gun control when it comes to my immune system.) Next, I take Cold EZ "Created by a teacher." Now there's one teacher who knows what she is doing. I bet that she wouldn't put up with any of that start school in August crap. Finally, I use it as an excuse to sleep an extra half hour; after all, doctors advise bed rest for colds, and who am I to argue with doctors? Boom! The cold is defeated the way the Chicago Bears defeated the Redskins 73-0 (Sorry to bring this up again.)

So how did I come by this good fortune and Carlin-like experience of swimming in shit? My friends in Forest Heights, less than two miles from my house and smack dab on the DC line, had a secret swimming hole. It wasn't really a swimming hole but an inlet of the Potomac River. The Potomac was not exactly the pristine waters of Lake Tahoe. To make matter worse, or better depending upon your perspective, it was near the Blue Plains Sewage Treatment Plant. The cool water, along with who knows what was in it, produced a refreshing sensation on a hot August day. Hose yourself off at a friend's house and stop by the 7-11 on the way home for a Slurpee and you were refreshed.

Now I could take advantage of mud baths in Calistoga, CA an easy day trip from where I live. I haven't tried them but I wonder if they provide a similar relaxing, cooling sensation. The problem is that you have to pay for them, and I don't know if there is a 7-11 nearby. By the way, the swimming hole is within view of National Harbor Place a new entertainment complex on the Potomac with shops, hotels, restaurants, the MGM resort and casino, and other attractions. Some things do change.

I've mentioned before our "staycations." There was an exception in August. The family friends, Myrtle and Earl, owned a small cottage on the Potomac at Fairview Beach, VA. The cottage was small but free and we would spend a week there.

There was a daily routine which I came to love. In the mornings we would shop or sightsee in Fredericksburg. One of the town's claims to fame was that George Washington supposedly threw a silver dollar across the Rappahannock River thus establishing the tradition of politicians throwing away good money.

There were lots of things to see and do but Doug and I didn't care for stores hawking back-to-school clothing and supplies. We usually ate somewhere in town and returned to the cottage.

Afternoons were spent on the beach on the Potomac. By the time the pollution made its way the fifty miles or so from DC it was pristine by our standards. No one seemed to get sick from eating the fish and crabs from the area. After beach time, Mom and Dad would take a nap and I would go down to The Beach Pavilion to explore. Fairview Beach had been a hopping place back in the 1940's with a dance pavilion and other attractions. Some of that still remained and it was enough to keep me occupied. Today the pavilion has a thriving restaurant, Tim's II that I someday hope to visit.

The evenings were filled with burgers, corn on the cob, home-grown tomatoes, and card games. The routine wasn't exciting, but it was different from life at home. Most of all, Mom seemed to find solace there during her troubled times.

I came to love the Potomac. It wasn't the Mississippi, Colorado, or Rogue, but I consider it my river. My brother-in-law Jim and I want to do a book on the Potomac: he with the photography and me with the words. It's on our bucket list, and maybe we will encounter a few buckets of crabs along the way.

August, a time of heat, calm, preparing for fall, burgers, prime-time fireflies, and a buffer before school. That's the way it should be now. That's my story and I'm sticking to it.

OXON HILL HIGH

I've mentioned before that 1968 must have been one of the worst years in the second half of the twentieth century. The assassinations of The Rev. Dr. Martin Luther King, Junior and Robert F. Kennedy, riots in most major U.S. cities, and the war in Viet Nam were just some of the headlines. In our small world of Oxon Hill there were other less significant events.

The summer of '68, just before wonderful Labor Day, I noticed that the guys were less interested in pickup football games or the usual late- August activities. More time was being spent at the clothing stores at Hillcrest Heights Mall, one of the first indoor malls in the U.S., and other suburban department stores. This was in preparation for the guys' big debuts at Oxon Hill Senior high School. I joined the group in pursuit of a proper school wardrobe using the earnings from my Star route to fund the effort. I probably needed fewer clothes than other guys because I was getting a steady stream from Cousin Billy. Cousin Billy was always in style and it was no longer a matter of him out growing his clothes he just tired of them and I was the beneficiary. By this time, he was in full swing with this band, The Magnificent Men, and was driving a candy apple red Corvette.

The pick-up baseball/football gang and others would be the sophomore class of '68. For me, Oxon Hill High was familiar yet strange. I had walked past it hundreds of times, attended the football games which were a big deal with good community attendance, and attended the fund raising carnival and donkey basketball games. The fact was that besides the gym I had never set foot inside the school.

The building was relatively new and had won several design awards. Most of the building was light red brick with colored panel windows which would be labeled retro. The gymnasium looked like a futuristic airplane hangar with large arches running from the ground over the building and returning to the ground. The cornerstone read "1959," so the building was less than a decade old.

I don't know if my classmates share my perceptions but Oxon Hill had many unique qualities. In many ways it was a Noah's Ark of education because it drew from such diverse areas and groups. The primary areas served were Southlawn, Forest Heights, Birchwood City, and what was unofficially called Proctorville because so many Proctors lived there. Proctorville was a black community and the majority of our black students came from "TheVille." Oxon Hill also served communities farther down Indian Head Highway past Super Chief Drive-In. Students came from Fort Washington and Tantallon and were known as "The rich kids." Tantallon kids' parents were doctors, lawyers, liquor store owners, anyone who made money and lots of it. We actually had a couple of congressmen's kids as students.

Oxon Hill was unique because it was the only high school in Maryland to offer ROTC. One day a week the ROTC guys would wear their uniforms and go through drills. Other schools around the nation would have called them geeks or protested because the Viet Nam War was heating up. Not so at Oxon Hill. Military parents made up a significant block of parental support. Many students were following the paths of their parents. Some, with no military ties, were lured by the promise of college financial aid. Others, led by forward looking parents, saw that Viet Nam was on the radar screen for their sons. If drafted, the ROTC kids might receive better treatment than those who were non ROTC.

The concert band was one of the best on the east coast. It was directed by William Johnson, who hailed from Ohio where they take their bands seriously. We played everything from Sousa marches to Wagnerian operas. The band was patterned after military concert bands and we substituted for them with Capitol steps concerts during the summer months.

High school started with approximately 500 of us trying to find out butts with both hands. It was a little easier than junior high, because we had experienced changing classes from period to period but Oxon Hill was a larger two-story building. The building was configured as a square with a courtyard in the middle. This was esthetically pleasing but a nightmare as to mobility.

In the 1700's, Frenchman and designer of DC, Pierre L'Enfant, thought that it was esthetically pleasing to place circles throughout the city. This was fine in the 1700's but poor Pierre never anticipated the automobile. Circles are one of several factors contributing to DC's horrific rush hours and they are the nemesis of tourists. For cheap fun my friends and I would go to Dupont Circle and watch tourists go around the circle while they attempted to figure out how to escape. We knew they were tourists by their license plates. There was another aspect of the attraction; seeing how many states we could identify and which state had the dumbest drivers. I will not reveal our findings so as to not offend drivers of that state. Esthetics, circles, and squares did not work for DC or Oxon Hill High.

As sophomore boys, we soon discovered that we were at the bottom of the pecking order regarding members of the opposite gender. We had fallen from the top of the heap as ninth graders to becoming invisible in high school. All the clothes shopping and pre-school preening failed to pay off. This became real to us within two weeks of the start of school with the Back to School dance.

The major obstacle was not so much the female vs. male maturation process, although guys could be emotionally immature, it was one simple fact—Juniors and Seniors could drive. This was a distinct advantage for upperclassman and even the homeliest of upperclassmen could attract attractive female sophs. This was an angst producing situation for the soph guys because we had a number of "princes" in our class; however, the "toads" with wheels won out while the princes sat on their toadstools.

There were three ways for sophomore guys to get dates. Some guys resorted to dating ninth grade girls.

There were numerous ninth grade females who were flattered to be asked to a high school dance. This was an entrée into the social life of high school so dating a sophomore guy was a step up. They could always return to school and say, "I'm dating a sophomore," to their collective wide-eyed peers.

A second way, and this required a bit of strategy and patience, was to go stag. This was a waiting game where you watched the sophomore guys with the upperclassmen guys to see what developed. Inevitably, there would be some upperclassmen that would do something stupid such as ignoring their dates and hanging out with their friends to engage in locker room banter. Some guys would want to dance with other gals and this was another turn- off. If you were a keen observer of nonverbal communication you could see the coming train wreck in slow motion. This method of observation was known as "bird-dogging." At the right moment you would ask the jilted person to dance. Ninety percent of the time this worked. In many cases the guy would be so engrossed with being self-important that he didn't know what was happening. After a few dances you made the suggestion of going to Pistone's for pizza. In many cases the upperclassman guy had not considered food for his date so the answer from the young woman would usually be "Yes." I was at a distinct advantage because my house was two blocks from the school. I'd call on a pay phone, Dad would pick us up and drop us at Pistone's, then he'd kill some time at Dart Drug a couple of doors away. If there had been cell phones in those days I would have been deadly. I would have gone to the rest room, called Dad, "Hey, I have a date who wants to go to Pistone's. Please meet me out front," sneaked in another dance, then out the door to Pistone's. The upper-class dude would not have known what hit him until later.

There were major advantages to this. First, you didn't have to buy a dance ticket for your date. Second, no corsage purchase, so the money could be better spent on pizza. Third, you had your choice of women from a fairly large field.

A third technique was to ask the guidance counselor's daughter to the dance. I never resorted to this—enough said. If all else failed you could adopt the philosophy of The Redskins and Senators of "Wait until next year."

As the first few weeks of the semester progressed, it became evident that Oxon Hill had some stellar teachers, while others were Cooter Preference Test drop outs. It seemed as if the humanities, English, History and Writing, had quality teachers. The Science department varied between the sublime and ridiculous. You could have the next thing to Marie Currie teaching one class and Mr. Hyde teaching the next.

Math was a complete joke. My first Math teacher looked as if he should be in the casting call for one of those L.A. based TV shows such as Surf Side Six or an extra in the next Gidget film. Trying to learn Math from him was like trying to learn a piece of jazz without having an instrument. He also had an eye for attractive female students. It became a female badge of honor to say that they had been asked to stay for "special tutoring" from Mr. B.

Other Math teachers could care less about "special tutoring" or anything other than drawing their next paychecks. As long as you turned in your homework you passed the class. Seeing as how I wanted to be the future radio voice of The Washington Redskins I could have cared less about the Pythagorean Theorem.

Perhaps the most serious scandal occurred in my French class. One of my friends asked for serious tutoring from our French teacher. The teacher began reviewing French adjectives with my friend. At one point he pulled out a pornographic magazine with a picture of a well-endowed nude male, and pointing to the male's "endowment," "Il est gros." said the teacher. My friend responded, "No, that's gross!" and left the classroom. My friend struggled with whether or not to tell school authorities about the incident. He eventually did and the teacher was fired as fast as you could say, "Sacrebleu!"

My first quarter was rough because I was taking all requirements with the exception of band which was my escape. It didn't help that I tried out for and made the JV football team. Football wasn't in my future despite the fact that I was the best placekicker on the team. Part-time jobs would win out if I was to have money for college. It was obvious that I wasn't going to get a football scholarship.

Things got better for me academically but I was shortsighted in many ways. Mark Twain once said, "Education is a wonderful thing. Too bad it has to be wasted on young people." That described me point and period. To me education should have been a big smorgasbord where I could pick or choose what I wanted. We didn't have that freedom.

I loved literature and had read many of the great American and British novels. I knew The Great Gatsby chapter and verse. George Orwell was a literary hero for me as well as J.D. Salinger, C.S. Lewis, and J.R.R. Tolkien. We read none of that.

I believe that my literature teachers all suffered from major depression or had failed in their attempts to become the next Jane Austen. Everything we read was depressing, not that Gatsby is an uplifting walk in the park, but at least there was some variety.

One teacher seemed obsessed with the sea and had us read Billy Budd and Moby Dick. Moby Dick was OK but overrated in my book and in my opinion I thought that someone should have nipped Billy in the bud. I kept thinking, "Why can't you throw in a little Steinbeck or Kerouac just for laughs?" Perhaps the literature police where on patrol.

Socially, I was not a big man on campus, probably a couple of notches down from the jocks, cheerleaders, and student government people, but I got along with almost everyone and owed some of my social skills to being a paper boy. For most of us going to high school was not only an exciting ritual of passage it was an escape as to what was going on in the real world just a few miles from us. Having DC in your backyard was both a blessing and a curse. You could try to escape its real world but it was always on your radar screen.

Dances and schoolwork aside, the 1968 Presidential Election was on the horizon. Richard Nixon was going for his second try at the Presidency while Hubert Humphrey had survived the mess in Chicago to land the Democratic nomination. There was an attractive girl in my first period English class named Ann with blonde hair and freckles. After speaking with her numerous times I discovered that she was the daughter of a Democratic congressman.

Fifteen-year-olds couldn't vote but the school was divided between the two candidates. I was leaning towards Humphrey and after numerous conversations with Ann I knew that I wanted him to win. In many ways Nixon seemed more stable to me but there was something about him that turned me off. I couldn't put my finger on it and it was purely gut feeling.

Polls showed Nixon leading throughout the summer but as memories of the Chicago convention dimmed. Humphrey began to catch up. Our school reflected the national trend and there was lively discussion in the hallways regarding the two candidates. School administrators decided to get into the act and they allowed political posters around campus. A few days before the convention all the activity was capped off by a political pep rally where students representing both candidates presented their platforms to a packed gymnasium. Ann was the representative for Humphrey. In a school wide vote Humphrey won by a forehead which may have been unfair given his rather prominent one.

The night before the election, the election polls showed the candidates to be in a dead heat. The next morning's results showed Nixon winning by a narrow margin. The discussion concerning the election continued in History classes and in the hallways. There was one thing for sure; nothing was for sure.

My social stock increased at the same time as the election process and it was purely a chance thing. It happened at a Saturday afternoon football game; Oxon Hill vs. Surrattsville. I got to the game early and there were a handful of students scattered throughout the stands. A couple of guys from the audio/visual group were connecting a microphone to the system and doing an audio test. After the test and into the live mic I hear the one guy say, "Who's going to announce this?" I looked at the two and it was obvious that they didn't have anyone to announce the game. Confidently, I asked, "Do you need an announcer? I'll do it." They looked at me and asked, "Do you have any experience?" "Sure! I know Warner Wolf." I didn't know Warner Wolf any more than I knew Mickey Mantle, but I had listened to him and other sportscasters enough that I knew I could do it. This would be an adventure; besides, what could they do, fire me?

I already had a program and knew all the numbers of the Oxon Hill players. All I had to do was learn Surattsville's numbers and my photographic memory went to work. I memorized the so-called skill players first: the quarterback, running backs and receivers, then I memorized the linebackers and defensive backs because they would be the ones making the most tackles. This would be a piece of cake. Washington Redskins' announcers watch out because here I come.

The stands filled and it was game time. An assistant wrestling coach was at my side and said, "Don't forget to announce the National Anthem. The last jerk announcer always forgot to do it!" "Of course." I replied acting as if I had been doing this for years.

Everything went pretty much as planned. Plays were called, players identified, and all was going well. Out of the blue someone hands me an announcement that the Key Club was having a car wash next Saturday. Suddenly, the floodgates were opened and I'm getting pieces of paper promoting everything from bake sales to dog washings as club fundraisers. Years later when I hit the Midwest I noticed the great Chicago Cubs announcer Harry Caray did the same thing only with birthdays, anniversaries, and other events.

It was almost halftime, and things were going well when someone handed me a card with something like, "Mary has the hots for John." I looked at the card and said, "I can't read this crap!" The mic was on and fortunately pointed away from me, but people in the two rows in front of me heard what I had said, as well as the wrestling coach yelling, "You can't say that." I turned off the mic, regained composure, and continued.

The rest of the game went well, and I reminded the fans of the next home game. The school principal told me, "Nice Job," and the AV guys said, "We have a new Voice of the Clippers." Clippers being our school nickname and not a personal foul.

I walked the couple of blocks home and when I arrived Mom was watching TV and getting ready to prepare dinner. "It's strange. I heard a voice coming through the air and I thought it was you." Mom thought that she was going off the deep end. "Mom, that was me. I announced the football game at school." She didn't believe me so I had to do a demo—"Bullock carried the ball, tackle by Dempsey, gain of four, First Down OXON HILL!" "Oh it was you," she said and that was about it. It was a nice humbling experience.

As "Voice of the Clippers," I did football, basketball, wrestling, and donkey basketball games. I'm not sure if they still have donkey basketball but years ago it was a big deal as a school fund raiser especially on the East Coast. Someone at Oxon Hill, and they always remained anonymous, made a connection with a donkey touring company. Every year, usually in February, a large truck rumbled onto the campus with twelve donkeys. I guess two were off-the-bench donkeys. The NBA gives a "Sixth Man Award" for the best bench player. I wonder if they gave a "Sixth Donkey Award" in donkey leagues.

There were posters everywhere promoting the event and it was as close to being a small-town event as you could get. The gym was packed SRO with students and community people. Additional chairs had to be added in the balcony and the fire marshall tended to look the other way for the event.

We always knew when the donkeys arrived. Even though it was winter and the windows were closed you could still smell the essence of donkey permeating the air. For some reason they always parked the truck and trailer near the school's left wing so if you had class in that wing, there was no escaping it.

The teams were faculty and coaches vs. the school's lettermen. The Faculty/Coaches team was the villain team. Community fans obviously had some pent up grudges from their high school days because they always sided with the Lettermen, plus there was a huge student turnout.

The basic premise was two five men teams on donkey back. You had to be on your donkey when you had the ball but a player could dismount from a donkey when attempting to retrieve a loose ball. The problem here was that you were pulling a stubborn beast as you were trying to retrieve the ball. One resourceful letterman had some success with his donkey by luring him with a sugar cube. The referee spotted this and issued a personal foul. I never understood the reason for the foul and I'm sure that sugar use is not listed in either NCAA or NBA rule books.

Of course there were donkey "accidents," much to the delight of the crowd. Each team had to produce a person who was designated as a "Pooper Scooper." This was a rigged game. The Lettermen would pool their money before the game and pay off the donkey handlers to feed Exlax to the faculty/coaches donkeys. An ample supply of Exlax was purchased at Dart Drug, which probably puzzled any senior citizens waiting in line and administered to the four-legged players. The poop ratio was about five to one in favor of the medicated donkeys.

Doing the P.A. for the games was part play-by-play, demolition derby, and WWF Wrestling. It was all about adding to the show and the show was for good causes. Part of the money from ticket sales and concessions went to the school's athletic fund, with the other portion going to a selected charity.

The announcing gig was my entree into other opportunities. One day I was leaving P.E. class when the basketball coach, Mr. Magnotto, called out to me. I immediately wondered what I had done wrong during P.E. "Gary, I've been meaning to talk to you." said Mr. M. This always brought out my reaction, "Am I pleased or frightened?" "Yeah, I wanted to talk with you about being our SID." I didn't want to appear ignorant, but I still didn't know if I was pleased or frightened. "Yeah, the Sports Information Director calls the newspapers with the scores and stats. Newspapers call you guys 'stringers.' You'd be responsible for calling The Star, Post, and News. What do you think?" Mr. M's offer sounded great, and it sure beat using donkey basketball games as a resumé builder. "Sure! I'd love to be the SID." I was already hip to the lingo..

Mr. M. gave me the contact info and I was off and running. The Post's contact was a man named Leonard Shapiro. The reason I remember is because I continued to read The Post through the years even though I moved from the DC area. He progressed a long way from coordinating the high school info. Leonard Shapiro became one of The Post's top sports writers, covering The Redskins and other major sporting events, as well as winning numerous awards.

Another opportunity came on the academic side with my journalism course. Journalism was one of my favorite high school courses and it met my English writing requirement. We had to do more writing than creative writing classes but it beat writing drivel about "My Most Unforgettable Character." That sounded too much like a Readers' Digest feature. I was able to dovetail my announcing and SID work into the class and at times I was writing the entire sports page of the school paper.

Our Journalism teacher was Mrs. Duncan. I never knew her background, but she seemed to know her stuff. We learned "The Five W's—Who, What, When, Where, Why, and How," the inverted pyramid of putting the most important information first in your story with the lesser details at the end, and fact checking.

One day she approached me with the, "Gary, I've been thinking of you..." lead in which of course set off an alarm for me. I had been working my butt off in class and always made my deadlines so I wondered what was up. "We got this letter from WTOP-TV, and they are looking for high school students who are interested in broadcasting to become WTOP Fellows. I immediately thought of you." I'm thinking, "Well that's nice Mrs. Duncan. I know what WTOP is but what is a fellow? This sounds pretty formal to me like I'd be working at the BBC." She answered my question with, "Yes, fellows get to go to WTOP and see the inside workings of the station and meet the station's personnel." This was right up there with going to Atlantic City to see the diving horse. "Sure sign me up! Who else is going?" "Oh, it's only one per school so you would be Oxon Hill's fellow." she responded. Wow this was great; not only the experience but exclusivity.

The only obstacle was transportation. We were a one car family and Dad drove it to work, so I had to figure out how to get to WTOP in N.W. DC. I didn't tell this to Mrs. Duncan and I gave her an enthusiastic, "Yes!" There was a DC Transit stop about a block from my house so I studied all the bus routes to N.W. As long as I could get close enough to the station I could walk or splurge for a cab.

I broke the news to my folks over dinner. Mom wanted to know if it cost anything. Dad was more enthusiastic and said that he would pick me up late at night if I could catch the bus there. He saw this as possibly leading to a career and he had given up on the idea of me becoming a pharmacist.

WTOP Fellow Day came, and I received special permission to leave school early to make it to the studio by 5PM. I received all the introductory information in official WTOP documents which included a special ID card to show to security. We would have orientation then watch the local evening news in the studio. There would be a surprise guest to speak to us. This really sounded official.

I left school to hop the bus. The first leg hit S.E. DC and went through some "iffy" sections. We went past my old neighborhood in Anacostia

hings had changed: more litter, abandoned businesses, and people congregating on street corners looking as if they may be engaged in some illegal activity. I transferred to another bus near Capitol Hill, then to another one Downtown traveling to Georgetown. From Georgetown to Wisconsin Ave. I was a block away from the WTOP studios, known as Broadcast House.

There was a guard and receptionist behind a large desk. Suddenly I panicked. Here I was a snot-nosed kid trying to enter the CBS affiliate for Washington, DC. Who did I think I was? All my info and ID were in order and I showed them to the receptionist. "Oh, you're one of our fellows. Welcome! Take the elevator to the second floor and our coordinator will meet you. You're one of the first ones here. Glad you could come." You would have thought that I was Walter Cronkite's son.

Someone greeted me on the second floor; I didn't even have to look for the room. I was led to a large, well- furnished room where I was met by the program coordinator, given a folder with the WTOP logo and familiar CBS "Eye," and told to help myself to refreshments. The "refreshments" were sandwiches, various snacks, soda, all enough to feed the Russian Army. Three high school students, all females weren't eating but sipping cups of coffee. I was starving but decided to follow their lead. The three looked as if they were Ivy League bound.

249

Eventually some guys entered ranging in looks from class nerds to jocks. They saw the food and with the finesse of hyenas plunged in to it. That was my cue to eat, but I tried to be less hyena-like. We were still eating when the coordinator introduced herself and gave us an overview of the program. Tonight we would be in the studio watching the news. "But before we watch the behind-the-scenes action we will meet with our special guest, Warner Wolf." WARNER WOLF! First hand carved roast beef sandwiches, salads, chips, a fine female fellow from Montgomery Blair High School and now Warner Wolf. What more could I ask for?

Warner entered in less than five minutes. He had prepared his sportscast and could back to the office to check for updates. He was a little shorter than I imagined but was dressed as if he had just walked out of a Brooks Brothers' catalog. His smile seemed even bigger in person than on TV. Warner greeted us and eyed the food table. "Wow, look what you're feeding these guys!" He laughed and then grabbed a cookie.

He told us that by being a WTOP Fellow we were off to a good start but not to expect to walk into WTOP and get a job following college graduation. He talked about his early career at a radio station In Pikesville, KY where he did everything there was to do at the station. Eventually, he landed at WTOP in his hometown of Washington, DC. He emphasized flexibility and hard work as being the keys to landing a big time TV position. It was a realistic but encouraging presentation.

Next we went to the booth overlooking the news set and there were two of my other heroes; Gordon Peterson and Max Robinson looking over their scripts. We were seated in front of the director and technicians. The newscast began and it was a surreal world. You could see what the viewers were seeing at home on an on-air monitor. The anchors were steady with their deliveries, but behind the scenes it seemed like the floor of the New York Stock Exchange. The director spoke a language known to his crew and fired it at a machine gun pace. He was not afraid of peppering his command with a variety of expletives. I don't know if this was the coordinator's plan but we were seeing the real world of television uncensored. Commercials were about the only time that the pace slowed but not by much. Material was added and deleted on the fly and we learned that a television newscast seldom went as scripted.

Following the newscast, we were given a tour of the studio. The news set was smaller than it appeared when watching it at home. The coordinator explained that television exaggerates size and distance. We returned to the meeting room and the jock types finished off the cookies.

The coordinators told us that the station was looking for election night volunteers. We would be doing fetch, tote, and carry jobs, and some of us would be turning the numbers on the big election results board. Because this was work we were not required to do we would be classified as volunteers thus avoiding union problems. Most of us volunteered and we were assured that there was work for everyone.

The next day Mrs. Duncan asked me to give a report to the class about my adventures. My report was straight up with no embellishment. I told everyone to be watching on election night because I would be working it.

Waiting for election night was like waiting for the opening of the baseball season. It was the off-year elections so the offices to be decided were congressional and local. WTOP covered DC, Maryland, and Virginia, so there were numerous results to report.

This time the food spread was in both the meeting room and the studio. The studio food was for the anchors and crew to eat when the station had a break and went to network coverage. I was assigned the task of one of the numbers turners on the results board as the results came in.

There was a trick to turning the numbers or putting numbers in the correct slots. The audience's left was my right. If a vote tally was 15,425 I would place the "1" on my right hand slot. You had to pull numbers out of their containers and quickly place them in the proper slot. The results board people all had headsets so we could hear the producer and director.

All this sounds easy, but under the heat of time and a hyper producer and director it was nerve wracking. At first I kept forgetting that my left was my right and vice versa when placing numbers in the slots. This was corrected by the producer and director yelling in my headset, "No, you're other left, dummy!" while spicing things up with a few choice expletives. Gradually I got the system down and I was slotting numbers like a pro. A couple of fellows were asked to relinquish their duties to other volunteers because they couldn't get the hang of the system. They didn't seem to care and went over to the food table.

We were to work until 10PM because of labor regulations. Dad picked me up a little after ten but not before I grabbed a couple of brownies on the way out. Number turning had been a "gofer" position, but I felt energized and didn't sleep well that night. The school newspaper carried a front page story concerning my exploits.

Other things were happening on the social front. Football coincided with my WTOP Fellow's experience. The football team had been mediocre my freshmen year winning only three games. Junior year the team gained a new quarterback, Mark W., when his military parents transferred to the area. Add to this a halfback, Donnie B., one of the few blacks on the team, and you had a team that could light up the scoreboard.

The team won eight games my junior year and looked to be even better for the senior year. The DC papers ranked Oxon Hill in the Metro Top Twenty which was highly competitive because it included schools from DC, Maryland, and Virginia. All this made my jobs of SID and announcing even more exciting.

The team adhered to a true team concept. Most of the player were not physically imposing, with at least two being under five feet six inches; still, it was a group that got the maximum effort from each individual. Off the field it was a tight knit group with the unofficial team song being The Jackson Five's I'll Be there. The team sang it in the locker room before home games and on the bus before away games. Donnie B. did Tito Jackson's solo better than Tito; "I'll be there to comfort you..."

The team was tightly knit and sometimes just plain tight. Team parties bothered me at times because there could be a large consumption of "Nectar of the Gods." I didn't drink and certainly did not considered myself to be a choirboy but I was concerned that people would get home in one piece. Fake IDs were plentiful as well as liquor stores. It was also easy to give a wino a buck and have him purchase the goods. It was not unusual to see some of the cheerleaders and pom pom girls sticking their toes in empty bottles and having balancing contests. I became a designated driver long before the term was in use.

Other out-of-class interest included a garage band, The Crystal Ship, which came from the haunting song by The Doors. The band could play just about anything that was on the charts at the time, but the floor always flooded with slow dancers in a death vise whenever we played The Crystal Ship. Due to popular demand, we usually played it at least three time a night.

I started on keyboard and as a fill-in drummer, but other more talented musicians took over, and I became the band manager. My responsibility was to book dates and place ads in the teen section of local newspapers. For some reason, we became a hit in the Maryland suburb of Silver Spring as word of mouth got us weekly dates.

The musicians were pretty good by garage band standards. Tom F. on drums could twirl his drum sticks with the best and got about as much sound from his small drum kit as The Stones' Charlie Watts. Glenn B. played AAA if not major league base. Joe K. was band leader and lead guitar with Danny L. on keyboard. Danny went on to playing pro gigs all over the DC area. It's sad to say, but similar to big time rock bands, Joe and Danny passed away long before their times from natural causes.

The world beyond the friendly confines of Oxon Hill High was unfriendly. Richard Nixon was President most of our junior year and all of our senior year. Based upon military reports, there was confusion as to whether or not we were winning the Viet Nam War. The media continued to paint a gloomy picture led by CBS and Walter Cronkite. As we entered our senior year, thoughts of a winning football team were intermingled with thoughts of going to Viet Nam, either voluntarily or otherwise. Not only was there concern from the guys about their futures but there was also concern about the vets returning home from the war. More and more vets returned not as heroes but as villains as there were numerous anti-war protest just a few miles from our high school doors. Some of our classmates had siblings returning with various injuries and traumas.

Many at Oxon Hill chose to immerse themselves in class activities. Despite the fact that protests were close by the general attitude seemed to be similar to The Cuban Missile Crisis: just ignore the problem because we were helpless.

My media pursuits diversified when five of us decided to use the school's P.A. system as an ersatz radio station; WOHH. The P.A. soundboard had a turntable so we could play records, but we couldn't play music back to back unless someone was quick on the record changing draw. Most of the music we played was Top 40's stuff, and we mixed in school news, weather, and sports. The school administration seemed pleased with what we were doing and it was better than the traditional boring reading of announcements.

As the war progressed we slowly mixed in war protest songs. There were no protests from the administration because they weren't listening to the lyrics. Eventually, a teacher, and we suspected a young Spanish teacher, told the administration what we were playing, and they tried to censor us. I made the argument that the top radio stations in DC were playing what we were playing so what was the problem? A compromise was reached that as long as we didn't blow out the classroom speakers and there was no profanity we could play whatever we wanted. I played Jimi Hendrix which was immediately deemed off limits; otherwise, things went smoothly as we promoted the positive aspects of our school.

That was no problem regarding football. Most of our key players were back and we were in a new division. The DC papers predicted that we would be the division champs. The Clippers had a new head coach, Victor Savoca, who had been the line coach. Coach Savoca had played his college football at The University of Miami, Florida, on the same offensive line as the great Oakland Raiders' Hall of Fame center, Jim Otto.

If Jim Henson had designed a football coach Muppet it would have looked like Coach Savoca. Coach was built like a Frigidaire and sounded as if he had gargled with Drano. Besides coaching, he also taught Driver's Ed and was notorious for bringing female students to tears while guys would shake like a Polaroid picture. Once when I was having difficulty merging into traffic he called me "a one dimensional guy." What in the world did that mean? Had I suddenly lost two dimensions?

The insults were just as creative and much more brutal. One Friday night a group of us went to see the film The Green Berets starring John Wayne, which turned out to be a piece of pro-war celluloid. At one point in the film, John Wayne addresses his troops as "gutless wonders." Coach Savoca and the rest of the football staff were sitting near the front of the theatre after gorging on Tony Roma ribs which was part of their Friday night tradition. We were sitting near the rear of the theatre and the coaches never saw us.

254

The next day was game day and Oxon Hill was holding on to a slim lead at halftime. Coach Savoca was not pleased with the team's play and in his locker room speech he addressed the team as "gutless wonders." Those of us who had been to the movie were holding our sides trying to keep from laughing. Coach slammed the door as he left with such force that items fell from lockers. I could imitate Coach's gravelly voice and yelled, "Did you hear that, you gutless wonders?" The team erupts with laughter. They went out and scored twenty-one unanswered points for an easy victory. The Gutless Wonders came through.

Coach Savoca struck fear into Driver's Ed students and football players alike, but the team loved him as did I. It wasn't long until he started calling me "Warner" after Warner Wolf. "You're kinda like that Warner guy on TV." he said.

The name stuck. Most of the people who signed my high school yearbook addressed me as "Warner." My ability to imitate Coach's voice came in handy. We were playing a road game and Coach was nursing a cold but still yelling at the top of his lungs. Laryngitis hit at the beginning of the fourth quarter. I was along for the ride and assisting team managers with their tasks when Coach came to me and croaked, "I can't talk. tell them to gimme the defense." I yelled "Gimme the Defense" in his voice, and he continued to issue commands to me to relay throughout the remainder of the game.

Oxon Hill went on the win the county championship. I never played a down of varsity football, but Coach Savoca gave me a football letter for my contributions to the team. One unfortunate event occurred during a road game with Central High School. Oxon Hill won the game and the team busses were leaving the grounds when a young fan, too young to be a high school student, threw a rock and smashed one of the bus' windows. The bus stopped and the driver surveyed the minimal damage. No one was hurt but it was a portent of things to come.

There were problems when we faced Central in a home basketball game. The game was interrupted by violence in the stands and police were called. Slowly, violence became a part of high school sports in the D.C, area, and it was the end of peace at sporting events. Following graduation I returned to watch various athletic events at Oxon Hill and gradually the police and hired guards increased in presence. It was sad to see what used to be good natured pranks by both schools were no longer the norm. Oxon Hill was a popular mark because we were the Clippers so opposing teams would burn Clipper ships at Friday night pep rallies. One time we foiled a burning by swiping every fire extinguisher at Oxon Hill High and crashing an opposing team's pep rally. The opponents were caught off guard, and we saved the ship's burning before hightailing it off to Pistone's. Today guns and not fire extinguishers would be the preferred weapons.

Senior year continued with more subversive acts. One of these was the conversion of an old custodians' storage space and restroom to an informal library dubbed "The Head." This was accomplished by some of the more forward thinking students and teachers who contributed the first books to the cause. There was everything from Alan Ginsberg and Jack Kerouac to The Rev. Dr. Martin Luther King. It was a Georgetown bookstore on our doorstep. Most of the literature teachers supported it.

On the other hand, I was stuck with one of the worst teachers I've had at any level, Mrs. J. She would have benefited from a visit to The Head. We started out with the poetry of Emily Dickenson. I never got into someone whose thrill was, "I heard a fly buzz when I died." Sorry Dickenson fans, she was really difficult to get into on a spring day during your senior year. We went on to Edgar Lee Masters' "cursing the silence of the waterlilies" and it was downhill from there. Carl Sandberg's Chicago as "hog butcher to the world" was Disneyland in comparison.

Mrs. J. could sense the class' discontent and decided to throw in the towel and introduced a new "relevant" project. No matter the level of education, I have always viewed the term "relevant project" with a great deal of suspicion. This usually means that the class is going to hell in a hand basket so the instructor has pulled something out of their back pocket in an effort to save it.

Since we were seniors, she figured that we were going out into a world not our own and that we needed practical skills. She assigned us to groups of three as "hypothetical roommates." We were given a sum of money to find an apartment, place a security deposit, furnish it, and come in under budget. One of our trio voted to take the money, buy a tent, and live on the beach at Ocean City. We could take the leftover money and buy Nathan's hot dogs and Phillip's crabcakes. He got my vote. I also voted out of this silliness and started skipping class in favor of covering the school's baseball team for our school newspaper The Searchlight.

One Sunday night I was attending a church pizza party when our youth leader, Pat Hansen, came to me in a concerned voice and said that my parents had called and that I was to return home IMMEDIATELY. I jumped in the trusty Ford Falcon and hurried home. My thoughts ran wild and I began to think the worst—something was wrong with Mom.

When I returned home it was obvious that Mom was OK. She was more than OK. She was hopping mad and she didn't hop well at that point. She did most of the talking with Dad adding stern looks and some occasional verbal back up. "Your literature teacher, Mrs. J, called and said that you are in danger of not graduating. She said that you missed ten of her classes and that is enough to flunk you. You might have to go to summer school to graduate."

My just-turned-eighteen-year-old mind raced. First, anger, You gutless witch! Why didn't you tell me instead of doing an end around and calling my parents? Who calls someone's parents on a Sunday night? Is this the extent of your personal life: getting your jollies by calling parents on a Sunday night? Is the problem with me that I wrote the entire sports page of The Searchlight without splitting one infinitive? Is the problem with me that our housing trio wants to camp on the beach at Ocean City and eat hot dogs, fries, and crab cakes, an idea which won universal approval from our classmates? Do you have a problem because you don't hear flies buzzing around you head and you're not dying?

Then I took a deep breath and thought that summer school might not be so bad. I had been accepted by Wheaton College for March. It was only one class in the morning so I could work in the afternoon. The major advantage was that I could skip Mrs. J's class, because I was flunking it anyway, and cover guys' baseball or women's gymnastics. The second was very appealing because it was Spring.

Then my cooler head prevailed. Maybe I was thinking of Rudyard Kipling's poem, "If you can keep your head when all about you..." Now that's poetry one can use. First there would be the embarrassment of not graduating with my class, not that there would be a major outcry of "Where's Dreibelbis?" but some would notice and most of all I would

257

notice. Second, there was the stigma of going to summer school. Today, all kinds of people attend summer school for a variety of reasons. Then, summer school was either for "smarties" or "dummies," and I was afraid that people would think I was the latter. Being the good soldier seemed to be the best route. A few years later Paul Simon came out with the song Kodachrome, with the lyrics, "When I think back to all the crap I learned in high school." Whenever I heard the song I thought of Mrs. J.

I took the high road and started attending class. The deal was that if I didn't have any more unexcused absences I would pass. I did the bogus apartment house keeping assignment which was the kind of thing one would do in Home Ec class. There was an elderly woman on my paper route who was renting rooms. She could take three people for $300 a month plus kitchen privileges. I included my employment figures from G.C. Murphy's plus all my Wheaton College information to show that this was only a temporary arrangement. In actuality, I was going to live with my parents until I went off to Wheaton, but I guess our teacher thought we were a bunch of losers doomed to work at Mc Donald's for the rest of our lives. I turned in the assignment, attended all classes, and nodded when she said the word "grand" which she tended to overuse. Graduation was in my future.

After dodging the non-graduation issue, there were other senior/spring things to consider. Someone, and I don't know whether it was a student government thing or something that someone saw on a Woodsy Owl public service announcement, suggested that we celebrated Earth Day. This was the first Earth Day and we were supposed to celebrate it to raise environmental awareness. The problem was that nobody knew what to do. Someone made a huge sign and some eco-minded students planted a tree in the school courtyard. That was the extent of our Earth Day celebration. Years later I went back to campus and couldn't find the tree. A longtime school employee told me that the tree had died years ago and was dug up to be taken to places unknown.

Another element of business was selecting a class song. This usually turns out to be some pabulum off the easy listening charts that will appeal to the "goody-two-shoes" students, the school administration, and parents. The choice: The Carpenters We've Only Just Begun. Years later at the thirtieth class reunion I was the emcee and asked who was responsible for this travesty. The D.J. played a few bars of it and laughter filled the room. No one confessed. David Blackwell and I had three nominations: Knock Three Times on the Ceiling if You Want Me by Tony Orlando and Dawn, She Came in the Bathroom Window by Joe Cocker, and The Beatles' Why Don't We Do It in the Road. None were considered.

Then there were the "Most Likely to..." awards. You usually knew who was going to win these before the results were made public. Of course there was always the "Most Likely to Succeed" awards to both male and female students. Noting that several of the males were already experiencing male pattern baldness, I put forward a "Most Likely to Recede" award. This was immediately struck down by a student government member who would have been a prime candidate for the award.

There were other events leading to graduation but the most important for many was the senior prom. Past proms at Oxon Hill High looked like a scene from the movie Grease where the multi-purpose room or gym was decorated. Some enterprising students were able to book a ballroom at The Washington Hilton Hotel, the same hotel where there was the assassination attempt of President Ronald Reagan by John Hinckley. You can say what you want about President Reagan's policies, but I always had to admire a man who had been shot being wheeled in on a gurney not knowing his fate who looks up at his wife Nancy and says, "Honey, I forgot to duck." Now that's no dime store cowboy.

My prom date would be a young woman named Debi from a rival high school who was now my steady. We had met at a church retreat and had been dating for about a year. Prom would be a last hurrah for us. Debi was a nice enough person but there was a little bit too much of a drama queen quality about her which was the last thing I needed in my life. Mom's bouts of depression were continuing so things were on edge on the home front. I was also feeling uncertainty in my life following graduation. There were daily announcements that the administration had us make every day as to which senior was going to which college. I knew that I was not going to be in the first wave of college attendees so I was down.

I was also feeling separation anxiety something that I still experience today. The high school curtain was going down and no stage manager could stop it. Prom was a celebration but it was another reminder that the show was very late into Act III.

For some reason, I can't remember the name of the prom band and I can usually remember things like that. I do remember that Debi wore a slinky blue, form-fitting dress and looked great. For some reason prom was more of a formality for me and not the big deal that others made it. After prom we went to a post-prom party which was dark, quiet, and uneventful. It seemed as if kids had been mandated to throw post-prom parties. Following this, many of the students went to Ocean City, MD but Debi and I declined. The next day we went duck pin bowling—a romantic way to cap off prom weekend.

Our graduation was at The University of Maryland's Cole Field House. Prince George's County schools had made a deal with the university for all the high schools to have their graduations at the field house. Our speaker was Maryland U.S. Senator Charles Mathias, and he gave the usual graduation pep talk that this was not an end but a beginning for us. As I walked across the stage to receive my diploma, I wish I could have agreed with him but I felt as if it were the beginning of the end.

THE NINE MONTHS OF
MY DISCONTENT

One of my favorite writers, John Steinbeck, wrote of his "winter of discontent." My "winter" spanned nine months or three seasons. While others anticipated leaving for college in the fall, I knew that I would not be going with them. I began spending a lot of time with Thomas Jefferson—Don't worry, I'll explained this later.

Clipper alums went like lemmings to Ocean City. Perhaps they weren't lemmings because they all came back alive. Following graduation, I began working full-time in the stockroom of G.C. Murphy's in order to raise college funds. I could have made more money elsewhere but I was a known commodity at Murphy's, and it was close to home. Lunches at the snack bar were free and certainly better than a certain national diner chain.

The experience was pretty much like Prince's early '80s hit, Raspberry Beret, "Working at the five and dime doing something next to nothing, my boss was Mr. Mc Gee..." Murphy's, like Woolworth's and Kresge's, had its origin as a "five and dime" store but they now called themselves "variety" stores.

There was a lot of hurry up and wait with the job. When the delivery trucks came in it was all hands on deck for the three of us in the stockroom. After unloading the truck we had to price the merchandise. This was long before bar codes so we had to price each item using old fashioned price stickers. If we worked quickly and accurately there was a lot of time for goofing around. The stockroom door had a special security signal so whenever the door opened we knew someone was coming in the stockroom. This was designed to keep out thieves but it didn't discriminate. We always knew when the boss was coming by the signal and his distinctive walk which was like a duck wearing shoes.

Another great perk was the candy room in our stockroom. Murphy's had an old fashioned candy and popcorn counter in the center of the store: heaven for kids and headaches for parents. We had access to the candy storage and all the bulk candy we could eat.

WPGC was our constant companion in the stockroom. Carole Kings' Tapestry album had just been released and would be on Billboard's Top 100 album listings for hundreds of weeks. King's "It's Too Late" played at least five times a shift, and it made me think of Debi.

A couple of weeks after graduation I was sitting at Murphy's lunch counter enjoying the Chopped Beefsteak Special, a bargain at $1.89 and even better when it was free, when the manager of our next door neighbor, Dart Drug, came to the counter with several of his stock clerks. The stock clerks were always making flirtatious comments to the women working the counter so I didn't care for them because I had my eye on one of the servers. Part of my feeling towards the Dart Group was that I saw them as competition. They sold some of the same merchandise we did at lower prices. Dart was a wholesale drug store and they threatened to put the other drug chains and variety stores like ours out of business. Their unofficial slogan was, "Don't fart with Dart."

Dart's manager, Harold Dawson, came over to where I was sitting and said, "We need help. What are you making here?" "$1.65." I responded. $1.65 was the minimum wage in 1971; please remember that gas was 29 cents a gallon at the time. "I'll raise you a nickel and there's lots of overtime." Dawson said. "Give me a day to think about it." I responded. "OK, but let me know by tomorrow. We really need the help."

I had pretty much decided to go to the dark side, or more accurately, the Dart side. I told Murphy's manager that I'd be leaving in two weeks, because I thought it was the customary thing to do. "Go ahead and leave now! Clock out! You can pick up your pay on Friday." I clocked out and thought about immediately going to Dart but decided to get a slice of pizza at Pistone's to celebrate my decision.

I walked into Dart the next day and they wasted no time in putting me to work. The place was a mess—a minefield of boxes. There were unopened, unmarked boxes of merchandise in the aisles. Most of this was the stuff on sale. Customers would open the boxes and grab what they wanted before it was priced leaving the cashiers to look through fliers to see the sale price. It was either that or take the customer's word for the price. In many cases the cashiers would say, "The hell with it!" and take the customer's word.

Dart was a lot more work than Murphy's so I was more than earning my extra nickel an hour. It was not unusual to unload a couple of eighteen wheelers a day in the oppressive DC heat We had no ideas as to where to put the merchandise, because there was no stockroom. The standard answer was, "Put it in the aisles." The customers didn't mind because they were getting their stuff on the cheap so they were forgiving. I've seen flea markets and garage sales that were better organized than Dart. Perhaps that is an insult to flea markets and garage sales.

Our manager, Mr. Dawson, was a peculiar fellow. He was short with a pot belly; blue eyes—one of them glass, and seemed to be indefatigable. We received weekly updates as to the sales' standing of Darts in the DC/Baltimore area. We were always in the top three and many times number one.

Dart appeared to be Mr. Dawson's life. He had no family and he didn't expect us to have one either. When he asked if we could work overtime, the subtext was, "You will work overtime." Overtime was the solution to the constant piles of unopened boxes in the aisles waiting to be priced. Overtime was assisting in raising college funds, but I thought that someone had said, "Everything in moderation."

One week I logged ninety hours. My parents were convinced that I was spending part of my time shacking up with some woman. One night it was approaching 10 'o clock when Dad came to Dart to pick up a prescription for Mom. Mr. Dawson had taken me off the floor to service the prescription counter, and to my surprise, here was Dad making the pickup. He reported to Mom that I was indeed spending my time at Dart.

One of the reasons that our Dart was always near or at the top of earnings was that we attracted a large black clientele from nearby DC. There were numerous apartments and smaller homes near the DC line and many black families settled there to flee less desirable, crime ridden sections of the city. Shopping options in DC were not as plentiful and those that existed gouged customers with high prices; consequently, our Dart was a great shopping option and just a couple of miles away. Sundays were huge for us because there was a twenty-page Dart circular in the local newspapers trumpeting sales. It was not unusual to see customers carry out four or five cases of Quaker State Oil when it went on sale.

Three of our stock clerks dubbed themselves "The Young, Gifted, and Black" stock clerks. Blake, Richard, and Clyde kept the place running and humming and they shared a small apartment just over the DC line. Richard, who became one of my best friends, confessed to me that there were nights near the end of the pay cycle when the three had popcorn for dinner. When I found this out I would always invite him to share my pizza with me at Pistone's.

The trio hailed from New Bern, NC and were part of a continuing exodus of blacks from the south. A number of the new DC residents were able to obtain good paying jobs in government positions. Others met various needs in the Metro area. Retail jobs were seen as plums compared to the condition they left in the south. The black population in DC swelled in 1950 to the '70s, and DC became known as "Chocolate City."

Richard was tall and thin with a dry sense of humor. Mr. Dawson referred to us as "The Salt and Pepper Twins," because we worked well together and tried to make work fun for everyone.

Blake was Richard's cousin. He had a modest Afro, tinted glasses, and in his words was "One clean dude." Almost everyone agreed. Blake could have played Richard Roundtree's sidekick in the movie Shaft, and it would have been a better movie. Long before sexual harassment policies, Blake broke all the rules but did so in a sly manner where no one could object. If an attractive female customer passed him in the store he would wait two beats and exclaim "GRACIOUS!" in a voice that filled the store. Most female customers never realized that the comment was intended for them. The stock guys knew and slyly went to the aisle where the "gracious" person may be headed.

Clyde was the other cousin in the trio and by far the most morose. Never smiling, he offered criticism to everyone. His secret came out one day when I asked Richard why Clyde always wore long sleeves even in blistering weather. Richard's response, "He doesn't want you to see his arms." Clyde was a serious drug user which explained his behavior as it became worse as the day progressed.

After a few weeks, I discovered that Mr. Dawson was a serious alcoholic. There was no evidence of his drinking on the job but I learned his secret from Richard and Blake who were Dart veterans. Mr. Dawson had been drinking and driving and was involved in a serious accident. His driver's license was taken from him and he rode in cabs. Many nights after the store's closing, he and another stock clerk, Russell, would buy a couple of pints, call a cab, and pay the cabbie $40 to drive them around while they drank. The cabbie would alert them as to when the fare was about to expire so they could be dropped off to crash at one of their apartments. Each had a spare set of work clothes at the other's apartment for the next workday. Alcohol never got in the way of Mr. Dawson's work ethic but I'm pretty sure that he spent a significant percentage of his bonus money on booze and cabs.

His drinking did cause him to miss some details. In-house thievery ran rampant at Dart. This was before security cameras and for a long period of time we had no security guard. There was a short hallway which opened to a trash room and alley. A large sliding door and a Masterlock were the only barriers between the trash room and the alley, and the Masterlock key was readily available to stock clerks. One stock clerk specialized in "Polaroid film marketing." He had the Polaroid film section and was the stocker/pricer. Of course he felt he needed a commission for his services so he would conveniently stash whole cases of film just outside the trash room door at a specific time so a friend could drive by and get the loot. Get the picture?

Store employees didn't know about the Polaroid caper for many weeks. Dawson and others got wise around the Thanksgiving season. People wanted Polaroid film for the holiday season and I think we ordered a Baltimore and Ohio Railway box car full. Suddenly, we were running out of supply and those of us who were cashiering knew we couldn't be selling that much; this plus our Polaroid, "Roid," seemed to be constantly carrying boxes of the stuff. An undercover security guard was hired and nabbed the guy his first night on duty.

The security guard called the cops and "Roid" was arrested in less time than it took to shake a Polaroid picture to develop. The guard and cops decided to have some fun. They could have taken "Roid" to the county jail but instead took him to the DC jail. The DC jail fits the definition of Bedlam. It was and is a cross between the casting call of a Fellini film and the cantina scene in Star Wars.

Dawson decided that we didn't need the services of the security guard following the Polaroid caper. The guard couldn't have been making more than $4-$5 an hour. Do the math and figure that there were forty-eight units of Polaroid in a box worth over $200 a box; we had lost thousands of dollars.

One night, the guy who had been our guard was shopping in our Dart when he saw a young employee taking merchandise to the back room behind the prescription counter. The guard knew that there were employee lockers in back so he waited until the employee returned from the room. She was empty-handed, and there was no reason to store anything in the back. The former guard told Dawson that he thought the employee had taken merchandise to the back and stored it in her locker, but Dawson didn't believe him. The employee was a young woman attending community college and tending to her ailing mother. Dawson decided to rehire the guard, and he caught her doing the same thing the next night. She was fired, charged, and released for a court date. Thank goodness she didn't have to go to the DC jail.

The biggest fiasco and mystery came on Washington's Birthday, which was one of the biggest sales days in all Metro stores and is now rivaled by "Black Friday." I think we were selling Quaker State oil for twenty-five cents a quart and rubbing alcohol for eight cents a bottle. Dawson hired a young woman the night before the sale and put her on the cash register the next day. A reminder here—this was before bar codes and simply sweeping the merchandise to register the price. There was a steel box next to the register where you put $20 and larger bills. At the end of the day you unlocked the box, put the bills in a bag, and counted the bag and drawer to cash out.

On Washington's Birthday, we had at least ten customers in each line with ten operating registers. It didn't help that Dart ran sales without advance warning so cashiers had to look in the circular for the sales price or take the easy way out and trust the customer.

The poor "newbie" was finally released from this torture and went to cash out. Now here's the mystery. Dawson and his assistant toady discovered that the "newbie's" cash out was over $2,000 short compared to the sales tape. When questioned, the poor "newbie" had no explanation. She thought that she had opened the steel box but wasn't sure. She couldn't remember counting a paper bag full of money. There was no money in the steel box. She had worked ten hours straight with no break and a couple of candy bars and a soda for lunch; all against labor laws.

Dawson phoned Dart headquarters just a few miles up I-495 and within an hour there were Dart officials at our store. The Spanish Inquisition and Gestapo had nothing on these guys. We could hear the employee being questioned in the back room for over two hours. Dart pressed no charges against her. She was dismissed after working one horrible day. We all thought that this was the end of the issue. WRONG.

We started noticing someone parked outside the store with binoculars. He was really obvious when we were outside unloading trucks. We figured out that he either came from Dart headquarters or that he was some weirdo bird-dogging our attractive employees. The whole thing became a store joke and we started calling him "Guy the Spy."

One day I decided to bring a pair of binoculars to work. Guy the Spy was there in the parking lot with his pair. I whipped out my pair of binoculars and started looking at him. He started his car engine and drove off, so we thought that this might be the end of Dart's version of Mad magazine's "Spy vs. Spy."

A couple of days later the "Young, Gifted and Black Trio" and I were taken to Dart Headquarters. It didn't bother me in the least and it relieved me from catching up with pricing and unloading eighteen wheelers. Dart was playing hard ball at this point, and we submitted to a polygraph test. We were given instructions before the test and some questions to determine a "baseline." At first I considered the experience to be a break, but I was getting grumpy now. It was well past lunchtime, we hadn't been fed, and I couldn't get My Murphy's beefsteak special along with onion rings. I would have killed for a couple of onion rings at that point.

It came my turn for testing. The interrogator, who appeared about as competent as The Pink Panther's Inspector Clouseau, began the question. "Is your name Gary Dribble biz?" "No, I'm not Gary Dribble biz, I'm Gary Dra Bell bus." He tried several times to pronounce my name before skipping the question. He asked more baseline questions: Did I work at Dart Drug? Was I eighteen? and other basic questions.

Then he dropped the bomb. "Have you ever stolen merchandise from an employer? Oh! Inspector Clouseau may have me here. Did taking candy from the candy room at G.C. Murphy's constitute stealing or was it a perk of the position? Everyone did it including management. President Bill Clinton's testimony concerning Monica Lewinsky came twenty-five years too late because I could have used him as a model for ducking this question. I said, "Yes." Oh, now he had me where he wanted me. He asked the question three times and each time I responded with.

"Yes." He stopped the machine. I told him about the candy at Murphy's and that I felt that technically it was stealing. I also mentioned the free lunches although this was an unspoken perk given to employees. I cleansed myself. It was as if I was testifying before Congressman Wilbur Mills and the House Ways and Means Committee, the same Wilbur Mills who chased Fannie Fox, "The Argentine Firecracker" into the Tidal Basin (Gee, Wilbur, you could have at least chased her into the reflecting pool at The Mall. It was far less polluted.)

I could tell that Inspector Clouseau's heart sank. He was looking for a BTO, Big Time Operator. I was a TWO, Teeny Weenie Operator. "Well Mr. Dribblebiz, besides the candy and lunches, have you ever stolen anything over $10?" he asked. "No!" I answered emphatically. The rest of the questioning was tame after that.

The Trio and I returned to Dart and announced that we were going to lunch. The store had managed without us for five hours, and it could jolly well manage while we took a long lunch break. If we had been Manhattan business types we would have had a three martini lunch; instead, we split two large combo pizzas with three pitchers of coke at Pistone's. Satisfied, we returned to work and did "something next to nothing."

As I recall the Summer of '71, it seemed as if I had no life outside of Dart Drug. August melted into September and Rod Stewart's "Maggie Mae" flooded the airwaves—"Wake up Maggie, I think I've got something to say to you. It's late September and I really should be back at school." Every time I heard the song I sank inside. It seemed as if everyone at Oxon Hill High was college bound and those who weren't drifted off into oblivion. Many would head to The University of Maryland to become Terrapins.

Many Terrapins came home for the weekend and shopped at Dart for munchies and school supplies as well as other types of "supplies." Guys purchased Trojan prophylactics in mass amounts as if they were intimate with the entire female freshman class. One discriminating freshman requested a box of Fourex Skins from a young woman cashier working the prescription counter. She thought that it was a type of Kodak film and she went searching through the film supply. I had to relocate her to the condom shelf. The look on her face would have made a "Kodak moment."

Women were very subtle with their contraceptive needs. When I worked the prescription counter, I encountered many co-eds who were familiar faces from high school. They would quietly ask me which aisle was the one with the contraceptive foam. My reply, "Oh, no problem. I'll take you there." We'd head over to the aisle and I would slowly recommend certain brands. The look on their faces was, "Would you just shut up and give me the foam, DAMN IT!" My other sales technique was if a woman who had treated me shabbily in high school asked for the foam aisle, I would raise my voice and in an authoritative tone ask, "Contraceptive foam. Why that's in aisle twenty-seven. Is that what you are looking for? CONTRACEPTIVE FOAM?" This was especially satisfying when there were ten people in line. One time I did this, and unbeknownst to me the customer's mother was at the end of the line. Had I known this I wouldn't have pulled the stunt. Even I would not sink so low to sooth my ego.

Perhaps my worst stunt was when an innocent co-ed asked me for the whereabouts of said foam. I led her over to the aisle and quietly suggested a brand. She thanked me, but before she left I said, "You know, this stuff is really good on Ritz Crackers for a late night snack." She appeared to believe me and said thanks. I guess everything tastes better when it sits on a Ritz.

OK, you've been patient enough concerning my Thomas Jefferson reference at the beginning of this chapter. It got to a point where one could achieve only so much satisfaction from Pistone's pizza and embarrassing co-eds. Rod Stewart's "Maggie Mae" haunted me. I knew that I was going to college in March, but it seemed as if that were an eternity. I'd been left behind in a world of eight cent alcohol, rubbers, and contraceptive foam.

One night, and I don't know why, I hit the drive through of the Jack-in-the-Box near Dart. This was when they actually had a Jack in the box and you placed your order by speaking into his mouth. I placed my order and headed Downtown in the trusty Ford Falcon. For some reason, I didn't go home but drove towards the Woodrow Wilson Bridge to Alexandria, VA. I could see the lights of The Washington Monument as I looked to my right over the Potomac River. I drove through Old Town Alexandria passing The Christ Church which had been the home church for George Washington and Robert E. Lee. Continuing on, I passed

National Airport and crossed the Fourteenth Street Bridge. To my left were the Tidal Basin and a parking lot facing The Jefferson Memorial. I drove to the nearly vacant lot and parked my car. The Tidal Basin water was calm, and the lights of The Jefferson Memorial bright. I turned the radio dial to WMAL and the jazz guru, Felix Grant, and listened to the jazz in silence while looking at the memorial. I became melancholy, not only because of my situation, but because I always felt that Thomas Jefferson was lonely over at his memorial. Dad had said that it was the least visited of the memorials because people couldn't figure out how to get there.

I sat there for about an hour thinking about the great President Jefferson and listening to the jazz offerings of DC's own Charlie Byrd on Felix' show. I started for home, but not before stopping at the Little Tavern in Alexandria for a couple of sliders and coffee before heading to the Woody Wilson Bridge. I continued this routine for many nights and my parents had no idea that I was spending quiet evenings with President Jefferson and Felix Grant.

My pre-college time became a prolonged American Graffiti night. I've already mentioned my lamenting the loss of The Senators. Logically, I knew that they were gone, but I also knew that next spring it would be strange to open up the sports section of the newspaper and not see "Washington" at the bottom of the American League standings, but a very foreign "Texas."

I began spending more time with Thomas Jefferson and Felix Grant, but eventually I began to diversify my routine and the nights became later. I visited the great music venues of Georgetown, such as The Cellar Door, The Bayou, Blues Alley, and others. I heard guitarist Charlie Byrd live as well as other artists who were on the rise. I didn't drink or smoke and I was always alone so I was often able to get close to the performers. Movies at the Georgetown Theatre were also my solace. It was an escape from Dart Drug and the dreaded Maggie Mae.

Georgetown in the early '70s was one of the coolest and most fashionable places to be on the East Coast. Stoners and Hippies were hanging out on the street, and live rock and roll could be heard from the doorways of bars and nightclubs. There was also Georgetown University, a few years before they would become a basketball powerhouse. One evening I was on Wisconsin Ave. and M Street in the heart of Georgetown, when I heard a unique voice that seemed to carry down the entire block saying, "They're big. They're BEAUTEEEFUL. Pick them out. Get them now. BEAUTEEEFUL balloons. Make the ladies happy. Make the children happy. When you make the children happy, everybody's happy." Here walks up this man with an assortment of colorful balloons for sale. Once again he repeated the same hawking refrain in a mellifluous voice. He was recognized as the one and only Balloon Man of Georgetown. The Balloon Man became so famous that he did station identification announcements for alternative rock radio station WHFS. Alas, I did not have a lady to be a balloon recipient.

I thought that dating someone might help my mood instead of spending my time with Thomas Jefferson. The one advantage of visiting TJ was that he didn't talk back and he was a cheap date. I started noticing a Dart employee named Ellie who worked at the cosmetics' counter. We started going out to eat after work and walk the few feet to the Oxon Hill Plaza Theatre to catch a movie. The red flags went up one night as we passed a jewelry store next to the theatre and she insisted on stopping and looking at rings. My visits with Thomas Jefferson sans Ellie resumed shortly thereafter.

There was another woman who caught my interest who worked the snack bar at Murphy's. Her name was Pat and she served me numerous times. She had graduated from a rival high school the year before and was attending a local community college while working part-time at Murphy's. She was attractive, friendly, and had a Colgate smile, but there was only so much that one could see when she had her hair pinned up and was wearing her snack bar whites.

One Sunday afternoon, I was working at Dart and missing another Redskin's game. I had to work most Sunday afternoons just when the 'Skins were getting exciting with their "Over the Hill Gang." I looked up from pricing something and saw Pat gliding by me. "Hi Gary!" and she flashed me her smile. Her brunette hair was shoulder length with blonde streaks, and her dress was form fitting much more flattering than her whites. She looked s if she had just come from church or some other function.

I started hanging out at Murphy's more often and eventually asked her for a date. We did movies, dinners, and shows Downtown. The strange thing was that we were both shy with one another. Her shyness made me shy as well, but we continued to date until I left for college.

271

The pre-college, American Graffiti weeks continued on to the Christmas season, which would be a huge deal for Dart. For years the running retail joke was that down came all the Halloween candy and decorations, and out came all the Christmas stuff. Not so at Dart. We started sneaking Christmas items into a couple of the aisles shortly after the school supplies were off the shelves. Pencils, notebooks, and Crayola crayons morphed into Christmas ornaments, lights, and outdoor decorations. We ran a Christmas on Columbus Day Sale and we had to restock the aisles that night due to the pre-Christmas locusts.

By Thanksgiving there were fully decorated Christmas trees and every Christmas item that Santa could imagine. We had five store length aisles devoted to Christmas candy. There was one whole section devoted to the Life Savers Christmas Storybook. This was a book -like container with ten different Life Savers flavors. It was a huge hit with stocking stuffers and for kids giving gifts Christmas gifts to their fellow students at school Christmas parties. The gift spending limit was usually a buck so The Storybook was a steal at fifty cents.

Each year there are non-toy items that seem to be gimmicks to me but stores can't keep them on the shelves. The Christmas of '71 was the year of the Hot Comb. This was a plug-in comb that assisted in the styling and drying of your hair. Dawson intended to order a gross. He made a mistake on the order form, and 1,440 Hot Combs arrived the day after Thanksgiving. We thought that there was no way in Hell we were going to get rid of them. We were mistaken.

There was the first wave of Hot Comb buyers, and that put a dent in our inventory; still, we had enough of them to stock every barber shop in DC, Maryland, and Virginia. Delaware being a small state we could have handled them as well. In one of my creative fits of marketing I told Dawson, "Look, the other Darts are going to run out. Put the word out that the Oxon Hill Dart has them in stock." There were people coming from Baltimore, Richmond, and the entire Metro area to buy Hot Combs. One customer from Baltimore bought fifty. We were pretty sure that he was a Hot Comb scalper.

Christmas Day approached. The eight- track tape of The Jackson Five's Christmas seemed to play nonstop and it was slow Yuletide insanity. I begged on my hands and knees for some Bing Crosby for variety. Christmas Eve came and the store was jammed. It's amazing how good those Chia Pets look at 9PM when you haven't started your Christmas shopping.

I told Dawson that I was leaving at 8:30. I had been there before 8AM when the store opened. He begged me to stay, but I wanted to go to our church's Christmas Eve service. He ducked out to get a quick bite at Murphy's around 8:00, and I punched out and escaped through a side door. I resented having to sneak out of work after a twelve hour shift in order to attend church.

There was a change of clothes in the Falcon and church was a minute's drive away. I have attended church services in almost all fifty states. For some reason this was one of the most meaningful services I have ever attended. My family decided not to attend. I sat in church in total peace, having escaped the mayhem of Dart.

I believe that Christmas and Easter are the most difficult times for clergy. How do you create a different spin each year for something many people already know? Pastor Warford's message focused on Christmas as being a season of peace. In spite of all that was going on around us and half a world away in Viet Nam this was the time that we could give the gift of peace. Wow, what a concept. Give the gift of peace instead of a damn Hot Comb.

The final hymn was I Heard the Bells on Christmas Day. I am filled with sorrow when I sing the lyrics and remember the Christmas Eve of '71...

And in despair I bowed my head,
"There is no peace on earth," I said,
"For hate is strong and mocks the song,
Of peace on earth good-will to men!"

but then I'm renewed by the final verse.

Then pealed the bells more loud and deep,
"He is not dead, nor doth he sleep.
The wrong shall fail,
The right prevail,
With peace on earth good will to men."

The service ended and there was hot chocolate and cookies. Some asked me what I was doing for Christmas, "Working." I responded. I left the church knowing that I had approximately eight hours of "the gift of peace."

I arrived at Dart about a half hour before opening. There were at least one hundred people outside. I've seen Black Friday crowds but I was shocked by this one. We were offering fifty percent off on Christmas merchandise—a good deal, but what were all these people doing bargain hunting this early in the day? When had they open their presents? Had they already styled their hair with their Hot Combs? Did they have lives?

Dawson was nowhere in sight. The assistant manager and a hand full of us were there to hold down Dart from the hordes. I offered the assistant manager $50 to let me kill the lights and put up a sign, "CLOSED! POWER OUTAGE!" For a hot couple of seconds he thought about it, then refused.

The doors opened promptly at 8AM. In recent years, I've heard of people being trampled at places like Walmart. No one lost their lives but some were on the verge of throwing punches. They could have used a strong dose of Pastor Warford's Christmas Eve "Peace" sermon. Some people were barely inside the door when they started making purchases. We had fully decorated trees near the cashiers and people wanting to buy them "as is." I did the math as to the tree and lights. I had no idea as to the price of the ornaments so I just threw them in. Fortunately, most of the remaining Christmas merchandise was priced.

One person asked if cigarettes were on sale. "Hell no!" was my less than Christmas-like response. I asked him why he thought they were on sale. "I give cartons of them for stocking stuffers." he replied. I almost gave them to him for half price but I didn't want to add fuel to the Yuletide fire.

The flood didn't let up. The later in the morning, the greater the crowds. It was as if everyone had opened their presents, discovered that their Hot Combs worked, but now needed batteries for toys. The theatre didn't open until noon, so instead of doing the civilized things such as conversing with family members or watching It's a Wonderful Life on TV for the twentieth time someone said, "Let's go to Dart! Those idiots are open! Maybe we can get a Hot Comb for Uncle Fred in Kalamazoo."

A major problem arose around lunchtime. Unless you had the foresight to brown bag it, Murphy's and Pistone's were closed. A couple of creative employees ran down to the movie theatre and bought loads of popcorn from the snack bar. Evidently, the people minding the theatre were three teenagers, who were also getting time and a half, who took pity on us and gave us free popcorn, extra butter included. Meanwhile back at the ranch, employees slyly lifted snack food items and Whitman candy samplers off the shelves. We sold Dak Danish canned ham which was slightly better than the quality of SPAM. Some employees grabbed can openers from the hardware aisle and had ham and potato chips for their Christmas lunches. It was sad to think that some of our less fortunate customers might be having the same fare for lunch because it was all they could afford. Two others ran across the parking lot to Seitz Liquor Store, "WE'RE OPEN 365 DAYS A YEAR," and split a twelve pack of National Bohemian in less than thirty minutes. They reeked of Natty Boh for the rest of the afternoon, while making repeated trips to the employee's restroom.

I found myself behind the prescription counter ringing up whatever people brought me for merchandise, while also ringing up prescriptions. Carpal Tunnel was not publicized back in the '70s, but my entire arm ached from ringing up sales. We had old NCR cash registers with the stick shift on the side for adding sales tax so you felt as if you were driving a cheap stick shift automobile.

The entire day felt like a Tim Burton film and this was long before Tim Burton began making films.

When things couldn't get any worse, in walked Dawson. Apparently he had discovered that he had slept through roughly half of Christmas so he decided to throw on yesterday's shirt and tie and wish us a "Merry Christmas." He looked as if he had one foot in the grave and another foot on a banana peel.

It was the first time he had ever come to the store in this condition. We knew that he drank but he had never entered Dart's doors five sheets to the wind. He was a functioning alcoholic. I've always said that being a functioning alcoholic is like playing golf with only a nine iron and a putter—You can do it, you just won't be very good.

He went to his office and closed the door, oblivious to the store's chaos. A few minutes later a woman brought a kitten to the prescription counter. "I found this kitten in the Hallmark aisle. What should I do with it?" I was at the end of my rope just like the kitten in the popular poster, "When you think you're at the end of your rope, hang on." Suddenly Dawson's office door opened and he reared his ugly head. "Get that G___D___ cat out of here!" he bellowed. Everybody froze. The woman replied, "You can't put it outside in the cold. It's just a baby!" I told the woman that we would take care of it. "Put that G_____D_____ cat outside!" Dawson bellowed again. I said that I would escort the cat outside. Instead, I took the kitten to the cosmetics counter where one of our more senior employees held forth. I asked her to tend to the kitten until things calmed down.

"Oh, so you think I'm an old lady who will take care of a cat just like that." she said. That's exactly what I was thinking but I lied. "No, we just need a place for it until things calm down." I assured her. "OK, I'll look after it. Get me a litter pan and some treats." The kitten had a temporary home hidden behind the cosmetics' counter.

Dawson, meanwhile, was trying to operate the prescription counter cash register. It was mid-afternoon, and things were calming down. The theatre was open, and others were at home busy preparing their Christmas feasts. Soon it was four 'o clock and I was exhausted. I stopped by the cosmetics counter to check on the kitten. She said, "I'll take the kitten home tonight along with the cat stuff. Don't charge me." "Don't worry, it's our secret." I responded. Knowing the kitten was in safe hands, I punched out. I had told Mom that I would be home by six.

It occurred to me that I didn't know much about the cosmetics person except that her name was Dot and that she drove an old Buick. I had no idea if she was married or had family; also, why had she chosen to work on Christmas Day? She had seniority and could have chosen not to work. Maybe the kitten was the gift of peace that she needed.

I had a couple of hours to kill until dinner at home. Peace is what I needed, so I decided to pay a Christmas visit to Thomas Jefferson. Within minutes I was on the Woody Wilson bridge with the sun setting over Northern Virginia. It wasn't long until I hit the historic row houses of Alexandria. The houses had large wreaths on their doors and no garish lights. Some had tasteful white lights. The shops were closed, but The Little Tavern was open. It had to be a "Roy Orbison" clientele—"Only the lonely." The traffic was sparse. The monuments were visible from the 14th Street Bridge, and their lights had just come on. A couple of planes were landing at National with people who may be coming home for the holidays.

I did not pay an immediate visit to President Jefferson but took a detour to The Mall. There, the National Christmas Tree with its hundreds of lights was in its glory as well as over fifty smaller trees representing each of the fifty states and territories. I did not stop to visit the eight reindeer they had on sight or warm myself at the Yule log.

The Tidal Basin and President Jefferson were soon in view. Some radio stations had stopped playing Christmas music at noon and had returned to their usual formats. WGMS, the classical station, was playing Handel's Messiah. I stopped by my usual spot and the sun had almost set. I thought of Pat and what she might be doing with her family. I wanted to be alone, but not alone.

My mind wandered to the Christmases that Thomas Jefferson may have had. I'm sure that many of them were grand, but there must have been lean ones during the war. It was soon time for me to return the way I had passed. A few of the lonely were still at Little Tavern as I passed back through Alexandria.

Back at home we had ham and the usual side dishes. Doug went to a friend's house and my folks retired to watch TV. I told Mom that I was not going to work tomorrow. My holiday ticket had been punched. They didn't call them "mental health" days back then, but that was what I needed.

As I drifted off to sleep, I thought of the cosmetician and the kitten. I wondered if she was eating Dak Danish Ham and watching Perry Como's or Andy Williams' Christmas Specials. Maybe she had to work on Christmas Day because she needed the time and a half. Maybe she lived in her Buick and needed a feline co-pilot. Then again, maybe she was rich, eccentric, and got her jollies watching the loonies at Dart. The truth was somewhere in the middle. She was a widow and lived alone. Her husband had a good government job and had provided for her. She received his pension and health coverage. Her home was across the river in Alexandria, and I had passed it many times. The Redskins and The National Symphony Orchestra were her two passions. She wanted Jurgensen instead of Kilmer at quarterback, and she wanted the symphony to play more Russian music. Perhaps she wanted to rock with Rachmaninoff.

277

Sometime in early February, Dot the cosmetician left Dart for a better paying and more tranquil job at The Hecht Company's suburban store. This was like trading a Pinto for an Impala as to pay and serenity. Before she left we passed around and signed a card. There was no going away present as that was not part of Dart's culture. I asked how the kitten was doing. Dot smiled and said that he was growing and happy. "He's a great cat. He follows me around like a puppy." She had named him "Alex" after Alexandria and Alexander Borodin the Russian composer. Dot left that night for the last time as a Dart employee and headed home to Alexandria and Alex. Perhaps Alex was the gift of peace she needed for Christmas. I never saw Dot again.

New Year's came, and I was now psychologically a short-timer at Dart, with less than seventy-five days left. In a strange way, I had developed some loyalty towards Dart perhaps because they had a profit sharing plan where you could have money deducted from your paycheck and profit as Dart profited. This turned out to be a good supplement to my college fund. There was The Great George Washington's Birthday fiasco along with some other bizarre events along the way. But I was feeling the home stretch of my "Season of Discontent."

Pat and I were going out on weekends because we were both busy and the only time available. She was my companion as we explored DC's nightlife, and maybe it was meant to be that she was only companionship. The problem was that I was falling in love with her but still had my guard up. What would it be like to leave her in March? My biggest fear was that if I told her I loved her she would not respond in kind. Woody Allen once said that if a shark doesn't continue to move it dies. We didn't have a dead shark, but it was on life support.

Back at Dart, the new year signaled inventory. We were to take stock of our merchandise and show headquarters that we were a well-oiled machine. All the Quaker State oil and WD 40 in the store would not be enough to lubricate us. Sales were good, we were still at or near the top of stores, so we just had to look like we knew what we were doing and we would pass with flying colors. Corporate didn't want to fart with a money making Dart and we were a cash cow for the chain.

The keeping up appearances strategy required a major house cleaning and organization. In reality this was like putting lipstick on a pig. We would have to get stock out of the aisles or on floor displays to demonstrate a semblance of organization. This meant another Dawson marathon session on our parts. Years later I saw a coffee mug with the message, "A Lack of Planning on Your Part is No Cause For an Emergency on My Part."—my exact feelings. Dawson decided that we would begin our marathon inventory quest on the Sunday before the brass came, and we would pull an "all-nighter," concluding sometime on Monday and the brass coming on Tuesday.

Things started out well enough after closing Sunday night. People were motivated by the time-and-a-half pay, and there was a rumor of bonuses if the store performed well and looked great. Sometime around midnight things began to fall apart. Russell, Dawson's drinking buddy, kept taking breaks. It became obvious that these were "nectar of the gods" breaks. Russell decided that he would try his unsteady hand with the floor buffer. We hadn't waxed the floor so I don't know why he thought this was a good idea.

Russell had firm control of the buffer for a New York minute when he lost his grip and the buffer crashed into a floor display pyramid of Turtle Wax. It seemed as if the entire display exploded on the floor, but it was probably only a couple of dozen bottles; still there was green goo all over the place. In his infinite wisdom, Russell decided to pick up every piece of glass out of the goo and use the Turtle Wax to buff the floor. Obviously he had heard the commercial jingle, "Turtle Wax gives that hard gloss finish—TURTLE WAX." He spent nearly an hour picking glass out of the goo. Satisfied with his work, he pulled out an old Gene Pitney eight track tape from someplace and put it one the store's P.A. system. With Gene Pitney blaring throughout the store, Russell manned the buffer and maneuvered it in such it way that it became a dance partner. The whole event was becoming more surreal by the moment. The more Russell and the buffer danced the greater the spread of goo. Someone pulled the plug of the buffer and told Russell to take a break. He was more than willing to refuel on more "nectar of the gods." We scooped up the wax and buffed the best we could.

About 3AM we saw the futility of what we were doing and that neatness counted so the heck with accuracy as to taking inventory of stock. We discovered one employee with excellent penmanship so we had her do the inventory slips while we counted. Neatly written inventory slips had to count for something. At one point, we were doing inventory of Kotex when the counter said, "Eighty boxes of Kotex." The woman recorder said, "Right, eighty manhole covers." It took us about five seconds but we got the reference. At 3AM we were slow on the uptake.

The sun rose, and we knew that we were burning daylight because we had to get as much done as we could before the opening at 8AM. We prayed for a light day of customer traffic so we could work. We broke for breakfast at Murphy's, and it was the first meal many of us had eaten in over twelve hours. We made a "to hell with it pack" where we would guess the number of merchandise items without counting and put numbers on slips. This system took about six hours, and we clocked out at 3PM. Some of us had worked thirty straight hours.

Following inventory, things began to calm down at Dart before the Washington's Birthday Fiasco, and I was able to work more reasonable hours: most of them 8AM-8PM. This meant that I had more time to explore Washington's nightlife and I entered an approach-avoidance syndrome as to college. The thought of going to college was exciting on a variety of fronts but I feared change. Instead of prepping and trying to find out as much as I could about Wheaton I did nothing. I decided that I was just going to let college happen.

Movies and music became my friends. The visits to President Jefferson were interspersed with visits to hear jazz guitarist Charlie Byrd and Chuck Brown, the founder of Go Go music, at various clubs in Georgetown. Nightlife was beginning to pick up in the wake of the riots following the assassination of Dr. King; however, many suburbanites were hesitant to explore the city after dark. Georgetown continued to be a hub of nightlife for young adults and teeny boppers.

Motown ruled the radio airwaves and there was a regular diet of DC product Marvin Gaye. I loved Motown, but there were nights when Elton John's Levon and Harry Chapin's Taxi matched my melancholy mood. For some reason Taxi is the music I remember the most from the period, and after hearing it a few times I could recite the six-minute plus lyrics.

When I wasn't listening to live music or DC radio I'd attempt to dial in WCFL or WLS from Chicago. The stations' signals came in strong at night, and I considered this to be college prep. It was important for me to know who would become my airwave friends once I hit the Midwest. It's ironic that the first time I heard DC's Roberta Flack sing The First Time Ever I Saw your Face was on Chicago's WCFL.

Whatever strange emotional state I was in must have rubbed off on Mom. I wasn't working the crazy shifts any longer at Dart, and there were some days when I was at home. Mom decided to open up to me in a manner she never had at any other time. This self-disclosure provided some dropped bombs.

First, she told me that she and Dad had previous spouses. Here's where the mystery of our family friend comes into play (See, after two hundred pages you forgot about Myrtle, but I promised you I'd get around to her.) Dad married one of Myrtle's sisters at the start of World War II. The story was that Dad was drafted and went to serve in England. In the meantime his wife was enjoying the company of other stateside DC Dandies. She wrote to him about her adventures and asked for a divorce.

At about the same time, Dad's father committed suicide by cutting his throat with a barber's razor. Dad returned stateside for his father's funeral only to boomerang back to England. Dad had a full head of hair before he entered the service but returned to the states completely bald. Doctors believed that it was due to stress. The story goes that sister Myrtle felt sorry for Dad and he became an unofficial member of her family. The friendship between Myrtle and Dad was platonic even though life between Myrtle and husband Earl was tense due to Earl's drinking.

Mom's story is a little more bizarre, but what do you expect coming from a background of moonshine and voodoo ("Moonshine and Voodoo" sounds like a great title for a ZZ Top album.) After my grandmother took Mom out of school following the eighth grade she stayed on the farm and helped where she could. Somehow, in her late teen years, Mom got involved in a pen pal club and started writing to a guy in Canada. The Canadian pal was part of a family of farm owners and was fairly well-to-do. He wrote and asked if he could visit Mom in North Carolina, and she said yes.

Here's where the story gets a little murky. The Canadian gentleman "came a callin,'" and I'm not sure if he asked to stay on the farm for the visit or what transpired. My grandmother said that if he was going to visit he would have to marry Mom. I'm not sure if there was any hanky panky involved, but Mom ended up marrying the gent and moving to Canada. Mom's story was that the Canadian was a less than energetic farmer, in her words "lazy," and this became grounds for the divorce.

Mom moved to DC to live with her cousin, who got her a job as an operator with The Chesapeake and Potomac Telephone Company. It would be the only job she ever held outside the household. The cousin's husband knew Dad, played matchmaker, and Mom and Dad married after several months of "courtin' and sparkin'." For some reason they married in South Carolina instead of DC or North Carolina. I never bothered to do a Sherlock on this issue. This was the first time I had heard all this information and I was nearly nineteen-years-old.

Many years later when I was in my forties and Dad had passed away Mom told me that when I was an infant and we were living on D Street, some Royal Canadian Police came to the apartment and claimed that Dad was not my biological father and that the Canadian gent wanted custody of me. If all the dates I've been told are true, my parents wed on June 17th, 1952, and I was born April 17th, 1953. I may have come along quickly but the time frame was realistic. Somehow the Canadians were sent packing and I didn't end up rooting for The Montreal Canadians or Toronto Maple Leafs although I do like Canadian bacon and have been known to drink a Molson's.

It wasn't so much the information which disturbed me but the timing of Mom's disclosure. Perhaps she thought that I was leaving for college soon and this was information I needed to know. I'll never know and I gave up trying to analyze Mom years ago.

Today the non-traditional family is accepted, if not de rigueur. We don't raise eyebrows over divorce and various combinations of parental units. I love Robin Williams' words at the conclusion of the movie Mrs.Doubtfire, where he talks about the various combinations of family members.

During the Baby Boomer era, family "make-up" was less open and in many cases not discussed. I had at least two close friends, David Blackwell being one, who were foster kids. I knew a couple of kids from single-mom households, and no explanation was given, plus we were to mind out own business. Due to the fact that DC was a military town I had numerous friends whose Dads had married women from different countries and brought them back to the U.S. We kids didn't think this was strange.

In short, the kids in Oxon Hill and throughout DC did not grow up in a Leave it to Beaver/Father Knows Best world. We knew this; we just didn't talk about it.

I survived family matters and Dart throughout the month of February. February has always been a "blink" month for me—you blinked and it was gone. I blinked through the weeks with Dart, Pat, pizza, music, and Thomas Jefferson. March came and college was a perceptible thing. In the lyrics of Judy Collins, "Who knows where the time goes..." I didn't know and I wasn't ready to know.

COLLEGE BOUND

The Ides of March came and it was time to go. The Dart gang gave me a going away card and broke the tradition by giving me a gift—a shaving kit. I'm not sure that anyone from Dart had ever gone away to college. You would have thought that I was going to Mars.

Everything was packed on the Saturday of my departure: suitcase, trunk, and briefcase. Dad was the master of cramming the most stuff in the least space. My train was departing early that evening so most of the day was hurry up and wait. My buddies, The Merry Pranksters, came to visit me early in the afternoon, and nobody knew quite what to say. They gave me a card, and I put it in my briefcase along with the Dart card and one from Pat. Pat and I had gone to see Dr. Zhivago a couple of nights earlier and it was almost like any other date except we drove to The Jefferson Memorial after the movie. We said goodbye, and she gave me a card with instructions not to open it until I was on the train.

Dad packed the car that was Union Station bound while I said goodbye to The Pranksters. I've never mentioned their names because the group was fluid in membership. It was similar to the original Rat Pack. The story of the original Rat Pack was that a group of entertainers were at the home of Humphrey Bogart and Lauren Bacall, partying and causing minor havoc. Lauren said, "Look at you guys. You look like a pack of rats." The name stuck. The Rat Pack settled into Jerry Lewis, Dean Martin, Sammy Davis Jr., Joey Bishop, and Peter Lawford.

The Pranksters' core was Gordon, Bob, Jimmy, Mike, and Bob W. They all attended Forest Heights Baptist Church but at the time you would never have known them to be "Good Baptist Boys." The last I checked with the group, most of them were church deacons.

The time came to head to Union Station, which was then a dark and dank train station. Today it is one of most welcoming station in the country with boutique shops, food court, and movie theatres.

For some reason, Mom stayed in the car when we got to the station. Dad helped me with my ample luggage to the train. The porter took everything except for my briefcase. The call came for all aboard, and I did something that I had never done before—I shook Dad's hand. It was as if neither one of us knew how to say goodbye. There was no hug and not much more than an exchange of goodbyes. Maybe it was the stoic Pennsylvania Dutch blood in both of us or the fact that we were a family that did not show public displays of affection. It was another surreal moment in my life that I have difficulty explaining.

The trip to Chicago would last all night. The train pulled out of the station slowly and headed north to Maryland, then Pennsylvania. It was not the scenic route and so unlike departing from National Airport. I would not be able to say goodbye to the sites of the city I loved including Thomas Jefferson.

We were in Northern Maryland near the Pennsylvania line and it was getting dark. I decided to go to the dining car and order a full dinner. Dad thought that I should wear a sports coat and tie on the train, and it helped me to feel like a seasoned traveler as I entered the dining car.

I ordered a small steak and probably would have ordered a martini if I drank and had been of legal drinking age. The order came and it was my first experience with dining car fare—expensive, but not bad. Suddenly, word came over the train's P.A. system that the dining car would uncouple from the rest of the train in Pittsburgh. Pittsburgh was a good three hours away with several stops but I panicked. I swallowed the rest of my dinner whole because I was afraid that I would be left behind in the dining car.

Rail travel is supposed to be scenic but I saw little in the darkness. I fell asleep and awakened to the flat lands of Western Ohio and Eastern Indiana. Mid-morning we hit the Southside of Chicago. The first impression was not inspiring. Factories, smoke, and junk were most of what I saw, and then we passed the White Sox' Comiskey Park. I thought that it looked run down with white paint and stenciled letters, COMISKEY PARK.

The train pulled into Chicago's Union Station, and I had been instructed to cab it to Northwestern Station for the train to Wheaton in the west suburbs. I made it to the station and was immediately met by a panhandler. Welcome to Chicago, "The City That Works," or perhaps more accurately "The City That Works You."

My adventure continued as I found the right ticket booth for The West Line. Fortunately, it was a Sunday morning and not a weekday rush hour or who knows where I would have been headed. The train going to Wheaton had numerous stops, and it would not be long until I could recall each stop from memory. We headed due West for the twenty-five miles to Wheaton. It seemed more like 250 miles. The towns and stops seemed to be unending: Villa Park, Oak Park, Melrose, Elmhurst, Lombard/ Glen Ellyn, and the hits went on. The conductor told me that it was best to stop at the College Ave. station instead of the Wheaton station, because it was closer to the college. He was right.

There were pay phones at the station so I called the college. Dad told me that someone would pick me up and take me to the dorm. WRONG! It's amazing how much incorrect information I received from my parents regarding my college entrance. It was difficult to fault them because neither had been to college; also, they lived in a very small world of their own. I had lived in that world as well having never been more than 400 miles from home. As I stood at the phone booth, it hit me that I was in another world.

The college operator said that no one would be in the dorms until Monday but later in the day I could contact the dorm's resident advisor and he would open the dorm doors and show me to my room. Scared, cold, and not knowing what to do, I attempted to haul my 100 pounds of belonging towards the campus. I had progressed about a block when a car stopped, and a middle-aged couple asked if I was a student. I must have had it stamped on my forehead and the 100 pounds of luggage had to be a giveaway. Answering "Yes" they invited me to their car. "The dorms aren't open yet so you can come home with us for Sunday dinner." The couple was the De Vettes, both foreign language professors at Wheaton. Mrs. DeVette's mother was with them as well.

The De Vettes were my first impression of Wheaton because I had never visited the campus. I was one of those odd cases where someone decides to attend a college or university sight unseen. The De Vettes served dinner, talked about the college, asked questions about me, and then it was time to head to the dorm. Today, there is lots of discussion as to whether or not there are angels among us. The De Vettes may not have been angels but I would say that they were "angelic" people.

They dropped me off at the freshman dorm, Fischer Hall after giving me a brief tour of the campus. I was in awe of it. The main building, Blanchard Hall, is a limestone castle with a milk bottle-like tower. The campus was compact and scenic. It was mid-March, and I wondered what the campus would look like in spring.

You may be wondering why I have taken this detour as to writing about my college life. The fact was I was never so lonely in my life. President Jefferson, where were you when I needed you? The next day I met with an advisor and chose classes for my schedule. My first day of classes was a disaster and I had no idea of what I was doing. Everyone else had been there the previous two quarters and I considered them to be veterans of the college game. I was a complete rookie, and at the end of the day I retreated to my dorm.

It was early evening when my dorm room phone rang. It was my parents wondering how things were going. I lied and told them that things were going great. Mom dropped the bomb, "Well, you can always come home and work at Dart if things aren't working out." Go home. Part of it sounded inviting and the other part meant I was a failure doomed to price eight-cent alcohol for the rest of my life as a Dart stock clerk.

I looked at my cash and travelers' checks and discovered that I had enough money for train fare and a couple of burgers for the trip home. Union Station never sounded so good.

Enter three more angels. "Hi, we heard that there was a new guy on the floor." The trio introduced themselves and invited me to go for pizza. If I was going back to DC I might as well do so on a full stomach. I was good for the offer and we headed to Jolly Roger's Pizza near campus.

It turned out that the trio had many of my concerns during the first classes of the quarter and they had been students since fall. One guy who was in by literature class asked, "What was all that stuff about King Lear had to become blind in order to see?" Another guy in my history class asked, "What's that about The Ottoman Empire? I thought an ottoman was something you put your feet on." Laughs all around the table.

I discovered that my more experienced classmates had questions about the first day of the quarter as well and it was new information for all of us. Thanks to the trio I decided to stick it out. I made respectable grades for the quarter, a B- average, but the important element of the quarter was learning to appreciate new people, places, and things. The professors were experts in their fields as well as being benevolent guides. My Oceanography professor, Dr. DeVries, had the corny line, "I always try to keep my students above 'C' level." After one got past his corny humor one discovered that he had explored the seven seas. He was also a survivor of intense brutality. Doc DeVries was part of a missionary family in the Philippines prior to and during World War II. He and his family were captured by the Japanese, assigned to a prison camp, and tortured. Doc was in his late forties when I took his class. His snow white hair made him look ten years older.

Colleges and universities use promotional catchlines such as "Capture the Whatsamatter U. Experience." Institutions attempt promote their images in a few pages of a brochure, flashy websites, or a few seconds of video. For me, Doc and many of his colleagues were major parts of The Wheaton Experience.

I was still homesick for DC; I never opened the card from Pat. For some reason I didn't want to see it and experience the closure. My closure was heading off into the West on a steel horse. As the days passed and I became more confident, I began to look at Wheaton as my second home.

Besides the academics, I began to develop on the social front as well. One of the first things I did when I hit campus was to visit WETN, the campus radio station. WETN was a low power FM station serving both the campus and nearby community. When I met the student program director I gave him the spiel about being a WTOP Fellow and announcing all the high school sports events. He smiled and nodded, then gave me the morning "baby-sitting" job of playing taped programs and announcing Wheaton's chapel broadcasts. It was entry level but at least it was a start.

My passion was doing play-by-play sports so I started thinking of how I could get my foot in the door with the sports staff. Without permission from the sports department, I called the Chicago Cubs and White Sox to ask for a press pass so I could interview players. The Cubs promptly dismissed me saying that they did not give passes to college radio station personnel. The Cubs were on 50,000 watt blowtorch WGN radio and had an extensive radio network. They also telecast most of their games on WGN-TV. In short, they needed no assistance from weak squeak college radio stations.

My next step was to call The White Sox. The Sox were an improving club but had experienced some recent lean years in wins and attendance. A couple of years earlier, The Sox drew fewer than 500,000 fans. Their radio station, WEAW in Evanston, IL, had a signal that barely covered Chicagoland. The legendary announcer, Harry Caray, had come on board, and he was a one-man promotional machine for The Sox. I called The Sox, and I think they were in a position of accepting any publicity no matter what. "Sure, press pass; no problem. Give us your station and name." BINGO! I was on The Sox press list.

I arrived at Comiskey Park armed with a cassette recorder and reporter's notebook. The press gate had my pass which allowed field access. "Now, since you are a college station, you will be in the auxiliary press box down the third base line." I could have cared less. My pass gave me access to the field before the game and that was all that mattered. If I came back with some interviews that would increase my stock at WETN.

Gameday came and I took the Northwestern train then the EL to Chicago's Southside and Comiskey Park. Sure enough, my press pass was there at the press gate with my misspelled name. I could have cared less.

I was escorted to the field gate and started interviewing players from both the Sox and Kansas City Royals. After about six interviews it was time to hit the press box. The auxiliary press box was for the suburban newspapers and media outlets other than the major Chicago papers and electronic media.

There was a sign, WETN, on my table space, so I thought that I had hit the big time. I discovered that one of my press colleagues was a woman who wrote for one of the larger suburban newspapers. There had been a big story in The Chicago Tribune a few days earlier concerning the fact that she had been denied press credentials because she was a woman. I recognized the name and face as well as the fact that she was the only woman in the press box.

I asked for an interview and she was more than happy to oblige me. She was not a happy camper concerning the Sox attitude towards woman and the general attitude of the press in the male dominated world of sports. It was the best of the interviews I taped that day and a bit of a scoop because no electronic media outlet had interviewed her.

Back at the station, I gave the news director the tape. The director and staff were amazed when they heard the interviews and played one each evening during the sports segment. We received strong positive feedback from women listeners concerning the interview with the woman sports reporter. I was starting to make inroads at WETN.

Chicago was growing on me. DC was still my hometown, but Chicago was a totally different experience. As Carl Sandberg wrote, it is "The City With the Big Shoulders." The lights were brighter on the theatre marquees and the buildings taller. DC had a limitation on the height of buildings so that no building, with the exception of The Washington Monument, could be taller than the Capitol Dome.

The other thing that impressed me was that with all its problems Chicago was a livable city. The mass transportation in Chicago was far superior to that of DC and you could travel virtually anywhere in Chicagoland without a car. The people were another difference. For the most part, they were helpful and it was almost as if they took pride in giving you directions. It was an, "Oh good! Let me show you another part of our city" attitude.

Then there's the food. The seafood is C- at best, because there is only so much you can get out of Lake Michigan. I missed the crab feasts and the bounty from the Chesapeake and Atlantic. The steaks and ribs more than made up for this void. Other cities will boast as to having better fare, but give me Chicago steaks, ribs, prime rib, or anything "red" anytime. It took me awhile to appreciate Chicago steaks because I was on a student's budget, but I did splurge a bit when I had some extra coins. The other thing about Chicago red meat is that they know how to cook it. Mom had always prepared steaks as if she were going to cremate them. Chicago chefs knew what they were doing. Chicago also has the best hot dogs. A Chicago style hot dog is a feast in and of itself with various vegetables and sweet relish.

As mentioned, Chicago style pan pizza is the best, hands down. New York has good "slices," but if I really want to harden my arteries, give me a pan pizza. Gino's East and Lou Malnati's are still my favorites, and I order Lou's via the internet for special occasions such as The Super Bowl.

Food filled the void of some of the homesickness, but there was still the issue of no Senators. It was my first Spring without them, but being out of town took away some of the sting. The Sox press visit also helped and I adopted The Sox as my new team. As the weeks passed, I also grew interested in The Cubs because they were on the tube more often. They were even on kids' TV shows.

One morning, I was on my way to class when I passed several of my classmates in the TV lounge of the dorm. They were watching a kids' show with a guy named Ray Rayner and a puppet goose named Garfield who made noise by clapping his beak. I asked, "Why are you guys watching a kids' show with a silly goose who can't speak?" "The Cubs' highlights are coming on!" they responded. Sure enough, the Cubs were showing their highlights on the goose show. I was informed that this was why so many kids grew up Cubs' fans.

There would be some friction here, because in Chicago you are either a Sox fan or a Cubs fan. I thought that since I was without The Senators, I could enjoy the bounty of two local teams. My classmates, many of them from the Midwest, informed me that this was not the case. One student cited the Bible telling me that a man cannot serve two masters. Another student was more earthly, "You're either pregnant or you're not."

The issue became more complicated when our Greek language professor offered to take some of us to a Cubs game. Four of us accompanied him as he drove his old convertible down Clark Street to Wrigley Field. We eventually arrived at "The Friendly Confines" and went on a treasure hunt to find a parking space. When I entered Wrigley the first time, I knew that it was my new "Green Cathedral." Comiskey Park had been an experience, but the park was showing its age. Wrigley was truly a ballpark unlike the cement doughnut I had been accustomed to at RFK Stadium.

I rubbed my eyes because I thought that I had entered a time machine, with Mr. Peabody and Sherman taking me back to the 1930s or '40s. It was a day game, and Wrigley was famous for having no lights. There were vendors roaming the stands selling score cards; a simple card with the players' numbers for both teams and a scoring grid for fifteen cents. Vendors served hot dogs out of a cart that they wheeled through the main aisle. Other vendors served ice cream treats called Frosty Malts. One fan informed me that a special treat for Cub fans was to scoop out the center of a Frosty Malt and pour in Old Style Beer. I passed.

292

The Cubs were playing The New York Mets, and it was pretty much the last hurrah for the great Willie Mays. The San Francisco Giants had traded Willie to New York, and it was poetic justice that he would end his career where he began in New York. I had seen Willie once, and that was for a few innings at the 1969 All Star Game in DC.

The image of Willie I will never forget was when he got a hit into the centerfield gap and thought about trying to stretch it into a double. He ran half way to second, and the Cubs' centerfielder gunned a perfect strike to second base. Seeing that he had no chance for a double, he threw on the brakes, scampered back to first, and was safe on a head-first slide. Amazing; "forty-two-years young," I thought.

It was a difficult decision, but I decided to root for both teams. They were in separate leagues, so they didn't compete against each other. If they both made the World Series, I could decide my pick; of course, anyone familiar with Chicago baseball knows that an all-Chicago World Series is a sign of The Apocalypse and that one should seek cover immediately.

The quarter was progressing rapidly, and it was time for me to plan my trip home. Quarters went faster than semesters and a Wheaton quarter was ten weeks. Finals were on the horizon and it was time for me to focus on academics and tear myself away from baseball.

I called my folks, and they assumed that I was coming home on the train. After very little research and some advice from my friends I discovered a better option. "Do you like trains?" asked one co-ed. "I like them for special trips, but why don't you fly student stand-by?" "Student stand-by? What's that?" I asked. "You've never heard of student stand-by?" She looked at me as if I had never heard of Coca Cola. "Student stand-by is really cheap. You just wait to see if they have room for you on the plane. Go down to Wheaton Travel and they will tell you." This sounded too good to be true.

I took her up on her offer and discovered that the fare to DC was $35. My parents had paid at least double that for my train fare. It was an hour and a half home by flight as opposed to an all-night ordeal on the train. I booked the flight and had my ticket in hand.

When I called my parents with the news they thought that I was involved with some type of Chicago underworld activity. I used the "All the kids are doing it" line and they became more skeptical. Finally, I told them to call the airline and find out for themselves. I didn't want to play

"Joe College" with them, but I was discovering a new world beyond Oxon Hill and DC.

It wasn't as if I didn't love home and didn't want to return; it was that I had discovered something different. DC was still home; however, I didn't adopt Chicago; Chicago adopted me. Finals came and I felt a sense of relief as well as wanting to return home. I knew I wasn't an "A" student, but I wasn't chopped liver either.

It was the first time I had ever flown out of O'Hare Airport, one of the busiest in the world, and certainly larger than Dulles or National. A local student, who knew O'Hare like the back of his hand dropped me off at the American Airlines terminal and told me to follow the signs. It sounded pretty easy, and it was.

This was long before 9-11 and airport security so getting to my gate was no big deal, but then fear set in.

This was student stand-by with the emphasis on "stand-by." Where would I go? Where would I stay? —no" The attendant at the desk looked friendly, so I asked her these questions. She looked as if she had fielded similar questions from dozens of "fly babies." She smiled and said, "Not to worry. You are near the top of the list, so you should get on." My fears were relieved, so I went off to enjoy a Chicago Style hot dog and Coke as my final meal in Chicago.

The flight turned out to be similar to the Atlantic City flight— different scenery, but the same drill and slightly longer flight duration. Maybe I could become a seasoned traveler after all.

We began our descent over Northern Virginia; then I saw them. There were my friends, the monuments of Washington, Lincoln, and Jefferson, and they looked as if they were meant for a model railroad layout. As we continued our descent, I remembered the thrill of the near-water landing on my last flight to DC. The water got closer and closer as I prayed for terra firma. We landed and I resumed a regular heartbeat.

Dad and Doug were there to collect my luggage and we headed to the car for the short drive through Alexandria to Oxon Hill. There was a surprise passenger with us. A black collie mix named Duchess rode shotgun at my feet. She kept making a clicking noise with her mouth as if she was a mechanical dog. "She does that when she pants in the car." Dad explained. Duchess was an offspring of Sandy, Uncle Frail and Aunt Blanche's dog. Uncle Frail had quit experimenting with canine genetics, and Duchess was a much better outcome than Piglet.

294

Mom met me at home and we didn't do anything special—no killing of the fatted calf or anything like that. The Merry Pranksters arrived that evening, and in short order we were back in the groove of visiting our favorite dining establishments and traveling to nowhere special. Mike was now an assistant manager at a Roy Rogers fast food place with the famed Double R Bar Burger, Bob and Gordon were about to graduate from Oxon Hill High, and Jimmy, the human version of Alfred E. Newman, was doing who knows what.

I got to play a couple of church softball games during the two-week break before heading back to Wheaton for summer school. In all things had not changed very much in the last ten weeks.

Things had changed regarding Pat. She now had a beau which I had expected due to the dearth of mail during the past few weeks. It seemed to be for the best, and it would avoid trying to maintain a long distance relationship.

The two weeks went by fast and it was back on student standby again to The Windy City and summer school. It was time to play catch-up ball for the two quarters I missed earlier in the academic year. This time it was a little easier to head West.

YOU CAN GO HOME AGAIN

The great Southern writer, Thomas Wolfe, wrote perhaps one of the most famous lines in American Literature—"You can't go home again." I maintain that this is true to some extent, depending on the circumstances. Please be patient and I'll explain my reasoning.

The return to Wheaton was uneventful and the Summer school class was less than 500 students so you got to know everyone. I practically ran WETN due to lack of staff and management moved me to the more listened to evening spot. I emceed a radiothon for The Junior Olympics where I was on air for twenty-six straight hours then had to do an essay exam on C.S. Lewis the next day. It was a whirlwind eight-week quarter then back to DC for six weeks until the Fall quarter.

During the summer at WETN, bits and pieces of information were coming over the news wire services concerning a break-in of the Democratic National Headquarters at the Watergate Complex in DC. The information was sketchy and The Washington Post seemed to be one of the few news sources that thought the story had legs. As the late Paul Harvey would say, "And now we know the rest of the story." I probably knew more than most Americans, because of my "ripping and reading" of the news at WETN. When I returned home, I read the reports from Bob Woodward and Carl Bernstein in The Washington Post, and something nagged me that something wasn't quite right. Little did I know that Woodward would be getting information from a source known as "Deep Throat" in a parking garage.

I returned to Wheaton for the Fall quarter and it is here that I leave you as to a Boomer growing up in DC and going West young man. At nineteen, I was no longer a kid and I was slowly putting away childish things; after all, isn't that what the Bible tells us to do.

As for Thomas Wolfe, I believe you can go home again, depending upon people, places, and things. Who are the people who may have impacted your life and are they still around? That's the case with any person or city. It may seem like great insight into the obvious, but many people never consider why they return home to see certain individuals. In some cases it is to have your ticket punched. I'm sad to admit that this was the case as to visiting my folks when they were alive. It wasn't that I disliked my family but we did not experience the closeness of other families.

I've reconciled this by thinking that my parents, especially Mom, had troubled childhoods. In many ways they did the best they could. It's an old reference used by many: "We always had food on the table and clothes to wear." Dad was a firm believer that one could never have enough milk. One of Dad's co-workers went shopping with him, and Dad bought six half gallons of milk. The co-worker exclaimed, "Man, that's a lot of milk!" Dad's response,"I'd much rather buy milk than pay for doctor bills." Perhaps milk and swimming in raw sewage have been the reasons for my good health. If I did a gratitude list concerning my parents there would be numerous items. My wish is that familial love be on the list. Perhaps this is up to me even though my folks have long since passed away. I can't adjust the wind, but I can adjust my sails. As for my friends, most of them have scattered across the nation. I have been able to stay in contact with some via social media.

When I return to DC, it is because of the city itself and the memories. DC does not have many of the aspects of other cities but its history and monuments are unsurpassed. Every time I return, there is a familiarity with the tangible reminders of our freedoms.The National Archives Building, home of The Constitution and Declaration of Independence, has only two words inscribed over its archway, "Study History." That's all; point and period. I could not agree more.

I think that other cities have an advantage over DC in that there are numerous generations of families who have grown up in their hometowns. The DC Boomer generation was, for the most part, the first DC generation for many families who migrated from other areas for government and military jobs. Many from my generation have chosen to remain in and around DC, and their children have as well, providing two more generations of "Metroites."

It's amazing that I have so few snapshots of my childhood. They disappeared over the years after numerous moves; plus, my parents were not big photo takers. In contrast, Eileen has boxes full of photos of her childhood, daughters, and ex-husband. My snapshots are mental ones, vivid, never changing. Those who are experts seem to be in universal agreement that the long term memory is the last to go; it's the short term memory that jumps up and bites you in the butt. As was previously mentioned, the great Bob Hope once said that there were four stages of memory loss: "First you forget names. Then you forget faces. Then you forget to zip up. Then you forget to zip down." I'm at stage 3.5 but my long-term hard drive is still strong.

During the last ten to fifteen years, I've embarked on solo field trips throughout DC. There are places I've driven to, such as my old neighborhoods, where no tourist would venture to visit. Other times I've driven to favorite sites just on a whim. One example produced a personal jackpot.

For some reason I decided to drive to RFK Stadium for old time's sake. As I circled the stadium, I noticed that one of the delivery gateways was open, and I could actually see part of the field. I pulled into the parking lot, and no one was around, so I walked to the gate. To my right I saw an attendant in a glass booth similar to ones used by toll takers and parking lot attendants.

I went over to the booth and flashed a smile. "Excuse me sir. I'm here from California but I'm a native of DC and a Redskins fan. I was wondering if it would be OK for me to walk around the field and walk up in the stands. I won't vandalize anything and I can show you my ID." The attendant laughed, "Go ahead man. I can tell that you're no trouble. Take as long as you like."

It was the same gate the 'Skins would open to vex opposing placekickers with swirling winds when they were trying to kick field goals. I walked down the home team side of the sidelines. Here they had stood: Jurgensen, Huff, Mitchell, Taylor, Theismann, the great offensive line, The Hogs, Lombardi, Joe Gibbs, and the rest. The sod was partially frozen and crunched under my feet.

The field had been prepped for a big high school game, but it was configured the same. I ran across the field to where left field had been for baseball and where Frank Howard had stood. The pilgrimage took me through the stands to the press box where The Post's Shirley Povich cranked out his columns with regularity on a typewriter long before laptops. It was time to leave. I had no camera; only mental snapshots. There are few tangible artifacts in my home of DC and Oxon Hill. I have replicas of Griffith and RFK Stadiums that Mom gave me as birthday presents. Some pennants, photos, and bobbleheads remain in boxes in the garage.

My prize possession is an old industrial clock in a brown frame, given to me by my old buddy, Mr. Mad Magazine, David Blackwell. I was honored when asked to emcee my thirty-fifth high school reunion. David and I reconnected and we are kindred spirits as to DC and Oxon Hill history. A year after the reunion, news circulated that the old, decaying high school gym was being torn down to build a new one in its place. I don't know what possessed him to do so, but David drove to the school during the demolition and pulled out the gym clock from the rubble.

He e-mailed me that he was sending the clock to me because he thought that I was the one person who would appreciate it. The clock was delivered a few days later, and it resides in a place where I have easy access to it and no one will discard it. I've thought about having it fixed, but I prefer to have it frozen in time. I can look at its face and mentally reverse time. I can visualize school days, great food, movies, pranks and jobs. I can visualize the days when DC was a sleepy Southern town that just happened to be The Nation's Capital and how the city grew as I grew. On a sad note, I can visualize great Americans gone too soon due to senseless assassinations.

Wind it to the future, and I can dream for a Redskins' Super Bowl, a Wizards' NBA Championship, a Nationals' World Series, and that the Capitals not choke in the Stanley Cup Playoffs.

I can also dream that DC drivers will learn to drive in the snow, that Marylanders will not pronounce "Washington" as "Worshington," and for a more united city. Dream on, and I pray for less crime and drug use, and that the District gets representation in Congress. DC has a non-voting representative in Congress, but still pays taxes. That's the reason tourists see DC license plates with "Taxation Without Representation."

Then there is always the dream that I will return to visit the city I love that I will always consider my hometown. I know that I can come home again. In the words of a famous Washingtonian, Duke Ellington, "A dream is a wish yet fulfilled." True!

GLOSSARY

Many people who visit the D.C. area for the first time are baffled by the D.C. area dialect. "Washington" is pronounced "Worshingtin" or "Warshinin." For the newcomer or visitor to D.C. I offer some commonly used words with the transition. Yes, you too will be able to speak like a native

Aysters—A shellfish from the bay.
Ballmer—Baltimore
Merlin—The state outside of D.C.
Arn—What you do with wrinkled clothes.
Bulled egg—An egg cooked in water.
Chest Peak—A large bay near D.C.
Colleyflare—A white vegetable.
Downey Owe Shin—Down to the ocean.
Duddeney—He sure does, duddeney?
Err—A time measurement of 60 minutes.
Far place—Where we burn wood and hang out Christmas stockings.
Fard—The area between the eyes and hairline.
Farmin—People who fight fires.
Ford—Opposite of backwards.
Gummint—Government
Idnit—"It is, idnit?"
Ignernt—ignorant
Klumya—Columbia a city outside of D.C.
Meer—What you see your reflection in.
Mudlaw—The woman who married your fodlaw.
Natty Boh—National Bohemian beer.
Norf Abnew—North Ave.

Numb—Conjunctive first person pronoun: "Aw bin workin' six errors numb tarred."

Plooshin—Pollution. Let's get it out of the Anacostia River.

Sarn—The noise from a pleece car or farn gin.

Slong—"Goodbye"

Spearmint—Experiment

Yerp—Europe

Youz—You all

Zinc—Where you wash your hands or dishes.

CPSIA information can be obtained
at www.ICGtesting.com
Printed in the USA
LVHW072312060319
609809LV00023B/85/P